Continuous Practices

A Strategic Approach to Accelerating the Software Production System

Daniel Ståhl
Torvald Mårtensson

Every precaution was taken in the preparation of this book. However, the authors take no responsibility for omissions or errors, or for any damages that may result from the use of information in this book.

ISBN 978-1-387-25376-0

Cover design by Daniel Ståhl.

To my beautiful sons, their mother, and the moments we share.
- Daniel

To my wife. My whole life depends on you.
- Torvald

Contents

Foreword by Jan Bosch

The history of mankind can be viewed as constantly shortening feedback cycles. Centuries ago, caravans traversed the Silk road and goods took many months, if not years, to reach their final destination. Today, modern clothing retailers decide on new designs, order the manufacturing and then sell these clothes in a matter of weeks. Communication within and between governments, companies and individuals used to take weeks or even months whereas today the time to transfer messages can be measured in milliseconds. Many other examples, such high frequency stock trading, exist that illustrate this trend.

The central technology that has enabled this transformation is software. Traditional system engineering relied on mechanics and later electronics, but it was firmly rooted in atoms. This means that a design, once finished, enters manufacturing and can no longer be changed. The feedback cycle is concerned with the next generation of the product and consequently slow. Once software is added to the system, the equation changes dramatically. Especially for connected products, the software can be updated periodically or even frequently. This allows systems to constantly exhibit new functionality and behaviour.

Interestingly, consumers have identified the advantages provided by software updates and are increasingly expecting their products to improve over time. Mobile phones are an illustrative example, but also virtually all Web 2.0 and Software-as-a-Service (SaaS) solutions update often. And, as examples such as Tesla show, this development is spreading to industry at large. Soon, independent of the system or product being focused on the B2C or B2B market; independent of it being safety critical or not, customers and users will expect their systems to get better every day they use these.

The corollary of deploying new software in systems frequently of course is data. Once a system is connected, one can not only install new

---

software on it. One can also extract data from the system that provides insight into the behaviour of the system as well as its users. This data can then be used as input for the development process, allowing R&D teams to stop developing or even remove functionality that does not provide the expected benefits. And, alternatively, double down on functionality that provides more benefits than expected.

As we know from control theory, the shorter the feedback loop, the more effectively the process is controlled. Research in software engineering shows that perhaps up to two thirds of all features and new functionality in systems is never used or used so seldomly that it doesn't justify the R&D investment. Fast feedback loops where partially developed features can be deployed and the effect of these features be measured before committing to additional development improves the effectiveness of R&D significantly.

Having established the importance of fast feedback loops and the unique opportunity provided by software, the next question is how to realize this in practice in order to reap the benefits of continuous practices. This is where this book provides its key contribution. It starts with explaining the basic concepts of continuous integration, delivery, deployment, release as well as DevOps. It describes the notion of pipelines as well as factors influencing the design of a continuous pipeline, including organizational and business realities. Subsequently, it addresses various dimensions that influence continuous practices, such as hardware, scale, regulation and distribution models. From there on, it goes into the trenches of realizing the pipeline in practice, including testing, release candidates, traceability, technology solutions and the like.

This book is written by two dyed-in-the-wool practitioners from world leading companies who have, as the saying goes, seen the elephant. Their approach does not originate from the ivory towers of academia, but is based on years of experience with building software production systems in reality. Over the last several years, I have had the privilege to work with the authors and I have consistently been impressed with their deep insights, novel and practical approaches and professionalism. And you, dear reader, will experience the same when reading this book!

As the world becomes increasingly digital, it moves to shorter and shorter feedback cycles. Software is the core technology in realizing this development. Continuous practices and fast, largely automated software production systems are central and critical in accomplishing this. Companies ignore this trend at their peril, but those that proactively adopt these approaches maintain and even improve their competitiveness. And not only that, due to the markedly improved effectiveness, society as a whole is better off using continuous practices. And who could possibly be against that?

Jan Bosch
Director Software Center
Hovås, January 2018

Preface

Continuous integration as a software engineering practice has long ceased to be a curious novelty, but has firmly established itself in the industry mainstream. The precise moment of its birth is up for debate: depending on whether one counts the introduction of continuous integration as a term by Grady Booch [1], the definition of Extreme Programming or its subsequent popularization by Kent Beck [2], the concept has been with us since the mid or late '90s. Considering the fact that the inception of software engineering as a recognized engineering discipline is generally dated to the late '60s, continuous integration isn't a new kid on the block anymore.

More recently, continuous integration has been joined on the stage not only by continuous delivery and continuous deployment, but terms like continuous testing, continuous release, continuous security and more are being thrown around and often used interchangeably [3]. If one adds DevOps to that mix one can easily be forgiven for feeling overwhelmed: what are these practices, how do they relate to one another, and what are they really good for?

If you have ever asked yourself any of those questions, know that you are in good company. In fact, when studying implementations of continuous practices in the software industry, one finds that not only do they differ significantly in nature, but the engineers building and using them also report very different effects [4, 5].

In this book we disentangle and break down "the big three" of continuous practices: continuous integration, continuous delivery and continuous deployment. Then we proceed to consider their value, their implications and how best to implement them depending on your context. By doing so we attempt to answer the questions any professional should be looking to answer before jumping in with both feet and adopting a new practice:

- What is this, and what is it not?

- Which aspects are relevant to you, and which can you safely skip?

- What kind of value should you expect to derive from this, and what should you do to maximize that value?

- What kind of challenges should you expect to encounter, and how can you go about overcoming them?

- How do you know whether you're actually making progress? How do you set an attainable goal for yourself and your organization?

Rather than accepting continuous practices at face value and assuming that they are equally applicable and beneficial in every situation, this book acknowledges that different segments of the software industry operate under different constraints, and that these questions may hold different answers depending on who you are. In this sense, it takes a strategic approach, helping you realize the practices that will benefit your business.

Who Should Read This Book

If you have an interest in effective and efficient software production systems – be it from an engineering or a business point of view – then this book is for you. We use the term software production system for the entire process of transforming sources into in-service software systems, including compilation, analysis, testing, packaging, distribution and deployment, as well as the infrastructure, tools and behaviors that underpin that process.

That may seem like a bold statement, but we stand by it. Continuous integration, delivery and deployment are not fringe concerns for a few specialists in the back office. They are influenced by and greatly influence how we do business.

Regardless of what your role and your stake in your organization's software production is, this book has something for you: we will cover not just what continuous practices are and how one might go about adopting them and improving them, but also which practices to focus on and what ambition level to strive for.

Similarly, whether you are a novice or a grizzled veteran straight from the trenches, we hope that you will find something of value in this book. Through a structured and measured approach to adoption and improvement of these practices, we seek to help everyone map a clear path forward, regardless of one's starting position.

What this book will not go into depth on, however, is detailed application of the various tools that tend to surface in this area. For the most part, we will simply assume that you know it's a good idea to keep your assets version controlled – whether it's source code, configurations, test scripts or something else – and automating your regression tests can provide great value, or that you should try to automate as much of your infrastructure management as possible and that there are tools that can help you do that. If that is the type of information you are looking for, then there are much better books out there than the one you are holding in your hand.

On the other hand, if you ever wondered how to best apply continuous practices to your particular business, then we hope you will find this book rewarding. It is not difficult to find literature on successful implementations of continuous integration, delivery or deployment, or DevOps. What tends to be more challenging is to translate those success stories into reality at home. It is important to understand that this is not simply because some are blessed with the ability to see the virtues of continuous practices clearly, while others are not so blessed. Instead, it's primarily because we in the software business all operate under different sets of rules, depending on a range of factors. In other words, if you ever struggled to figure out how the success of somebody else might be translated to your organization, or if you implemented continuous practices but it didn't quite turn out the way you had hoped, then read on.

Why We Wrote This Book

Both as researchers and as practitioners we have observed, studied and participated in a multitude of software projects in a range of companies and segments of the software industry – projects which have enthusiastically taken on the idea of continuous integration, and later continuous delivery and/or deployment. We wish that these had all been success stories and that everybody involved had lived happily ever after. Unfortunately that has not always been the case. It's not so much that these projects crash and burn by any means, but rather that vast amounts of effort and resources are poured into an attempt to improve the efficacy and/or efficiency of the project. When one stops to look critically at the results, it not always clear what was truly achieved.

We find that the lack of a systematic approach to the problem is largely to blame [6], and that even though several excellent sources on individual continuous practices have been published over the years (such as the works of Jez Humble and David Farley [7] and Paul Duvall [8]) a broader picture is still missing.

As one result was added to another in our research, and one project experience was added to the next, we began to feel the need to connect those dots. Partly for the sake of others: so often do we encounter confusion regarding continuous practices and their meaning, value, prerequisites and consequences that we feel painting a larger picture in the form of a book would be a service to the community. But also for our own sake, asking ourselves, if we climb up on the shoulders of giants and build from there by putting all these findings and experiences together into a coherent whole, what does that actually look like? Writing a book can be a be a very worthwhile exercise in that it forces you to assemble and structure your thoughts in a disciplined fashion.

That being said, precisely because the issues encountered in continuous practices are so interconnected and multidisciplinary, when one sets out to write a book about them one easily ends up writing a book about the universe and everything in it – or at the very least about software engineering in general. Therefore we have had to make some tough choices and refrained from diving too deeply into certain related topics. We hope that the reader finds we have made the right choices.

> When we started working on this book, we soon become aware that it was like working on a complex software product: as soon as you pull on one string, that in turn pulls in all kinds of other stuff as well. We realized that we had to be careful about what to include and what to exclude in the book.
>
> *- Torvald*

Navigating This Book

This book is split up into multiple parts, to help the reader navigate it.

Part I provides a taxonomy and breakdown of continuous practices and puts them in a context: why are they, what are they, what are they not, and how do they relate to one another? This constitutes one of two cornerstones in the book.

Part II constitutes the second cornerstone. It discusses what the system that is continuously integrated, delivered and deployed actually is. Continuous practices are often presented in the form of a pipeline from sources to production, but reality tends to be more complicated than that: rather than a pipeline, there is an ecosystem of sources, components, libraries, third party products, services and systems delivered to one another, like a network of software food chains. From that point of view, what is ultimately the scope of the pipeline? Part II proceeds from there to examine the variability space of contextual factors relevant to continuous practices. What is your relationship to your customers? What is the safety criticality of your system? Are your requirements set in stone or do they change on a daily basis? To illustrate the differences, several archetypical software projects are described, occupying their respective parts of the variability space.

The scene thus set, Part III takes a technical perspective by looking at the tooling and infrastructure required to build a software production system. It breaks that system down into its elements and success factors, cutting across continuous integration, delivery and deployment, detailing the challenges you will typically face and how to tackle them, depending on your particular context. It returns to the archetypes laid out in Part II and explains the concepts and challenges from their respective points of view; explaining not just how to construct and manage a pipeline but how to navigate a network of pipelines.

Part IV is structured similarly to Part III, but leaves the realm of the purely technical and looks closely at the organization: enabling and encouraging the behaviors that make continuous practices work. Despite a state of the art pipeline and superior tooling, if developers are not convinced of the value of integrating frequently in small increments – or perceive themselves unable to – continuous integration is not going to happen. Like Part III, it discusses these challenges from the viewpoints of the archetypes introduced in Part II.

Part V is forward-looking. Whether one is just starting out on the journey, or is well underway but looking to take the next step, the question is how to improve and to succeed at continuous practices. This part is designed to help you do that by first assessing your current state and helping you determine where you want to go from there and what the delta looks like: which continuous practice success factors are lacking or need to be improved, and how does one go about doing that? Finally, we end on a forward looking note by contemplating the changes, opportunities and challenges we can see coming over the horizon, both in software engineering in general and in continuous practices in particular.

Acknowledgments

The talented engineers and researchers – particularly from the companies and universities that make up Software Center[1] – who generously spent their time answering our questions and participating in our case studies and thereby enabled the research upon which this book is based are unfortunately too many to name here. You know who you are, and we owe you our gratitude.

---

1   http://software-center.se

We would particularly like to thank *Kristofer Hallén, Inga-Lill Holmqvist, Ivan Pinheiro, Helena Holmström Olsson, Ola Söder* and *Roger Persson* for their early feedback on the book, *Lars Kruse* for sharing his experiences from dealing with regulations in a continuous delivery setting, *Anas Dakkak* for his insights on continuous deployment and *Peter Thorngren* for his input on development in an automotive context.

Figures in this book include icons by Eleonor Wang and Freepik, from www.flaticon.com.

About the Authors

Daniel Ståhl has a background as software developer and architect. He works as Subject Matter Expert and Product Development Leader at Ericsson AB, where he is responsible for the corporate strategy on continuous integration, delivery and deployment. He has been working professionally in software development since 2007, and has spent most of that time implementing and researching continuous practices in organizations ranging from single teams to tens of thousands of engineers. He received an MSc degree from Linköping University, Sweden, and a PhD degree from the University of Groningen, The Netherlands.

Torvald Mårtensson is Distinguished Engineer in System Integration and Test at Saab AB. He has a background of twelve years in the aeronautics industry and another eight years in the telecom industry. His work has primarily revolved around systems integration and system testing of large-scale software systems, and he has published several research papers on the subject at conferences and in journals. He received an MSc degree from Linköping University, Sweden, in 1997.

How to Contact Us

Daniel Ståhl can be reached at http://www.danielstahl.co/contact, via e-mail at daniel.b.stahl@gmail.com or via LinkedIn at https://www.linkedin.com/in/daniel-b-stahl. A list of publications is available at http://tinyurl.com/scholar-stahl.

Torvald Mårtensson can be reached by e-mail at torvald.martensson@gmail.com or via LinkedIn at http://www.linkedin.com/in/torvald-martensson. A list of publications is available at http://tinyurl.com/scholar-torvaldm.

Colophon

This book was written using LibreOffice Writer. Torvald contributed text, which was edited by Daniel and inserted into the LibreOffice Writer document. Gliffy and LibreOffice Calc were used to create the figures.

The book was self-published using lulu.com, with Daniel performing all layout work and conversion into print format using LibreOffice Writer. The book cover was designed and illustrated by Daniel, using GIMP.

Part I: Understanding Continuous Practices

Chapter 1

The History of Continuous Practices

The software industry is a fiercely competitive world where the fittest thrive, while others are mercilessly marked for extinction. Just as in natural selection in the wild, it is not those best adapted to today's environment who will rise to prominence tomorrow, but those most able to embrace and adapt to changing circumstances. Any trait that will help an organism make the necessary adaptations is a trait that will be selected for and preserved through generations. It is in this light we regard continuous practices – as genes in the software industry genome that make their hosts more responsive and adaptable, thereby increasing their robustness and survivability. The shortened feedback cycles and turn-around times provided by continuous practices have been found to serve as enablers for greater flexibility and responsiveness in face of changes in business and technology alike, explaining their rapid spread throughout the software industry, similar to the rapid spread of a beneficial gene throughout a population.

The idea that it is better to split a large and complicated task into smaller chunks and address them separately, one by one, rather than attempting to solve everything in one go is not a new one. Not in software engineering, and not in other realms of human activity.

In the late '90s and the early '00s, however, the concept of continuous integration gained attention and traction within the software engineering community. It was often advocated as part of a larger context, such as the Agile Manifesto [9] or Extreme Programming [2].

In the years that followed it largely came to live a life of its own – as any kid it grew up, moved out of the house, gained independence – and established itself in the mainstream.

The concept of continuous integration is appealing to a large group of developers. Any software engineer who has been involved in a project involving a total number of developers larger than one can relate to the difficult and often painful experience of trying to get their changes to work with those of their colleagues, and how that pain gets worse the longer one puts off dealing with it.

To someone who is not a developer, the fundamental issue may be difficult to grasp fully. We all use software in our daily lives, we are all dependent on it: software is the lifeblood of modern society. Yet it is easy to forget that all this software was written by software developers, and very rarely by one developer working alone, but by dozens, hundreds or even thousands, collaborating to create a solid, safe, coherent and usable end product. The fundamental question that continuous integration tries to address is this: How do you do that in a good way?

Again, if you are not a developer yourself, one way to picture the problem is to think of writing a novel. Actually, a very long novel, spanning thousands of pages. Writing such a long novel is a daunting task, and apart from the sheer effort, it's really hard to keep track of all the characters and plot twists and events, shaping them into a coherent narrative. But to make things worse, you are not writing alone, but collaborating with hundreds of other writers, all writing in parallel with you, and every time one of them makes a change you have to make sure that their change doesn't come into conflict with whatever it is you are currently working on.

This is the reality of thousands and thousands of software developers around the world, creating the systems that underpin nearly every aspect of our lives – from our coffee machines and our cars to our banks and our telephones. This is why it is very difficult to increase development speed by simply adding more developers: every extra person increases the coordination overhead. Obviously there are ways to make the situation less disastrous: you can make plans and split up the work, you can enforce a chapter structure that reduces the overlap between authors, but in the end you have to make the pieces fit together.

The core tenet of continuous integration is that the longer you wait and the larger changes you build up before integrating with your colleagues – "the bigger the bangs" – the worse it will be. As a rule of thumb, if you let two developers work in isolation for six months building separate parts of a system, you should expect them to spend at least another six months trying to integrate them, no matter how meticulously planned and well defined the interface between them appeared to be at the planning stage. To avoid this, continuous integration declares, developers should instead integrate very, very frequently: at least daily is often suggested (e.g. by Paul Duvall [8]). What happens then is that no longer do you have to worry that your colleagues might be making huge sweeping changes that are going to collide head-first with your work a few months down the line. Instead, changes become smaller, more manageable and transparent, and as you leave the office in the evening, you know that everybody's work up to that point has been integrated into a coherent and – hopefully – working whole.

This idea is very appealing and is easy to get behind, as any sane person would say yes to greater predictability in their work, avoiding nasty surprises, and not having weeks worth of work ruined by incompatible changes made by others. Actually achieving this practice of continuous integration is easier said than done, however. There are numerous challenges and bumps in the road which we will explore in this book. Some have to do with behavior, communication and psychology. Others have to do with technology, tools and infrastructure.

There are lots of ways to go about trying to solve these challenges, and often different solutions present themselves in different contexts. For instance, achieving continuous integration in a three man e-commerce development team is a very different experience from doing the same thing in an organization of 3,000 developers building a cyber-physical defense system. This is a significant reason why there has been a high degree of confusion and divergence as to what continuous integration actually means, with many authors and practitioners focusing almost exclusively on tools and techniques, leading to problematic questions regarding whether a certain technique is part of continuous integration, or if you can do continuous integration without a particular tool. We and many others, on the other hand, prefer a more holistic view which focuses on developer behavior – behavior which is in turn enabled and encouraged by tools and techniques, to which there may be many approaches.

While this confusion regarding the actual meaning of continuous integration has long been problematic, it was about to get much worse when a slew of additional continuous practices entered the scene.

Enter Continuous Delivery

Continuous delivery was popularized by Jez Humble and David Farley in 2010 [7], arguing for a way of working that essentially builds upon the idea of continuous integration: rather than just integrating frequently and ensuring that there is an up-to-date shared baseline where everybody's latest changes have been integrated, let us also treat every revision of that baseline as a release candidate to be automatically evaluated and progressed through an automated pipeline, to be potentially released and/or deployed depending on business decisions. The pipeline as a metaphor for the process of turning software sources into trusted, running and value-generating in-production software is wide-spread in the industry, and we use it extensively in this book. For a more in-depth discussion of the pipeline concept and when it is and isn't a useful analogy, see Chapter 6.

This may seem like a fairly straight-forward approach to developing software, but when introduced this represented a nearly diametrically opposed way of working to the traditional mainstream method. Whereas release candidates had previously tended to be a small number of versions identified fairly late in the product life cycle, carefully selected and manually tested, advocates of continuous delivery suggested that they should be mass produced, immediately, and automatically tested. One way to think of this is as a shift to a more heuristic way of looking at software development: let's not try to analyze our way to determining what might be the best version of the software to release, but automatically analyze all of them and select those that turn out to pass our criteria.

Unfortunately, if interpreting continuous integration has sometimes been difficult in the community, that difficulty pales in comparison to the confusion caused by continuous delivery (something we try to untangle in Chapter 2).

Even though some clarity is lacking with regards to the terminology, continuous delivery has become enormously popular, to the point that it is more or less expected for software development projects to employ it, or at the very least to strive for it. Arguably this is because in a way, continuous delivery is more tangible than continuous integration, and less dependent on the mindset and behavior of individual developers, something we will explore further in subsequent chapters of this book.

Enter Continuous Deployment

At about the same time as continuous delivery was introduced, the term continuous deployment was coined and popularized by Timothy Fitz [10], stating that "Every commit should be instantly deployed to production".

Since their inception, both continuous delivery and continuous deployment have enjoyed steadily growing popularity [11, 12] and are in fact often used interchangeably [3], even though a closer look reveals that they actually do carry very different meanings.

A noteworthy aspect of continuous deployment is that it implicitly assumes that the product is something similar to a website or a Software as a Service solution, even though this is rarely made explicit. What we have seen since then is numerous cases where engineers, inspired by the many benefits of continuous deployment, strive to apply it to a completely different domain, operating under very different circumstances, resulting in further divergence in interpretation of what the concept actually means in practice.

Enter Continuous Everything?

Even though continuous integration, continuous delivery and continuous deployment may be considered "the big three" of continuous practices, additional variants have been proposed. This is particularly the case where people want to broaden the scope: seeing the value that continuous practices bring to software development, there is a desire to bring the same benefits to other parts of the enterprise.

This is the case in the area of operations, often influenced by the popularity of the DevOps movement, where terms such as "continuous operations" are proposed by some, or in the area of software testing where terms such as "continuous testing" and "continuous verification" have been introduced. This is not without its problems, because there is clearly a great deal of overlap here: continuous deployment involves a high degree of operations aspects, and the ability to perform continuous delivery hinges on one's ability to continuously test and verify the software.

Similarly, extending the concept of continuous practices into other domains of the product development process, "continuous evolution", "continuous security", "continuous compliance", "continuous planning" and more have been proposed [10]. These have – as of the time of writing – not achieved the popularity of "the big three", however, and so are not included in this book.

Summary

In this chapter we have briefly looked at the history of continuous practices: how it began with continuous integration in the late '90s and early '00s, and how more and more practices have been coined since then, and also how the understanding of the actual meaning of the concepts has not always been crystal clear. In particular, we have looked into the three most popular continuous practices: continuous integration, delivery and deployment. In the next chapter we will dig deeper into what these terms mean, what they do not mean, which contexts they apply to and how they relate to one another – and we will also talk about why all of that matters.

Chapter 2

What's What?

In this chapter we discuss what the three most popular continuous practices – integration, delivery and deployment – actually mean. We also discuss a fourth continuous practice: continuous release. We do this because we find it essential in understanding the difference between continuous delivery and deployment, and understanding what they are not.

On Semantics

It is not uncommon to hear phrases such as "that's just a matter of semantics" or similar, arguing that some distinction or other is of little importance. Indeed, some will point out that any difference between, say, continuous delivery and continuous deployment is only a matter of semantics. And they would be right: it is a matter of semantics. Where they would be wrong, though, is that it is unimportant.

What is semantics, then? Semantics is simply the meaning and interpretation of a word, a sentence, a sign or a phrase. And, arguably, the meaning of the words we use is the single most important aspect of language: without agreed upon semantics, we may just as well utter random noises for all the good it will do us. And all too often, that's what we seem to be doing when we speak to one another about continuous practices.

Some readers may object to this gloomy picture of current state of affairs. Surely, it's not as bad as all that? Surely, we have a fairly good understanding of what these continuous practices mean? They're about speed in software development, for the purpose of better productivity, predictability, time to market and such. And that's right, it is about those things, but the devil is in the details. It's possible to imagine any number of actions one might take that would fit that description, and not all of them are necessarily very helpful. Indeed, looking at continuous integration implementations we see a great deal of divergence in interpretation and implementation [4], as well as – unsurprisingly – outcomes [5]. For instance, we have watched projects develop a severe case of tunnel vision, spending huge resources on constructing elaborate and advanced pipelines to build and test their software in order to achieve continuous integration. At the same time they have completely ignored all the other impediments actually keeping their developers from committing frequently and consequently changing little in terms of actual behavior.

Granted, definitions of continuous practices are not always as fuzzy as the example above, but in our interactions with industry projects trying to implement them the level of understanding is surprisingly often at that rather hazy level. It is also striking how often they are described in terms of what one hopes to achieve with them (this is particularly the case when it comes to DevOps, which we will take a closer look at in Chapter 3). There is even a tendency to deliberately avoid concrete definitions in favor of focusing on values, thereby allowing everyone to find the solution that suits their particular context best. There is a certain rationality to this: the software engineering community is indeed highly diverse, and one size will most certainly not fit all. But it is also highly problematic, in that it leaves each one of us to find our own path to salvation.

To illustrate the point, let us assume we were introducing a new diet, which focuses on eating nutritious food in the interest of being healthy and living longer. All of which is great – who can argue with that? The problem is that followers of this diet will inevitably end up interpreting it in very different ways. Some will stay away from meat, others will go low carb, others will eat nothing but carrots. They all share the same values and they all want the same thing; unfortunately they will achieve very different results, and some will end up hospitalized or worse as a consequence.

That part about carrots is not a joke, by the way. A distant relative of mine once tried an all carrot diet, and yes, he did wind up hospitalized for severe nutritional deficiency. My takeaway from that was that aiming for the stars is commendable, but figuring out your own unique way to get there isn't guaranteed to work, and may be downright dangerous. The road to hell is paved with good intentions, and all that.

- Daniel

This is why we need to be careful about words, and try to be as precise as we can. To exemplify, when we speak of *speed* in continuous integration, what do we mean by that? Time from an action to a certain outcome? Which actions, and which outcomes, exactly? Or do we actually mean frequency, rather than speed? Or both? May we end up in a situation where we have to weigh one against the other? Unless we take care to sort out the semantics, we may never find out.

To conclude, semantics matter a great deal. That's why we're going to spend this chapter on ironing out the semantics of continuous practices: what do they mean, what do they *not* mean, and how do they relate to one another? Unless one is very clear on semantics, chances are that any subsequent implementation will be equally muddled.

At a workshop with several different companies which all used continuous practices, it turned out that we had very different views of what a continuous integration and delivery pipeline was. One participant stated that the pipeline ends where the developer's code is integrated into the mainline. Another participant then argued the opposite: where the developer's code is integrated is where the pipeline begins. Yet another participant had never heard the term pipeline before. With the definitions we propose in this book, we hope to bring clarity in such discussions and ease communication around best practices.

- Torvald

Another consequence of being careless with semantics is that it can lead to a term being essentially synonymous with "good", which will guarantee that any impartial conversation regarding its pros and cons or whether it even applies to a certain case will not take place. Because if continuous integration equals "good", then if one suggests that someone might not in truth be practicing continuous integration, then they are by definition bad.

We have seen this first hand in companies we have worked with, where senior management buy into the idea of continuous integration, and all projects in the company are enjoined to adopt it as soon as possible. Unfortunately, as it turns out, without first defining what would actually be considered continuous integration, with the foreseeable result that each project ends up doing its own thing. Some very valuable tools and concepts can result from that process, but it also leads to a situation where continuous integration becomes an identity, and any constructive discussion on whether they are actually continuously integrating or not becomes an attack on that identity.

Going back to the simile of diets, it's like watching a self-proclaimed vegan eat dairy products while refusing to listen to any argument that they are therefore by definition not a vegan. Because to them, veganism permits dairy products. In other words, reckless treatment of semantics threatens to launch us straight into the realm of truthiness and alternative facts.

Continuous Integration

Even though we in the previous section deplored the fact that continuous integration and other continuous practices are often used carelessly, it is possible to identify what we would refer to as a mainstream interpretation. In the case of continuous integration, this can be traced back to the clearly formulated definition by Martin Fowler [13], which states that continuous integration is "a software development practice where members of a team integrate their work frequently, usually each person integrates at least daily – leading to multiple integrations per day".

In this definition it is noteworthy that the word "frequently" is used, rather than e.g. "quickly" or "speedily". In other words, it is the frequency with which developers integrate that is the crucial factor, rather than the speed of builds, duration of tests or latency of feedback. Neither are the defining factors of continuous integration things like the scope of automated tests or the means of triggering builds. That does not mean that such factors are irrelevant – on the contrary, they tend to be the difference between success and catastrophe, which is why we will look closely at them in this book, but they do not define the practice.

Indeed, as many will point out, in theory it is entirely possible to perform continuous integration without any automation at all. In practice, on the other hand, it depends. In trivial scenarios of one or a handful of developers, continuous integration without support from automation is certainly possible, but anything beyond that requires particular tooling and infrastructure. Precisely which tools and what infrastructure varies depending on you and your ambitions.

Think of it as mountain climbing. The definition of having climbed a mountain has nothing to do with the gear you used to get there, but is only about whether you reached the top or not. Easier climbs can be done with your bare hands, but the more difficult ones will require a

---

range of specialized tooling, as well as skill, perseverance and constitution. Pragmatically speaking, it's always a good idea to use a common version control repository, it's a good idea to automatically build and test your software, and it's a good idea to employ specialized tools for these tasks. There are already numerous excellent sources covering these aspects, such as Duvall's book on continuous integration [8], without us belaboring the point. In this book, we will instead focus on subsequent challenges you may run into once you have those bases covered, and to the best of our ability point you in the right direction to overcome them in your particular context.

In the end, returning to Fowler's description of the practice from 2006, we only encounter two minor issues with it. One is that we prefer naming it a *developer practice*, as opposed to a *development practice*. This is partly to distinguish it from continuous delivery – a term that hadn't yet been popularized at the time – and partly to emphasize the fact that this, unlike continuous delivery, is entirely up to the behavior of the individual developer. If the developer does not actually integrate frequently, then there is no continuous integration. The organization as such may have the loftiest ambitions and the fanciest software pipeline, but it all comes down to how the individual developer behaves. That being said, any conventions, processes or directives the organization (or the individual developers themselves) institute as part of integration become part of the scope of continuous integration. Not all such processes may be conducive to frequent integrations, but whatever steps we need to perform for whatever reason to commit to the mainline need to be considered part of the practice in the individual case. In other words, continuously integrating in one case may in one case involve nothing more than performing a merge operation in the SCM system, whereas in another case it may also involve code review, passing a mandatory central compilation and test activity and then signing a legal contract in blood. While all those things may impede frequent integrations, and while we may discuss their value and necessity, as long as they exist and are mandatory they, too, need to be addressed in any effort to continuously integrate.

The second issue is regarding *members of a team*. In a small scale scenario this is unproblematic, but at larger scales, in organizations of hundreds or thousands of developers split into a multitude of teams all working on the same software, it becomes ambiguous. What does "team" refer to in that context? One out of the hundreds of actual teams in the organization? Or is the "team" all the developers working on the same source code?

One may argue that such large scale setups are a bad idea and should be avoided, making the point moot. As Beck puts it, software should be split "along its natural fracture lines" [2] into smaller pieces to avoid this situation – and not just for the sake of continuous integration. This is a valid point, and in this book we will discuss the interplay between software architecture, organization and continuous integration at some length, but reality doesn't always look like that. In reality, the same source code is very often developed by more than a two pizza team, and in those situations it needs to be made very clear that continuous integration is not about frequently integrating only with your nearest colleagues, but with everyone who is collaborating with you on the source code. No matter how quickly developers commit to their team branch, if they only deliver from that team branch to the shared project mainline (or master branch, trunk, dev branch...) once a week, then they are not continuously integrating – at least not with everyone who coinhabits the source code, which is what really matters.

Hence, when we in this book use the term continuous integration, we mean a developer practice where developers integrate their work frequently, usually each person integrates at least daily, leading to multiple integrations per day.

Continuous Delivery

In the previous section on continuous delivery we stressed the point that it is a *developer practice*, as opposed to a *development practice*. That is because continuous delivery is exactly that: a development practice. It doesn't have so much to do with the behavior of the individual developer as with how the project or the organization decides to think about software changes and release candidates.

Similarly to continuous integration we identify a mainstream interpretation of the practice; an interpretation that goes back to the original description by Humble and Farley [7], who state that in continuous delivery, "every change is, in effect, a release candidate", whereas traditional approaches "identify release candidates at the end". Furthermore, while simply looking at a change in the product will only let you guess whether it truly adds value without introducing faults, in continuous delivery it is the build, test and analysis activities that make up the software pipeline that determine whether this is the case. In this sense, continuous delivery presents a mindset shift towards a heuristic approach to software development.

Similarly to the case of continuous integration, however, when applying the practice to large-scale development projects this definition becomes somewhat problematic. Simply put, if there are hundreds or thousands of changes to the source code, then fully evaluating each of them in the continuous delivery pipeline typically isn't feasible. In practice there tends to be high degree of batching of changes, often in multiple layers, throughout the pipeline. The first few activities, e.g. compilation and unit testing, may be done for every change. Higher level tests, meanwhile, requiring more time to complete, will pick up new changes as frequently as possible, but not frequently enough to test every individual change. Further downstream in the pipeline even longer running tests might pick one out of every few of those changes, and so forth. In this way, the release candidates that come out the far end up the pipeline are actually a sampling of the ones that entered it. Naturally, the less you need to batch, the better, not least for troubleshooting purposes. Also, there are parallelization techniques that help with this, as will be covered in Part III: Building the Pipeline. The fundamental principle still holds, however: which ones make it through is determined through a heuristic process, rather than through up-front analysis.

There are plenty of diverging interpretations, particularly in relation to continuous deployment and DevOps (which is why we have devoted Chapter 3 to discussing DevOps). The terms continuous delivery and continuous deployment are often used interchangeably [3], sometimes continuous delivery is said to enable DevOps, sometimes DevOps is said to enable continuous delivery. Sometimes continuous delivery is said to be a subset of continuous deployment, and sometimes the other way around. Much of this can be explained by the fact that continuous delivery is, arguably, a misnomer. Despite its name, as explained by e.g. Jez Humble [7] and Martin Fowler [14], continuous delivery actually has very little to do with delivering to anyone, but rather ensuring that one produces a steady stream of new product versions which *can potentially* be deployed and/or released.

This distinction may appear subtle, particularly in certain domains. If the product in question is a Software as a Service solution deployed to a cloud environment under your own control, then actually deploying the software is a relatively small step. On the other hand, in the case of a mechatronic embedded system in a highly regulated market, where the target environment is owned and controlled by a third party and moving around at high speed on public highways, going from producing a ready-to-go software version that *could* be deployed at any time and actually *deploying it* is a significant step.

It is important to emphasize that continuous delivery entails everything up to that deployment step, however: any testing, packaging, documentation, certification or digital signing required needs to be included in the practice of continuous delivery. In this sense it is analogous to the continuous integration. Just like everything involved in integrating is by definition part of continuous integration in the individual case, everything involved in creating a ready-to-go release candidate is part of the scope of continuous delivery. This means that these practices may express themselves rather differently from case to case, something we will dig further into in Part II: Understanding Your Context. Another possible explanation for the confusion regarding continuous delivery is the fact that as the popularity of continuous practices increases, new individuals are constantly entering the space: the finer points of the terminology and underlying concepts may appear less clear to new-comers than to old-timers, as hinted at by Andrew Phillips [15].

To summarize, when we in this book use the term continuous delivery, we mean a development practice where every change is treated as a potential release candidate to be frequently and rapidly evaluated through one's continuous delivery pipeline, and that one is always able to deploy and/or release the latest working version, but may decide not to, e.g. for business reasons.

Continuous Deployment

As noted earlier, the popularization of the term continuous deployment largely coincided with that of continuous delivery. In fact, its coining by Timothy Fitz predates the publishing of Continuous Delivery by Humble and Farley by about a year.

If continuous delivery is about ensuring you always have an evaluated and ready-to-go release candidate on hand, and are thus *able* to deploy at any time, continuous deployment is about *doing* it. Ideally, "every commit should be instantly deployed to production" [10]. One exception worth highlighting is the situation where the release candidate produced by the pipeline is not a deployable product per se, but something like a library or other resource that may be integrated into other systems. This scenario of pipelines feeding into other pipelines is covered in Chapter 6.

Implementing continuous deployment implies the same capabilities as continuous delivery, but adds a slew of additional challenges. Which challenges, precisely, depends on the business domain and risk profile of the individual case, something we will investigate further in Chapter 20. On the technical side of things, such challenges revolve around traceability and the ability to upgrade software in production with zero downtime – something that ultimately boils down to fundamental architectural choices in the design of the software. On the not-so-technical side, challenges one might face involve customer relations and trust issues, as well as purely contractual and regulatory hurdles.

It is worth pointing out that there are two main incentives for adopting continuous deployment in an organization. One is improved effectiveness in software development, while the other is the ability to rapidly and frequently bring value to the customers and/or users. In other words, continuous deployment can either be driven from within the development organization, or from business needs. While one incentive doesn't preclude the other, it's important to be carefully and explicitly consider why one adopts continuous deployment in the individual case. Without a clear vision and purpose it's easy be led astray. We would also caution readers that even when continuous deployment is driven from within for the sake of improving software development, it will inevitably affect the entire organization in a way that continuous integration or delivery don't. This is why it's critical to get not just the R&D side of the house onboard, but also e.g. sales and marketing, as we will discuss further in Chapter 25.

Proponents of continuous deployment also tend to emphasize the importance of failing fast and valuing mean time to recovery over mean time to failure. Indeed, one might argue that the practice embodies these values: it is better to deploy quickly, get feedback, and rapidly fix any failure (or, barring that, roll back) than to spend too much time and effort trying to avoid the failure in the first place.

If continuous deployment is about more or less instantly deploying to production, one obvious but often overlooked conclusion is that this practice is not applicable to every domain, mainly for two reasons. First, not all software is pushed to consumers. While the "X as a Service" trend promises to change this, a very significant portion of software is still user installed. Second, the premise that mean time to recovery holds sway over mean time to failure doesn't always hold true. In safety critical systems, where even a minimal downtime can literally be the difference between life and death, continuous deployment isn't necessarily invalidated, but a large part of its incentive is inapplicable.

On a slightly more pedantic note, let us consider how continuous deployment relates to continuous delivery. There are two main interpretations here: either continuous deployment is viewed as a superset of continuous delivery (and frequently continuous integration as well), or as something that follows on top of it – an extension to continuous delivery. The former view is expressed by Timothy Fitz, stating that "continuous deployment includes [continuous delivery] practices, and then some" [16].

Recalling an earlier simile, mountain climbing implies walking (and a great number of other abilities), but reading a book on mountain climbing one doesn't expect to go into any depth on the problems and virtues of putting one foot in front of the other (as fascinating a subject at that is, as any robotics researcher will tell you). To keep the scope of each practice manageable, we take the same approach to continuous deployment and delivery, regarding continuous delivery as a prerequisite, but not a subset, of continuous deployment. As Jez Humble puts it, even though "continuous deployment implies continuous delivery the converse is not true" [17]. This distinction allows us to cleanly separate the challenges related specifically to continuous deployment from those relevant to continuous delivery. It also lets us see that continuous deployment is not so much about software development, as it is about software operations.

To conclude, when we in this book use the term continuous deployment, we mean an operations practice where release candidates evaluated in continuous delivery are frequently and rapidly placed in a production environment, the nature of which may differ depending on technological context.

Continuous Release

This book is not about continuous release. Even so, we would spend a moment introducing the practice, if for no other reason than to delineate continuous deployment and clarify what it isn't.

Putting software into production does not necessarily equate making it available to users: consider practices such as limited deployments for feature experimentation, canary deployments and dark launches. Canary deployments and dark launches are similar practices, where deployments are made only to a small user base in order to test the software and collect feedback before exposing it to a larger user base – and to contain the damage in case of failures. The difference between a canary deployment and a dark launch, as we use the terms (just as with continuous practices, there is a certain level of confusion and careless use of jargon in the industry on this point), is that in a dark launch the feature is invisible to the end user. In other words, it is typically used to roll out the infrastructure and to monitor e.g. performance impacts in preparation of launching a feature.

In all of these practices, software is deployed to production without being made generally available. Conversely, as already explored, making software generally available does not necessarily equate deploying it to production, particularly in cases where there is no actual production environment under the producer's control.

This is where the continuous release practice comes into play. Continuous release is a business practice where release candidates evaluated in continuous delivery are frequently and rapidly made generally available to users and/or customers. From an engineering point of view there is really very little to it: assuming that continuous delivery is done right, continuous release should involve nothing more than pushing a button, if that. This is why we will not delve into any details on continuous release in this book – it is ultimately a question of business strategy and therefore outside of our scope.

Putting It All Together

Describing each practice by itself is all well and good, but we haven't so far considered the big picture – how those pieces connect to form a greater whole. If you will, we have so far identified the pieces of the jigsaw puzzle, but we haven't actually tried to put them together. Figure 1 shows how these pieces together form a continuous integration, delivery and deployment pipeline.

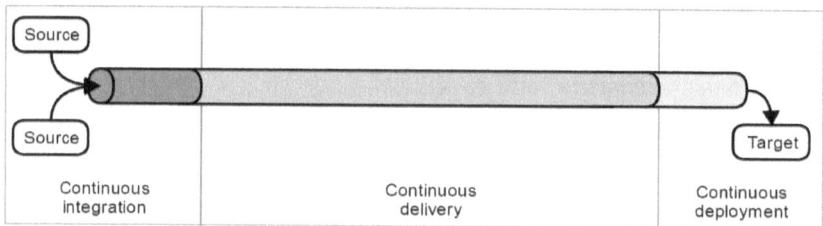

Figure 1: A continuous integration, delivery and deployment pipeline.

In this view, continuous delivery makes up the bulk of the pipeline itself; this is where the majority of testing, analysis, evaluation and promotion of the release candidate itself takes place. Continuous integration, on the other hand, is where those release candidates are created. In this sense it constitutes the instep of the pipeline, but continuous integration is more than that: it is the actual practice of frequently integrating the sources that go into making those release candidates, whether those sources are source code, media, third party libraries, component dependencies or documentation. Continuous deployment forms the very end of the pipeline, taking the release candidates and overseeing their deployment into the target environment.

Summary

In this chapter we started off by discussing semantics and why agreeing on what a word actually means is important. From there we moved on to take a closer look at continuous integration, delivery and deployment as individual practices and discussed the finer points of their definitions and how they relate to one another:

- Continuous integration is a developer practice where developers integrate their work frequently, usually each person integrates at least daily, leading to multiple integrations per day.

- Continuous delivery is a development practice where every change is treated as a potential release candidate to be frequently and rapidly evaluated through one's continuous delivery pipeline, and that one is always able to deploy and/or release the latest working version, but may decide not to, e.g. for business reasons.

- Continuous deployment is an operations practice where release candidates evaluated in continuous delivery are frequently and rapidly placed in a production environment, the nature of which may differ depending on technological context.

This has laid the foundation we need in order to tackle the challenges each practice represents, and to seize the opportunities they afford. Before we go there, however, there is one more definition we need to consider. Continuous practices do not exist in a vacuum of their own in the software engineering community. Often, they are mentioned in the same breath as another term, which is the subject of the next chapter: DevOps.

Chapter 3

DevOps

In the previous chapter we discussed each continuous practice in turn. Another popular term in the software engineering community is DevOps – often used in conjunction with or even interchangeably with one or another of the continuous practices. In other words, the same confusion plaguing the concept of continuous practices is very much prevalent in DevOps – particularly with regards to how it relates to continuous integration, delivery and deployment.

This book is not about DevOps; there are other excellent resources on that. Instead, in this chapter we will discuss the concept and what it means, seeking a point of view where it can serve to provide clarifying context rather than muddy the waters.

History

There are several accounts of how the DevOps movement originated and evolved [18, 19, 20]. In brief, DevOps was born out of frustration over the experienced divide between development and operations in most software projects. One early thought leader who identified this issue was Patrick Debois, who sowed the seeds of the DevOps movement at the Agile Conference of 2008 and subsequently began building a community around the need for "Agile System Administration", eventually leading up to the first DevOpsDays in 2009.

From that first DevOpsDays the community quickly expanded, drawing in practitioners from all over the world, sharing their experiences on integrating development with operations. A few years later this began to attract the attention of analysts and therefore large enterprises and tool vendors, who were eager to include DevOps in their service offerings and marketing messages. Since then the term DevOps has arguably become somewhat diluted, often used as a label to put on any tool, process or change program aiming at more effective, efficient, collaborative and/or simply better software engineering.

That being said, at its core DevOps is still an experience-based movement for practitioners, by practitioners [18]. As with the case of continuous practices, it is worth taking the time to define what we actually mean by the term, however. That way, at least within the context of this book, we can all agree on what we mean by DevOps and what falls inside its scope and what falls outside of it.

The Meaning of DevOps

Is DevOps the same as continuous delivery? Or the same as continuous deployment? A cursory reading of some sources will give the impression that this is the case. Indeed, usage of the term differs between sources [21] and some publications appear almost deliberately obtuse on this subject [11]. As Andrew Phillips puts it, "some people say continous delivery is the goal of DevOps, some people say DevOps is the [enabler of] continuous delivery" and "unfortunately [...] people use the terms almost interchangeably" [15]. A curious practitioner just entering the field, trying to understand what it all means, can certainly be forgiven for feeling bewildered.

We argue that just like the different continuous practices are in fact distinct from one another, DevOps should not be considered the same as – or worse, a vaguely defined expanded subset of – e.g. continuous delivery. In fact, there is what we would call a mainstream interpretation, where DevOps can be understood as a larger framework encompassing a number of principles, values, methods and practices, such as continuous delivery and continuous deployment [11]. This is similar to how pair programming is often described as an agile practice: there is more to Agile than pair programming, and you can do pair programming just fine without buying into anything else on the Agile smorgasbord. That being said, one's Agile experience may be more or less complete without the particular practice of pair programming, as the principles and values one aspires to may not be properly supported without it. The same holds true for DevOps and continuous practices: while DevOps is in theory entirely possible without continuous delivery and deployment, the rapidity, consistency and reliability those practices provide – when well executed – are an integral part of making DevOps possible (without making any point as to whether pair programming is equally integral to Agile). This view of DevOps is depicted in Figure 2.

Since DevOps is frequently described as a set of values, or even a culture – in fact there has been a great deal of resistance within the DevOps movement against defining something like a counterpart to the Agile manifesto – let's take a moment to reflect on the difference between a culture and a practice. Speaking of cultures and values is important, because they affect the decisions we make and the actions we take. What's more, culture can be very hard to change, and while the right culture can be a great asset, the wrong one can be fatal: culture beats strategy every time (while often attributed to Peter Drucker, slogans like "Culture eats strategy for breakfast" or "Culture trumps strategy" have a very long and not altogether obvious history). Consequently, the importance of adopting conducive values and fostering the right culture can hardly be overestimated.

That being said, as engineers and researchers we have a problem with culture and values: they are very hard to quantify, evaluate and ultimately to emulate effectively. Actual behavior, on the other hand, affects physical reality and has direct consequences. It can also be measured, analyzed and copied. From this point of view, culture is only important insofar as it influences that behavior. Conversely, one may exhibit a certain behavior for any number of reasons or based on any number of beliefs or values. To exemplify, a developer who integrates her work continuously may do so because of a culture that values avoiding big bangs, because she enjoys frequent test feedback or because she and her colleagues simply believe that code should never live long outside of the central repository. In the end it all leads to the same behavior.

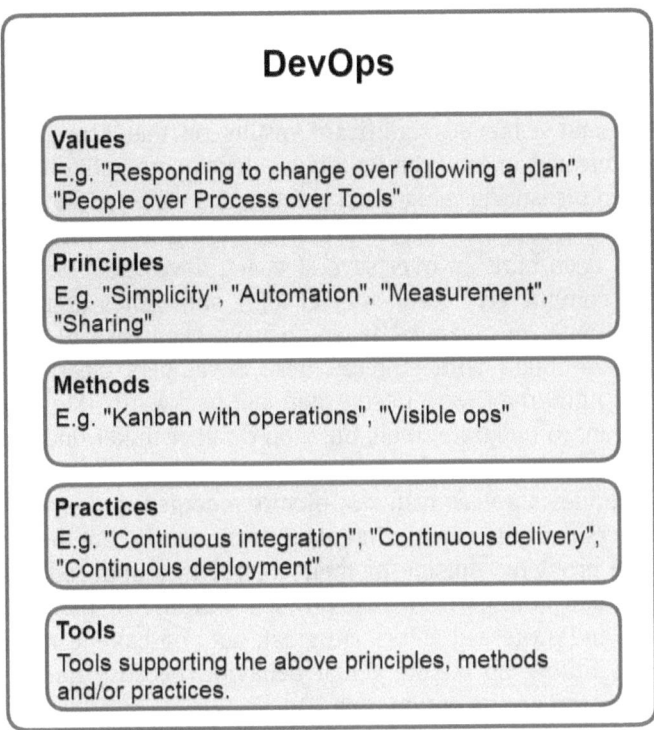

Figure 2: DevOps as consisting of values, principles, methods, practices and tools.

It is also worth pointing out that sometimes the best intentions and the most well meaning values in the world are not enough if the practical conditions are not right. That is why we in this book speak fairly little of cultures, and all the more about practices.

One very large project we studied had invested enormous amounts of effort and money into building their continuous delivery pipeline and achieved significant results on that score, but we were interested in how the individual developers behaved. When we began measuring integration frequencies we were surprised to find that despite the very impressive tooling and infrastructure that had been built up over several years, developers on average did not commit very frequently at all – sometimes as rarely as once a month, on average! It would have been easy to interpret this is a problem with culture: these developers clearly hadn't seen the light, they were uneducated and backwards, they simply didn't want to integrate often, but would rather tinker undisturbed in the comfort of their own private branch. When we followed up with interviews a very different picture emerged, however: these developers really wanted to integrate continuously, but there were all these problems outside of their control that impeded them. I learned many things from that project, and one of them is that cultures and professed values are great, but you have to make the effort to follow up on the actual behavior, because that's what ultimately affects the bottom line.

- Daniel

DevOps and Agile

Some will ask how DevOps relates to Agile: aren't the principles espoused by DevOps very similar to what Agile already established years before? The simple answer is yes, they are very similar. In fact, DevOps has been heavily influenced by Agile – after all, the original discussion group created by Patrick Debois before the first DevOpsDays was called "Agile System Administration".

One example of this is the DevOps Manifesto [22], one often cited take on what DevOps means (although as already pointed out, there are many who deplore such initiatives, and so it should not be construed as a universally accepted description of the phenomenon). It tweaks and slightly expands upon the Manifesto for Agile Software Development [9] to allow it to represent not only the Agile movement, but also the DevOps movement. This reveals that the underlying principles are the same, but while the Agile Manifesto is explicitly about software *development*, DevOps emphasizes the need to add *operations*. In this sense, Agile can be thought of as the older brother of DevOps, with the latter taking a similar approach but applying it to a larger problem.

Why Now?

An interesting question is why DevOps has become so popular now, and not before. Surely, smooth collaboration between development and operations is not a novel idea? Surely, organizations in the past ought to have seen the same issues and would have benefited equally as their counterparts today? It is of course difficult to determine the root cause of any historical movement with any certainty, but on a speculative note we would offer that the DevOps movement has gained traction due to several factors coming together to form the perfect storm – factors which are themselves closely connected to one another.

One such factor is the emergence of true cloud environments: environments where developers through a simple API call can gain access to and manage an environment matching their needs, if not in seconds then at least in minutes. The importance of this shift in how we go about engineering software can hardly be overestimated. As Adrian Cockroft puts it, "you can trivially do hardware experiments that last a few days on a huge scale, scattered all over the world, something that you wouldn't even think of doing if you had to tell your ops guys" [23]. It's a shift that also forces us to re-think what operations really is. It used to be that operations was about managing server racks and saving the day when an unexpected spike in traffic meant we needed an extra two servers configured and running, preferably yesterday. As cloud technologies increasingly generalize and hide that bare metal reality under layers of abstraction and put the controls directly in the hands of developers, operations becomes less a question of managing the environment and more about applying software development techniques to automating those tasks.

At the same time, the advent of continuous deployment has increased the need for developers to get directly involved and take greater responsibility for the production environment. No longer is it sufficient to say "it works in *my* environment" and hand the problem off to the operations side of the house: when your commit is automatically rolled out into production, any problem quickly becomes *your* problem. This drives the need for solutions that take a holistic perspective of the end-to-end process: from the point of view represented in Figure 2, it requires a larger framework of supporting values, principles and practices in which continuous deployment can function smoothly.

Last but not least, the rise of Software as a Service business models plays an important part. In the olden days, where user installed software was the norm, collaboration between development and operations was simply a non-issue: by definition, if someone else deploys and operates the software, DevOps is not applicable. In the world of Software as a Service, on the other hand, the tables have turned and suddenly operations and development share a common business goal, driving the need for homogenization and smooth collaboration.

Summary

In this chapter we have touched briefly upon DevOps: where it comes from, why it has gained popularity, what it means and how it relates to continuous practices and to Agile. Briefly put, when we in this book use the term DevOps we mean a set values, principles, methods, tools and practices – including continuous practices – used together to improve software development, delivery and operations. At this point we have gained sufficient an understanding of these practices and the context in which they exist to begin breaking them down into their basic elements.

Part II:
Understanding Your
Context

Chapter 4

Introduction

In this part we will discuss the importance of considering your context when adopting continuous practices. First we will discuss what the scope of these continuous practices actually is. While literature frequently presents a straight forward view of a pipeline transforming sources into deployed software in a live production environment, reality tends to be slightly more complicated: there are always libraries, components and third party products that are being pulled into that pipeline, and they in turn all have their own pipelines and in fact their own life cycles. Conversely, there is often some system (or system of systems) with which our software is integrating. Perhaps our software is a component integrated into a subsystem, which is then integrated into a full solution, which is then deployed into a larger network of products, which then forms part of the internet – a system of systems in its own right. Like a network of food chains, any continuous integration, delivery and deployment pipeline we choose to study is in effect interdependent on many other pipelines, and when we consider e.g. providing feedback to the developer we must also consider the complexity of traversing that network and how that may affect everything from tooling to behavior and expectations.

Following the concept of networks of pipelines, seven dimensions of contextual variability are introduced. These dimensions represent the fact that the software industry is incredibly diverse, and depending on which part of it you operate in, you will be constrained by different sets of rules. It is an often recognized fact that business-to-consumer (B2C) markets differ from business-to-business (B2B), but to capture the dynamics of continuous practices it is too crude a dichotomy to be meaningful. A software engineer in the B2C domain may find the challenges and constraints of another engineer working in the B2B domain very familiar, while at the same time having little in common with a third case in another B2C segment of the industry.

Instead, we find that there are multiple dimensions of variability, each of which impacts the feasibility, applicability and/or potential value of continuous practices in their own, unique ways. Together these dimensions form a variability space, into which any given case can be mapped in order to understand its possibilities and limitations. Only with that understanding can we hope to adopt practices in a strategic fashion based on realistic business value, rather than rushing into something out of fear of missing out. This is similar to the idea behind tools such as Business Model Canvas[2] – just as it's a good idea to map out your value proposition and your customers and your channels before setting up your business, it's a good idea to understand the context in which your software operates before deciding how to produce it.

Each of the variability dimensions is explained in a separate chapter. Note that we in this part of the book will not go too much into solutions to the challenges posed by specific areas in this variability space, but rather focus on highlighting and exemplifying the issues.

Before going into the details of understanding context, a number of archetypes of software engineering cases are introduced. These have been selected to cover as large an area of the variability space as possible. The archetypes will serve to exemplify the notion of networks of pipelines along with the variability dimensions and their significance for each archetype. We will then return to these archetypes and use them throughout the book, striving to explain new concepts through exemplification. Perhaps one or two of these archetypes will match your own experiences closely enough that you can learn directly from their struggles and achievements – if not, then regard them as a guide to analyzing your own context and adopting continuous practices that suit your particular needs.

Before moving on to these archetypes, we would like to point something out that is easily overlooked. Not all of the ways in which we differ – what we in this book think of as dimensions of variability – are

---

2   https://strategyzer.com

set in stone. They do not necessarily define us, even if we too often allow them to define our thinking. Too rarely do most of us challenge why things are the way they are, or whether they really need to be that way. If your current development project employs over a thousand engineers, and by reading this book you realize that this in itself is an impediment, then maybe, just maybe, there is a way for you to reduce the size of your development effort, or at the very least identify seams along which it may be split into more or less autonomous parts. And if your distribution model is not amenable to continuous practices or your customers are hesitant to let you deploy continuously, then possibly there might be a way for you to remove that obstacle, rather than adapting and building your way around it.

But then again, perhaps not. Sometimes we just have to make the most of the cards we're dealt. What we would like you to keep in the back of your mind when you continue on this journey with us is this: do not *only* read this book as a way of understanding how to make continuous practices work in your context, but *also* as a way of understanding how a slightly different context might better support continuous practices.

Chapter 5

Archetypes

In this chapter we introduce a number of hypothetical software developers, chosen to represent various segments of the industry. They are designed to cover as wide a swathe of the software industry as possible, and will be used for two purposes in this book. First, in the next few chapters, they will be used to communicate and elucidate the types of variability we see in the industry. Second, in Parts III and IV, they will be used to exemplify and highlight particular situations and challenges in adopting continuous practices.

Something we discussed a lot while writing the book was the use of these archetypes. We wanted to make them come alive almost like real persons, but at the same time not be identical to specific individuals or cases in the real world. Our archetypes are based on a mix of our own experiences, our previous research projects and other studies. As we have combined different bits and pieces from many different sources, none of the archetypes reflects the exact situation at any single company. This is important to bear in mind: the archetypes are realistic, but not real.

- Torvald

Jane

Jane develops part of the software of a military fighting vehicle. This vehicle contains a wide array of systems – communications, engine control, steering, sensors, target acquisition, countermeasures et cetera – which are all controlled by software in a distributed and highly redundant real time system. As such, the software tends to be tightly coupled: the changes Jane makes to her component can potentially impact any other part of the system, and therefore any one of her 150 colleagues.

Jane's customers are not individual consumers or even businesses, but national governments. As such, they are not numerous, but they have plenty of particular requirements and exert influence not only on the end result of the development, but also the nature of the development, which is strictly regulated.

The intense focus on complying with regulations, (many of them related to information security), leads to several effects on Jane and her colleagues. One is that repeatedly throughout the project, the overriding business concern becomes not only to develop a working product, but also to demonstrate compliance. Another is that certain parts of the product are classified, and access to information about them – how they function, what their requirements are, their source code – is restricted, making collaboration, troubleshooting and communication at a holistic system level even more challenging.

Furthermore, contracts are signed and requirements agreed many years prior to expected delivery. Even after delivery – despite support, updates and maintenance being part of the overall deal – daily deployments of software are not an option, as long term self-sustained offline operations are a strict requirement. Instead, the customer expects the system to not only function without faults but also to remain impervious to hacker attacks for several years without updates. The last part is particularly difficult since the vehicle is not an isolated entity, but an integrated part of electronic tactical and strategic command and control systems.

Testing Jane's product is both challenging and expensive. One challenge is that testing the full system on target requires an actual test vehicle – something that is not only very costly, but for a significant part of the software project doesn't even exist yet. Verification of several of the components, particularly human-machine interfaces, cannot be automated since the definition of correct behavior is not quantifiable, but up to the subjective perception of what feels right to the user. Consequently, software changes progress through a hierarchy of increasingly holistic and realistic tests: from unit and component tests through simulated environments all the way to eventual live testing in the actual vehicle. Meanwhile, the development of sufficiently realistic simulators represents a significant engineering undertaking in itself.

Bob

Bob is one of approximately 50 developers building an advertisement funded social media platform, available both as a web site and as a mobile device app, both served by the same cloud deployed backend service.

Bob's company values the ability to quickly push changes into production, receive real time feedback and then take rapid action based upon that feedback. In a typical working day, Bob tends to push at least one change into production, either to the web frontend, the backend service or both. Many of these changes revolve around implementing and acting upon A/B tests to optimize the service based on user behavior. The mobile device app goes through slightly longer update cycles, because it is distributed through third party app stores.

The users of the social media platform are individual consumers, who have little to say about the rapid pace of deployments to the web service, to the extent that they even notice. Despite some fairly rigorous automated testing as part of the pipeline, bad updates do slip through into production from time to time. This is not considered a critical problem, however. One reason is that the rapid deployments allows speedy recovery, and the other reason is the practice of performing canary deployments – every new version is deployed to a small fraction of the infrastructure, and only if that works is it installed across the board. In fact, due to the high frequency of deployments, at any given time there is a number of versions being rolled out concurrently. Bob and his colleagues tend to think of these updates as waves rolling across an ocean, and speak of them as "update waves".

Unlike some of our other archetypes, the software Bob commits is not integrated into any larger system context, but pushed straight into production. On a more philosophical note, though, that isn't entirely true. Just as the fighting vehicle developed by Jane is ultimately integrated into tactical and strategic command and control systems, Bob's software is integrated into another system of systems, albeit a rather loosely connected one: the Internet.

Mary

Mary works in a large scale project developing a networking solution. Similarly to Jane, it is an embedded software system running on custom hardware, but large parts of it are highly abstracted from the physical interfaces and written in programming languages that most developers would be familiar with.

The solution developed by Mary and her colleagues is split into a large number of components of varying sizes. Some of them are developed by a single team of four or five developers, while Mary's component is actively worked upon by more than 500. This means that even though the component is very frequently updated, producing dozens of new versions every day, Mary herself doesn't commit her code all that often. Instead, she prefers to integrate with the members of her immediate team and thoroughly test their changes before submitting them to the shared development branch, to minimize the risk of introducing any faults that would cause trouble for the in excess of 500 engineers co-inhabiting the same source code.

Even so, thoroughly testing the product is a lengthy and resource intensive process. Beyond unit and component testing, Mary's project relies extensively on simulators to test the system – and similarly to Jane's project, building those simulators is no small effort in itself. Testing on target is also required, however, and since the product is built on custom hardware it's impossible to simply throw additional generic server racks at the problem: test equipment is expensive, and there is never enough of it.

The customers of the system are a handful of network operators and government agencies. These have mixed feelings about software being continuously deployed to their live networks. On the one hand they are very enthusiastic about quickly and cheaply receiving new features and performance enhancements, but on the other they are deeply concerned about the quality of that software: a network outage, even for a few minutes or even seconds, is not an option. Indeed, some customers use the software in a medical setting where critical failures could be directly life threatening. As a consequence, constant compliance with FDA regulations is a significant concern to Mary and her colleagues, as they must always be ready to display satisfactory documentation and traceability in case auditors pay them an unexpected visit.

John

As a computer games developer, John may be the archetype that most closely resembles the stereotypical linear pipeline from sources to production. While game development projects come in many shapes and sizes, John's is fairly small and straight forward. It involves a total of eight people in mixed roles and responsibilities, of which three are predominantly software developers, four are predominantly content creators and one is dedicated quality assurance. Even though a number of libraries and frameworks for e.g. graphics and audio are integrated, they are very stable and rarely change through the project's life cycle. All the source code along with all media and other resources are stored in a single source repository, to which both developers and content creators commit several times on any normal working day.

The game is user installed and targets both the PC and the console markets, and is distributed through an online digital distribution platform. The game is supported post-release through a number of planned patches, content updates and purchasable expansions. The main event, though, by which the product is ultimately judged by both consumers and media, is the official launch date of the game.

By this logic, John's life working on the game is very clearly separated into two parts: pre-launch and post-launch. Pre-launch there is no such thing as release or deployment: the software is a strictly internal affair, and the closest thing to user feedback is that from quality assurance. Post-launch is different: user feedback and bug reports are streaming in, and the pressure is on to fix all the issues experienced by customers. There is no such thing as deployment, though: John and his colleagues can produce a steady stream of updates, but it is ultimately up to the users to download and install them. In this sense, John's case can be viewed as falling somewhere in a gray zone between continuous delivery and deployment. In Chapter 13 we will look closer at various modes of distribution and how their consequences.

Last but not least, John is keenly aware of the fine line between too many updates – where consumers are annoyed by the frequent patches and changes – and too few.

Alice

Alice is our final archetype. Like Bob and John she works in a business-to-consumer segment of the industry, but unlike them she works very closely to physical hardware in a mechatronic and safety critical system: she develops software for one of the electronic control units (ECUs) that forms part of the steering system in a car. The car as a whole contains dozens of such electronic control units, all running their own dedicated software.

Software development in Alice's case is strongly dictated by the AUTOSAR architecture and is strictly focused on managing the individual ECUs, their interfaces and their interactions. The overall system design is not so much a software concern, as it is a hardware concern. Rather than being integrated directly with the software of other ECUs, the software of each unit is instead integrated with the controlling logic built into its hardware, which then signals other units – signals which are interpreted and processed in the consuming unit's hardware before being passed on to its software.

The actual amount of software in these electronic control units is not large. Measured in lines of code, Alice's system is the smallest of all the archetypes[3], and there are less than ten in-house software development

---

3   This point may seem controversial to some. At the time of writing, the lines of code reported from the automotive industry vary by orders of magnitude. From studies and collaboration with professionals in the

teams for the entire vehicle system. Instead, the vast majority of the effort in the project is being expended on integration of and signaling between the hardware components, and their interactions with the mechanical systems.

The software Alice develops is built and unit tested by an automated continuous integration server, and Alice keeps a physical ECU on her desk to manually try out her changes before checking them in. Every other day a dedicated system integration team picks up their latest version, which is tested in conjunction with a selection of other ECUs. Then, further down the line, Alice's software is tested in an actual vehicle running the complete set of ECUs of the system on target hardware. This enables testing of the software and its interactions with all its collaborators in a complete system context under realistic conditions.

The exact configuration of both software and hardware is always in flux, however: there is no such thing as a stable set of units and software revisions that can be thoroughly tested and then reproduced in all produced units. Instead, every vehicle coming off the assembly line represents a more or less unique configuration of hardware and software – a variability space which is impossible to cover for every requirement.

In terms of pipeline network, Alice lives near the bottom of the food chain: there is very little in terms of software dependencies, and the code Alice develops is in the form of fairly short snippets processing and responding to specific signals from the hardware. From her point of view, she is unable to identify any particular make or model as her production environment – indeed, her particular ECU is not even included in every car. Instead, the closest thing she has is the system integration node in the pipeline network. That being said, Alice still requires feedback from that node and others further up the food chain to better understand her place in the larger solution, and how she affects the car as a whole through the changes she makes to her electronic control unit.

---

industry, we suspect that some figures are due to the use of differing measurement practices and reporting incentives. We find that actual numbers are likely in the very low end of the spectrum reported publicly, while granting that there is a high degree of variability.

To make things more interesting, not every ECU is developed in-house. Instead, many are pulled in – hardware and software – from third party vendors, many of whom in turn also supply other (competing) car manufacturers. This impacts Alice and her colleagues, because a large part of the day-to-day work is troubleshooting integration problems between these ECUs. This requires traceability from their sources into the system integration to help them pinpoint any problem in their own code, but also – in an ideal scenario – into the sources of collaborating ECUs, or at the very least quick and frictionless communication channels to their developers. For in-house units this is less of a problem, for two reasons. First, Alice can, at least in theory, easily walk over to their desks and start a conversation in front of a whiteboard. Second, because Alice and her colleagues can actually design the pipelines of all their in-house ECUs and build the needed traceabilitiy into it. That does not mean this is always done, however, more for reasons of mindset and engineering background than for technical reasons; we will have reason to return to this in subsequent chapters. But in the case of third party suppliers this can become a major hassle: what they supply is not software, but physical boxes with certain expected behaviors. The software running in those boxes is completely invisible to Alice and her teammates, and patching it can mean anything from downloading and manually flashing it themselves, to shipping it back to the supplier and waiting for an update to arrive by mail (not the electronic kind). Of course, this entire process becomes particularly enervating when all communication takes place via supply managers and bug reports and coordinators of one kind of the other, rather than engineer to engineer.

A Word of Caution

What we have described in this chapter is five archetypical software engineers, and by extension segments of the software industry, based on research, personal experiences and collaborations. They are not laws of nature, and they are not valid for every engineer and every case within their respective industry segments.

We wish to stress this point in order to avoid any misunderstandings. When we, for instance, discuss Alice's ordeals in integrating ECUs and dealing with third party suppliers, this should not be taken to mean that this is the case for every car manufacturing company, and always will be. Alice and the other archetypes are simply hypothetical personae to help illustrate, personify and elucidate the challenges and opportunities of continuous practices. Nothing more, and nothing less.

This note of caution equally applies to subsequent chapters, where we return to these archetypes to further elaborate on their challenges and opportunities, while adding more detail to their respective contexts. For instance, when we in Chapter 11 go into Mary's struggles with large organizations and unhelpful software architectures, that does not mean that all networking systems are poorly designed. Similarly, John's customer relations dilemma in Chapter 8 and his consequent inability to deploy too frequently does not mean that it is impossible to continuously deploy computer games.

Summary

In this chapter we have introduced five fictional software developers: Jane, Bob, Mary, John and Alice (summarized in Figure 3). They all work in different segments of the industry, and operate under very different rules. In the next few chapters we will look in greater depth at how they differ and what the impact of those differences are on the applicability, feasibility and value of continuous practices.

Archetype	Industry segment
Jane	Defense
Bob	Social media
Mary	Networks
Alice	Automotive
John	Computer games

Figure 3: Archetypes summary.

Chapter 6

Networks of Pipelines

Software developers who have never found themselves integrating software delivered to them by a third party or by a different group within their projects are few and far between, at least outside of artificially constructed and constrained learning environments. Similarly, most have at some point delivered software into another context, to be integrated into a larger system or environment or system of systems. We all pull in software made by others, we all hand software over to some other, larger context. Yet simply reading literature on continuous practices one might be fooled into thinking that all software development starts with a repository of source code and ends in a perfectly isolated production environment, with a neat sequential chain of steps in between, all with a clear one-to-one relationship. As is so often the case, however, reality is more complicated than that.

In this chapter we discuss what a system is. First of all, though, let us be clear that we believe there really is no such thing as "The System", in the sense of a neatly delineated entity existing in supreme isolation and independence from the surrounding environment. There's always something you deliver into, an environment with which to integrate, and almost always someone you accept deliveries from. Like predators and prey in a wildlife ecosystem, software also forms complicated networks of food chains, where each node may be considered a pipeline in its own right. In other words, a software production system is rarely so much a pipeline as it is an intricate network of pipelines. And for each such pipeline, receiving and giving feedback to others in the network is vital for understanding the full picture. And just as in nature, many such networks are extremely vast and complicated, while some are slightly less so.

In Chapter 1 we introduced the concept of a continuous integration, delivery and deployment pipeline. Figure 4 illustrates what a network of pipelines might look like. In this simplistic network of three pipelines, continuous integration, delivery and deployment are shown as as dark, medium and light gray, respectively. Note that the first two pipelines are continuous integration and delivery pipelines – they do not actually deploy, because in this example they do not produce any finished product, but rather libraries or components. This is an important point to emphasize. In literature, pipelines are often described as transforming sources to finished products, while in practice, these pipelines may produce any number of intermediate artifact types: libraries, media, textual documentation, executables and so on.

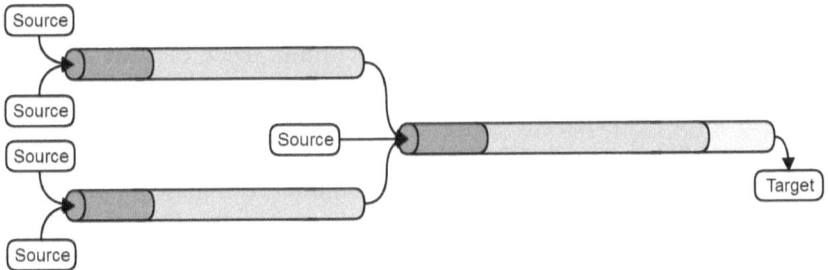

Figure 4: A network of pipelines.

The rightmost pipeline, on the other hand, includes continuous integration, delivery and deployment. It continuously integrates its own sources as well as the output from its dependency pipelines into release candidates, which are then evaluated in continuous delivery, and eventually promoted to be continuously deployed to the target environment.

Note that integration of software between pipelines (e.g. triggering the rightmost pipeline in Figure 4) can be based either on push or pull mechanisms. Schedule based mechanism are also an alternative, although they serve little purpose except being easy to implement. As a consequence, we generally advise against them. Which trigger mechanism to choose comes down to the relationship between the pipelines and how dependencies are identified, something we will return to in Chapter 16 and Chapter 21.

Furthermore, the pipelines are not independent in the sense that the activities performed – or not performed – in one pipeline affects which activities ought to be performed – or not performed – in another. This ties in with the concept of pushing test value down the pyramid of system modules [24]. What can be tested early in a small system scope doesn't need to be tested later in a larger (and presumably more expensive) scope. Translated to the idea of pipelines, the more testing is done in the leftmost pipelines of Figure 4, the less needs to be tested in the rightmost pipeline, and vice versa.

That software production systems are rarely so much straight pipelines as they are intricate networks may certainly sound like bad news, but it's not only a complication: it is also a tool. As we will look into further in Part IV: Onboarding the Organization, achieving actual continuous integration behavior in very large organizations is extremely challenging. This is why breaking a monolithic piece of software into separate parts with a higher degree of autonomy – in effect, expanding a single pipeline into a network of pipelines – is a proven method of circumventing those challenges. It doesn't come without its own problems and a certain degree of overhead, but it can untie the hands of developers and allow them to progress more rapidly. Doing that can never be an excuse to retreat from a holistic view of the solution, however: any developer worth her salt needs to understand her place in that network and how her actions affect others. That understanding doesn't appear magically, but requires traceability, a subject we will introduce in this chapter and then revisit in greater depth in Part III: Building the Pipeline.

Finally, it's important to understand that pipelines are not branches. Branching of source code operates in another dimension altogether, where multiple versions of the same asset exist in parallel. In a network of pipelines, on the other hand, every pipeline produces a separate part of one or more larger software systems.

A Case in Point

As we outlined in Chapter 5, this complicated web of pipelines is very much a part of Alice's day-to-day struggles developing one of many ECUs of a car. The requirements she receives and the expectations on her as a developer are for the electronic control unit she is working on – a unit which is integrated into the system not as a software component, but as an actual, physical box hooked up by wires to other ECUs and vehicle systems.

Alice's team practices continuous integration, committing their changes to their unit at least once a day and rebuilding and testing it for each commit. Furthermore, each one of those commits is treated as a release candidate in the sense that it could potentially be shipped off and deployed to a car – but that doesn't mean that it is continuously integrated with its collaborators or the larger system of the vehicle, much less released or deployed to actual consumers. Quite the opposite: a dedicated integration team flashes the ECU and tries it out in a system context, a process which takes three or four days on average. To circumvent this, a virtual integration environment that simulates the hardware and wiring has been created, allowing changes to be tested in minutes rather than days. These tests are used solely for feedback to the developers, however, not for promoting the software change towards delivery or deployment.

This begs the question, are Alice and her teammates practicing continuous integration and delivery? Clearly the answer is both yes and no, depending on the scope one considers. This is why answers to this type of questions so often need to be qualified to be meaningful. Within the limited scope of their electronic control unit – a scope itself larger than some complete products – they are. Zooming out, however, within the scope of the car as a whole, they clearly aren't. Moreover, it is quite conceivable for another ECU to not continuously integrate at all. In summary, it is perfectly possible to simultaneously practice continuous integration in one part of the network of pipelines, while not in another.

As a matter of fact, a significant portion of the lead time in getting a new feature into a car is resolving errors in integration with other ECUs, mainly because it takes time to receive feedback in case of problems. In other words, looking at Figure 4, Alice's main pain point is the later, right-most pipeline, which consumes the output of each ECU.

Another Case in Point

Let us take a look at Mary and her networking solution, instead. In some ways, Mary would be very familiar with Alice's situation. In others, their realities are complete opposites. Mary's product is similarly modularized, but first of all, the integrated entity is a piece of software (more precisely, binaries derived from the source code) rather than a physical box of metal and plastic. In addition, in Mary's case significant efforts have been spent building a continuous delivery pipeline on a system level. As a consequence, the next consuming node in the network of pipelines is much faster and operates at a higher frequency than in Alice's case. The moment a new component is published it is pulled in and tested with all its collaborators, and feedback is automatically sent back to the individual developers in real time.

This is great news, except the component Mary is working on is huge, and she doesn't commit to it very often, for a number of reasons. Although she and her teammates frequently commit to their team branch, several weeks will pass between their commits to the shared development branch. But when you multiply that with the hundreds of developers working on that component, you get a very steady stream of new release candidates.

Clearly, a relevant question to ask is why Mary only commits every few weeks, rather than daily, as prescribed by continuous integration doctrine. There are multiple reasons, which we will return to, particularly in Chapter 11. That being said, let us repeat that we merely present this as an illustrative example (albeit, in our experience, a representative one), and not as any law governing any one industry segment.

If we were to ask the same question as in Alice's case – does Mary practice continuous integration? – the answer is not obvious. Unlike Alice's case, in the larger scope software is frequently integrated and new versions are built, ready to be evaluated in the continuous delivery pipeline. Even so, what the individual developers are practicing is anything but continuous integration, as the merging of their changes with their colleagues is a very infrequent event (with the exception of those who happen to be located in the same organizational unit). While Alice can at least claim to practice continuous integration in a small part of the of the larger system, Mary can make no such claim. Instead, she frequently integrates the entire system with a small part of the organization, which is a very different way of working.

In terms of the simplistic network depicted in Figure 4, Mary's problems are localized to the left-most part. Once a change has been integrated into the first pipeline, the journey downstream is much smoother sailing than in Alice's case. Again, when talking about continuous practices we need to qualify that: continuous practices in what context?

A Counter-Example

Unlike Mary and Alice, John is not overly concerned with integrating with some larger system context from which he may receive angry mails at some point in the future. His closest equivalent is the guy in quality assurance, with the main difference that the end product that eventually ends up in the hands of the customer – and is sent over to QA – is something he can build, view and play with on his laptop. Therefore, continuous integration and delivery looks much more like a pipeline to John than it does to Mary and Alice, if only because he, unlike them, is at the top of a much shorter software food chain.

If one were to wax philosophical, one might argue that the game is in fact integrated into a wide array of larger systems at the customer: the particular combination of operating system, hardware and drivers of each end user. This is true, in the same sense that Bob's social media web service is integrated with the internet, but with the significant difference that these are very highly standardized environments. Therefore, it is perfectly feasible for John to simply set up a set of reference computers and test his changes on those, assuming they cover the vast majority of customer environments.

He is similarly unconcerned with his own dependencies, such as graphics rendering libraries and audio frameworks. At the start of the project he picked the latest and greatest of what he needed, and only on occasion had reason to change that. There is certainly no need for him to continually and automatically pull in new versions as they become available – he greatly prefers to keep his baseline stable. As for the in-house developed software, John and his team prefer to keep it all in a single repository, for the simple reason that they have seen little reason to split it up.

In other words, if we were to ask John whether he practices continuous integration and/or delivery he wouldn't hesitate the way Mary or Alice might. Of course he does, he would tell us – he commits multiple times a day to the central repository, and every commit is automatically tested and built into a new installable package.

The Importance of Traceability

In a complicated network of pipelines, it is of paramount importance to keep track of where your software is and where it is going. There are multiple stakeholders who require that information to work effectively. One is the software developer who needs to understand where the code she committed half an hour ago is, where it was deployed, if it was tested okay and whether it caused any problems downstream from her. Another is the product owner who wants to know where in the pipeline his prioritized feature is, and how close it is to being released to the customer who is waiting for it. A third is the manager who needs to monitor the performance of the development organization and discover any bottlenecks in the network where changes pile up without making their way through to production.

All of this comes down to traceability. Whenever you say traceability, different people may get different ideas, and there certainly are very distinct ways to think about it. At its core it's about understanding what happened why in a given process – in our case a software development process. The traditional approach to this, and what many think of when they hear the word traceability, is looking into documentation and meeting protocols and memos and logs and doing audits and, in a general sense, playing detective. That certainly is one way of doing it, but questions of cost efficiency aside, that simply is not sufficient for continuous practices. Continuous practices place a number of specific demands on your traceability methods [25], the most important of which is that the trace links – the data that tells you how something is related to something else, such as a source revision implementing a requirement – can not be be generated manually *ex post facto*, but must be automatically generated *in situ*. In other words, what is needed is a real time self-documenting pipeline that allows you and any other stakeholders, including regulatory supervisors, to answer the fundamental question of what the blazes is actually going on. We will have cause to return to this topic – what this form of traceability can be used for and how to build it into your pipeline – throughout this book. In particular, we will be looking into techniques to achieve this type of traceability and to derive insights from it in Chapter 15.

One developer I interviewed for a case study described his job like this: When you commit code it's like tossing it into a black hole; then you get angry mails back a few weeks later. We see variants of this theme over and over again in large-scale software development projects, and it all boils down to traceability: where did my change go, who picked it up, how was it tested, where was it tested, how did it go, was it deployed and so forth. In a continuous practices context, those questions need to be answered in real time, not in a manually compiled spreadsheet or a fancy slide deck at next week's leadership team meeting. This point can hardly be overemphasized, particularly as many like to espouse the importance of developers taking end-to-end responsibility for the software they produce. When they don't it's rarely because they're lazy or incompetent. Rather, it's because it's really hard to take responsibility for something you can't see. So if you want your developers to take greater responsibility, start by giving them the means.

- Daniel

Saving the question of concrete tools and techniques for Part III: Building the Pipeline, when starting out from a position of low visibility across pipelines, and consequently across the various parts and hierarchical levels of one's software, it is important to consider which questions are important to answer, and from which pipelines the information needed to answer those questions must be gathered. As a concrete example, one of Jane's colleagues is quality responsible for the rangefinder component in the military vehicle, and the majority of his day-to-day questions can not be answered by testing that component itself, but by testing the vehicle's weapon targeting subsystem to accurately track a target. In other words, to effectively do his job, the traceability he is in greatest need of is from the weapon targeting subsystem's pipeline – situated downstream from the rangefinder component. Mapping out such needs in the organization provides a good starting point on the journey towards cross-pipeline transparency and traceability.

A sometimes overlooked fact is that traceability is critical for regulations compliance. The core message of nearly any major regulatory body is this: We want you to apply sound Software Lifecycle Management practices to your software development. This means keeping track of what was changed, who changed it, when it was changed, why it was changed, and how you know it works as you expect it to work. To comply with the regulations, you need to show documentation to that effect, whenever the auditors come knocking at your door. We will delve deeper into this in Chapter 12.

Summary

In this chapter we have shown that even though we like to talk about the process of turning source code into live services in production as a pipeline, we must be aware that it is a gross simplification. In most cases, reality is closer to a network of interdependent pipelines, all feeding and being fed by one another, not unlike the network of food chains in an ecosystem. And just as in the wild, some ecosystems are much more intricate and colorful than others. All the same, though, when considering the question of whether you practice continuous integration, delivery or deployment, or to what extent you would like to, it's important to also consider in what context: which parts of the ecosystem should be continuously integrated, delivered, deployed and/or released, respectively?

In other words, we argue that continuous practices can't be simplified to developers committing to a mainline and building frequent release candidates from that – it also includes integration of subsystems, modules, binaries and libraries from any number of mainlines. This is why continuous practices are not a black and white phenomenon, but there exists a gray zone of varying degrees of adoption of continuous practices throughout the network of pipelines. Furthermore, that variability should not be brushed off as being down to the engineers being laggards, late adopters or generally dimwitted; there may be perfectly good reasons for it.

Over the course of this book we will frequently use the term "a pipeline," even though we have just established that reality tends to be much more complicated than that term implies. We do this for the sake of readability – rather than typing out "a network of pipelines" or "a software production system" or some other awkward term, we find that the shorter and more colloquial term of "a pipeline" makes for a better reading experience.

Similarly, though the term "release candidate" is used throughout the book, its meaning is not immediately clear given a network of pipelines. What constitutes a release candidate in a network of dozens of pipelines all consuming one another's output? For the sake of consistency, we will use "release candidate" to refer to the artifacts created and evaluated by any pipeline, regardless of its place in any larger context. In other words, a "release candidate" may refer to a component as well as a complete solution, unless otherwise stated.

In the next few chapters we will explore other facets of variability, which serve as a tool for finding answers to which continuous practices can be valuable or even feasible in any given situation. When you read those chapters, keep in mind that when considering an entire network or ecosystem of pipelines, those answers may not be the same across the entirety of that network.

Chapter 7

Safety Criticality

Sometimes you will hear developers or even researchers argue that testing is really for cowards (though using slightly less polite wording) and that the whole idea of trying to prevent faults from getting into production is outdated. Instead, under slogans such as "following the hacker way", in the brave new world of continuous deployment, developers should just get their code out there, and fix it if it breaks.

The ability to very rapidly deploy new software and study its effects – and therefore also to very rapidly react to any problems and deploy a fix – does open up new possibilities. The argument that this ability gives us reason to reconsider old conceptions of what quality is certainly has merit, but we would wager that anyone who espouses the view that testing is pointless and it's all about reacting to faults as they occur in production, has never worked on a safety critical system. Because when that fault that does occur in production doesn't just inconvenience an online shopper, but disconnects an emergency call or crashes an airliner, then the hacker way suddenly appears less glamorous than it does criminally reckless.

In fact, this is an excellent case in point why considering these dimensions of one's context is so important. If all you have experienced is one extreme of the spectrum, then it's understandable that you're not cognizant of what being at the other end implies. If all your software engineering experiences are from projects where the worst case scenario is that the web service goes down for a while and you lose out on revenue, then skipping tests in order to more quickly get into production makes a certain amount of sense. And if it works for you, then why would anyone else want to work differently? This applies to all of the dimensions of variability we present in this book.

The Archetypes

Let us consider safety criticality from the perspectives of our software engineering archetypes. If we were to plot the archetypes from Chapter 5 onto a scale from high to low safety criticality, it would look something like Figure 5.

Figure 5: The Safety Criticality dimension.

As we can see, this scale is highly polarized. While it is difficult to objectively quantify something as complex as safety criticality, what the scale shows is that at the far left we find the three archetypes where a software failure is likely to cause deaths, injuries and/or significant disruption of society. On the right hand side, on the other hand, we find the two archetypes where software failures can cause little beyond end user inconvenience and/or monetary damage to the company. The reason Bob is slightly farther to the left than John on the scale is that Bob's social media platform does handle sensitive information and account details of its users – information that wouldn't cause widespread devastation by any means, but that would be unfortunate if it ended up in the wrong hands. John's game, meanwhile, does not handle sensitive information at all – there's not even any handling of payment or licenses, which is all taken care of by the online distribution platform.

As a consequence, Bob's team have consciously split their pipelines, so that depending on the part of the product that is touched, more or less rigorous testing regimes are applied to it before letting it through into production. Anything that touches on the user information storage in particular is not only tested for known vulnerabilities, but also manually reviewed. Changes to the web frontend are subjected only to a bare minimum of sanity checks, though, in order to keep the time from change to deployment and subsequent feedback as low as possible. In fact, Bob performs regular testing in the production environment, not least in the form of A/B testing of new features and interface layout.

Jane, Alice and Mary face more dramatic consequences of software faults. Just as in Bob's case, however, not all parts of their respective products are as critical. Alice's car features a built-in infotainment system, any malfunction of which doesn't register much higher on the scale than John's game. Similarly, much of the software in Mary's networking solution doesn't revolve around the actual routing of traffic, but performs auxiliary functions such as network management, logging and self-monitoring. While bad, a temporary failure in these parts is unlikely to put anyone in physical danger.

A closer look at the industry reveals that this is in fact very often the case, and most of us have experienced this first hand: various functions of any given software system are more or less safety critical. This is one reason why Bob's approach of breaking that system down into parts with separate pipelines and separate testing policies can be very valuable, as it lets you test what needs to be tested where it is needed, and yet maintain speed and responsiveness where possible.

If you think back to Chapter 6, you will see that this relates to the network of pipelines and how the complexity of such a network is not only a challenge, but also a tool. Thinking of your software production system less in terms of a linear pipeline and more in terms of a network gives you the means of situating tests where they are truly required.

This is true regardless of whether that network of pipelines has one or multiple exit points – in theory, anyway. In practice, if the system is built into a single delivered entity, as in Jane's case, there are likely requirements to the effect that the holistic system needs to be tested for certain safety critical elements. This is particularly the case when operating in a highly regulated context. With that caveat in mind, let us consider Jane's military vehicle and Bob's social media platform, respectively. The backend, the mobile device app and the web frontend of Bob's product are all deployed separately – in other words, the network of pipelines has multiple exit points. In this case it is not difficult to see how different testing regimes can be applied to them. Meanwhile, Jane's software product is highly coupled and deployed to the target environment as a single package (although distributed across multiple real time computers spread across the vehicle), but before that integration point each component has its own test scope based on its potential to disrupt the larger system. In such a scenario, intelligent dynamic scoping of tests is a more suitable solution, which we will return to in Part III: Building the Pipeline.

Summary

In this section we have looked at how safety criticality affects continuous software engineering practices, and considered the challenges and opportunities of our archetypes. What we find is that a high degree of safety criticality means that a software system – or at least parts of it – require more rigorous testing than non-critical software systems, because no matter how quickly you recover from a fault it isn't quickly enough if the fault ends up causing death or serious injury.

Closely related to the contextual dimension of safety criticality is the question of regulatory compliance, which we will return to in Chapter 12, and producing and managing documentation (e.g. Functional Safety documentation), which is touched upon in Chapter 18.

Chapter 8

Power Balance

Developing and selling software for a living can be a curious experience, not least when dealing with highly intense and active customers. Unfortunately, not all customers are of a mind. For instance, what do you do in a situation where a large customer, upon whom the future of your business hinges, comes to you and tells you they are now all into this DevOps thing, and they want you to explain to them how you are going to be "working according to DevOps" and continuously deploying your enormous software solution to them within a year? And then you have another, almost equally large and important customer tell you that they have no interest in continuous deployment, they just want an annual release, but on the other hand you better make sure there are no critical faults in it, because they have zero tolerance for downtime and the FDA is breathing down their neck to demonstrate hazard mitigation?

Anyone who cannot relate to that predicament should count themselves lucky: chances are they are at one end of the Power Balance spectrum, where the software producer sets the rules. This could be either because the customers don't care or because they'll just have to live with it. Anyone to whom that scenario is familiar, on the other hand, might find themselves at the opposite end, where the producer is in the hands of the customers: they tell the producer how to develop and provide their software to them, and on a happy day they will at least agree with one another.

In this chapter we will look into how Power Balance affects your continuous practices and how to deal with conflicting requirements. As in the previous chapter, we will do it through the eyes of our archetypes.

The Archetypes

If we think of Power Balance as a scale, ranging from absolute producer power to absolute customer power, we can plot the archetypes from Chapter 5 onto that scale, as shown in Figure 6.

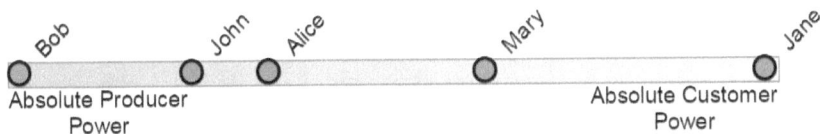

Figure 6: The Power Balance dimension.

At one far end of the scale is Bob, who is in complete control over how, when and if to deploy software to the service. This is not least the case because the users are individual consumers lacking the time, expertise and incentive to analyze the details of every new change. Indeed, most of these changes are so small and frequent that most users barely recognize them, but rather experience a gradual, almost continuous, evolution of the service.

John is in a similar situation, but has dramatically fewer and proportionally more passionate users. The people who play John's games care deeply about every single change made to its internal mechanics and reward systems. To them, too many updates – particularly back-and-forth experimentation – would be a nuisance and would likely trigger bad reviews and complaints. That being said, there isn't any major contract hinging a particular deployment schedule (at least not post-release of the game), and apart from the distribution platform's requirements John and his team have a high degree of freedom in what they release when.

Moving further to the right on the scale in Figure 6 we find Alice. While individual customers do not have any insight into or influence over how Alice's software ends up in the car they are buying, they are able to customize that car in great detail. This places specific requirements on the software deployment pipeline. Alice's case also demonstrates a simple rule of thumb: the more the customer invests in your product financially, the more they invest in it emotionally and the more they care about how you manage it – and the more power they wield over you. For instance, they might be likely to care a great deal more about how software is deployed to their car, than they care about how Bob updates his web service. Unfortunately, chances are they won't agree on how it should be done. For instance, whether continuous deployment of software updates to one's car is a good thing or not is one such potentially divisive question: either you love the idea, or you're terrified of it.

Somewhat unsurprisingly, on the right hand side of the Power Balance scale we find the two business-to-business archetypes. This isn't a law of nature, but a strong tendency. As mentioned previously, the product Mary works on is sold to a number of network operators and government agencies, some of whom use it in a medical context. To Mary's company, each of these customers is a big deal, and losing any one of them would be a tough blow, threatening to push them into the red. As a consequence, they have a significant incentive to meet any particular demands of those customers. The customers, on the other hand, are well aware of their power and are happy to wield it, and since the product is also a critical part of their respective businesses they have an inexhaustible supply of opinions and wishes. Unfortunately, they often collide. The network operators in particular are driving Mary's company to deploy continuously and bring down mean time to recovery, while the government agencies are pushing back and want to add ever longer and more comprehensive test suites before they are willing to accept any new update. This puts Mary and her colleagues in a difficult position, where on the one hand they need to speed up their pipeline and push software out as quickly as possible, and on the other they need to support and maintain a number of legacy tracks indefinitely, until they can persuade customers to upgrade to a slightly less outdated version.

In Jane's case, however, customer power is taken to a whole new level. In her case, selling the product – a military fighting vehicle – is more than just a financial transaction. It's a question of international politics. Not infrequently, deals are the subject of intense political debate, talks on government-to-government level and sometimes even referendums. They may also involve various forms of counterpurchases, or the requirement to place parts of the development in the purchasing nation. Requirements of this type affect not only how Jane's product is deployed to the customer, but potentially any and every aspect of how it is developed.

Dealing with Customer Demands

How, then, does one deal with customer demands on the style of deployment, or even development? Unfortunately there is no silver bullet solution to the problem, because the problem itself is so diverse. In this book we will try to give you the tools to establish this for your particular case in a systematic fashion, by describing the success factors involved in building a pipeline and onboarding your organization. When you read those chapters, we urge you reflect on your own experiences and your own context, and consider to what extent the individual success factor may be feasible or restricted in your particular case. Based on that, it then becomes easier to select the factors that are likely to bring you the greatest return on investment.

This may sound like obvious advice: think about what might work for you and focus your investments there. And indeed it is – or rather, it should be. Unfortunately, it's easy to end up in a situation where continuous practices are implemented for their own sake, without much consideration for or understanding of the market or the customers. As a result, the R&D side of the house invests heavily in continuous deployment capacities before the business side realizes what's happening and pulls the brakes because the market will never accept it.

That being said, if you find yourself in Mary's situation where you're getting mixed signals from the customers, or perhaps your market is in a transition period where some customers are lagging behind while some are open to or even requesting continuous deployment – or you think they will be in the near future – you will have to go for a hybrid approach. You will not be able to maintain just a single latest and greatest track and constantly roll forward on that.

The good news is that you can practice continuous integration, delivery and deployment in a multi-track environment as well. One approach to dealing with this hybrid solution is to maintain one continuously deployed track of the product, with its own pipeline, and separate maintenance tracks, also with their separate pipelines. We find this to be worth the overhead, because even if a particular customer doesn't want you to continuously deploy to them, it may well be a good idea to maintain continuous delivery capabilities. This is especially the case when that customer wants you to be able to rapidly deploy a correction when needed – free of any new features.

The bad news, of course, is that all this adds overhead to the software development. Overhead from sheer management of and working in a branched environment, but also overhead from building and maintaining multiple pipelines. Ideally, these pipelines can be constructed generically enough that all tracks can use the same build and test activities and the same infrastructure, only configured differently, something we will discuss further in Chapter 16.

Summary

In this chapter we have recognized the fact that the power balance between software producers and customers varies from market to market. In some markets, the producers have the power, and decide for themselves how to develop and deploy their software. In other markets, this is strongly influenced by the customer, and some find themselves in a gray zone, with contradictory requirements and/or room for negotiations. In the next chapter, we will look into another dimension of variability: Lead Time.

Chapter 9

Lead Time

Lead Time is a somewhat incongruous dimension. Some readers may be surprised by its inclusion, because surely one goal of introducing continuous practices in the first place is to reduce lead times? This is true, but the types of lead time we address here are not lead time in developing the software per se, but rather lead time forced upon the project by – depending on your point of view – external factors. These predominantly take one of two forms. One is lead time in the business domain, as part of the contract. This can be seen in major civil infrastructure investments or defense projects; the contract may stipulate that the product shall be delivered in three or five or ten years' time, not because it would necessarily be impossible to develop it any quicker, but because the customer is simply not ready to receive it sooner. The second form of lead time is where the larger system, as opposed to only the software, takes a long time to design and manufacture. This is arguably easier to affect, but as fascinating a subject as it may be, speeding up industry manufacturing projects in general is far outside the scope of this book. We will focus on software, and so from that point of view we will regard as a simple fact of life that it will, for instance, take a certain number of years to design and build a new high-speed train from scratch. Therefore it will also take some time before the software for that train can be fully integrated and deployed into its target environment.

Architectural Runway

This latter type of lead time, where you are unable to integrate the full system until the project has reached a certain level of maturity, is sometimes referred to as an architectural runway. The concept of an architectural runway is much better explained by Dean Leffingwell [26] than we can hope to do in this book. Briefly put, however, it's the system architecture and infrastructure required to implement new features – the platform onto which new stuff can be added. Much literature on continuous practices unfortunately assumes that you are already in that steady state, where the architectural runway exists and you continuously expand on it. But what about when it doesn't?

One approach, as laid out in the Scaled Agile Framework (SAFe) [27], is to start small with a single team tasked with constructing the runway, and then expanding by adding on more development teams. From a continuous practices point of view, the product's pipeline – or network of pipelines – would similarly expand, thereby keeping pace with the product development.

This isn't always an option, however. Sometimes the architectural runway simply takes too long to construct (typically because it's not a pure software project) and feature development, or development of the various parts of the system, can not wait until an infrastructure to build upon exists. This is one of those situations where one could argue that the reason you find yourself facing this problem is because you're not practicing continuous integration. By definition, if you had been continuously integrating you wouldn't be in the trouble you're in, ergo the solution is to continuously integrate. We don't think reality is that simple, however. It's never black and white, and despite the best intentions, software developers find themselves unable to integrate the full system for reasons beyond their control, and rubbing it in by quoting scripture won't help anyone. Instead, let us consider pragmatic approaches to alleviate the problem.

One path forward is simulation. By simulating the target-environment-that-does-not-yet-exist, you provide a way for the software components of the system to integrate and verify their interactions at an earlier stage, in a setting that is very close to the actual production environment. Having a good simulator also has the added benefit of providing a means of testing the whole system outside of the (potentially very expensive) target environment, something we will return to in Chapter 10. Besides, simulators also let you test things you can't otherwise test in an actual environment, by injecting faults and simulating catastrophic scenarios (see Chapter 17). It is important to note that in order to enable continuous practices, these simulators must cater to automated testing: by executing automated test cases in the simulator environment as part of the system's pipeline, you can get up and running with continuous integration before the actual architectural runway is in place. That being said, there's the one caveat that most simulators don't come free of charge, and developing them from scratch is a lot of work. Related to simulation is the practice of emulation, which can provide a simplified substitute for system components that aren't yet available, thereby allowing development of surrounding parts to proceed with a slightly higher level of confidence than without any integration at all.

The second approach is one of process and development practices. Even if you are in a position where you are not yet able to integrate the full system, ensure that each part of the system runs its own pipeline which can then be hooked into a planned common system pipeline. Then encourage development teams to write test cases for their collaborators, inserting them in their respective pipelines. To exemplify, even though Jane's vehicle does not yet exist, the target acquisition software and the sensors are already in development. To avoid the worst parts of integration hell once they are joined together, the target acquisition team writes test cases representing how they expect to interact with those sensors, and the responses they expect to receive back. Then, for every change made in the sensor components, the expectations from target acquisition are verified. The test cases thereby serve as a form of acceptance tests and facilitate concrete interface negotiations sooner rather than later in the development process.

Collecting Data Despite Long Lead Times

A project involving long lead times poses another challenge. Ideally, one would like to receive user feedback on features and functionality, but if the finished product is years away, how does one accomplish that?

In literature, we find that most accounts of continuous practices in general and data collection in particular assume that there is a live system exposed to users, where software can be deployed and changes to user behavior can be measured. But what if the product is still nothing but parts scattered across the factory floor? Attempting to answer that question in full quickly leads into the realm of industrial design and is also outside the scope of this book, but if we focus solely on the software there are some key concepts we need to address.

> When dealing with continuous practices you will constantly find yourself not just dealing with software engineering, but stumbling into the realms of business strategy, human psychology, social interactions, information visualization, change management and much more. Personally I always found that to be the main reason why the field captured and held my fascination for so many years; it will ceaselessly challenge your perspectives.
>
> *- Daniel*

Obviously, what one does when one is far away from having a complete product to try out on end users is to do the next best thing: try out whatever parts, or failing that, whatever simulations of the real thing are available, and get end user feedback on that. This is far from a revolutionary idea, but rather than basing such experimentation on the actual production software, we see some engineers build very elaborate mock-ups – including bespoke software – of the production systems. In the end, however, those mock-ups sometimes turn out to be so radically different from the true product that their findings weren't even applicable.

A continuous delivery pipeline has an important role to play in these scenarios, by preventing this type of experimentation to veer away down its own track, separate from and ultimately irrelevant to the rest of the system. As we discussed in Chapter 6, a pipeline is not a linear thing, but has many inputs and many outputs. Even though a point where a complete, fully integrated software product comes out the far end of that pipeline is a long way away, whatever pieces are produced can be deployed into simulated environments or mock-ups to run experiments at a very early stage in the development process, while ensuring that the software being trialed is feasible and consequently that the experiments are realistic and relevant.

In Figure 7 such an example is shown. It is an unfinished network of pipelines where each component has its own continuous integration and delivery pipeline, but they are not yet all integrated into a complete system to be deployed onto its target environment. This is because that target environment does not yet even exist (the dashed edges in the figure represent planned but not yet complete parts of the network). The bottom two components are integrated, however, and their output is continuously deployed into a simulated target environment. In this environment testing and customer demos of their functionality can be carried out, providing valuable early feedback to the development teams.

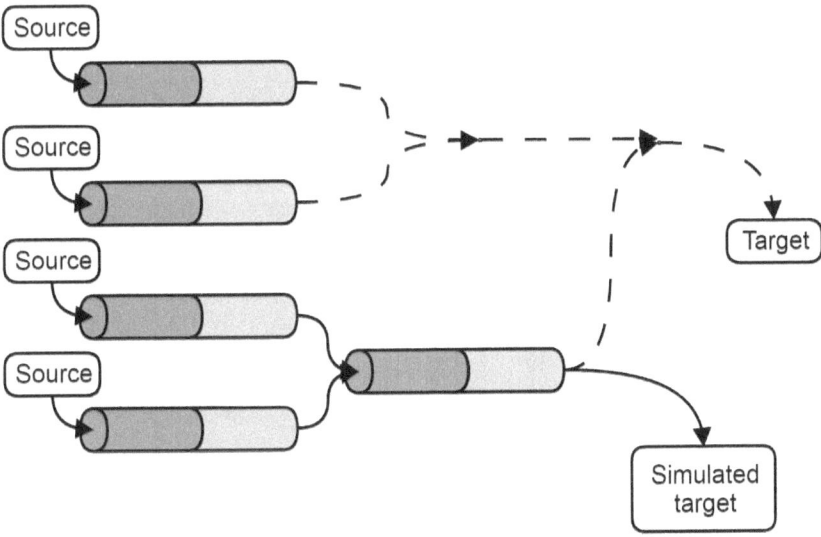

Figure 7: An unfinished multi-sink network of pipelines.

The Archetypes

Figure 8 maps each of the archetypes from Chapter 5 onto the Lead Time scale.

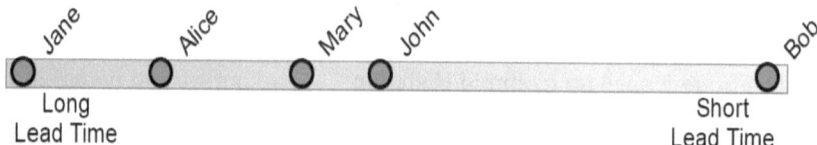

Figure 8: The Lead Time dimension.

Alice and Mary mostly face the second form of lead time discussed above: that of an architectural runway, as they develop very large scale embedded systems. Particularly in Alice's case, software development is not only highly specification driven, where actual programming tends to happen very late and the ability to integrate and test that software happens even later, but it is also dependent on hardware development. Consequently, for a significant part of the project life cycle, there simply is no software to continuously integrate or deploy, and no target to deploy it on. Moreover, the mindset of the project is not so much that of a software system of components to be integrated sooner rather than later, as of a physical system of physical items – which only happen to contain software – to be assembled on the factory floor. This means that when the integration of two ECUs fails, it isn't analyzed and solved informally at the developers' desks, but rather through escalation and rebooting of the interface specification process, which involves a completely different set of engineers and thus adds significant lead time to solving the problem.

Mary has it slightly easier in that her product is more software defined and driven by formal specifications to a lesser degree. As a consequence, the time before there is actual software, something to run it on and collaborators to integrate with is shorter.

Jane, however, is heavily affected by both types of lead time. On the one side, when the contract is signed the first delivery is still years into the future. Part of this is due to the fact that the purchaser requires time to ready themselves for the delivery. Acquiring a weapon system is more than just picking up the hardware and parking it in your garage – organizations need to be recruited and set up, and personnel must be trained to operate and care for the equipment. Mostly, however, it is due to the same challenges that Alice struggles with, namely that there is a significant amount of hardware development involved, but also because a fair amount of research is also included in that time: when the product is initially sold, a number of open research questions remain unsolved in order to design the promised product. These research questions are simply expected to be solved during the development process. As a consequence, Jane and her colleagues spend significant efforts on developing simulated environments, which are also used extensively for testing. These are used for several purposes: as part of the pipeline, where software collaborators can be tested early in an integrated environment, as well as for manual testing by the developers themselves on their desktops as they try out their changes against the latest available version of the system. They are also used to get feedback from the intended end users, even though the finished vehicle is nowhere near complete and they are far away even from a physical prototype. By constantly deploying the latest software to a simulated environment, however, Jane can get rapid feedback directly from users, particularly on displays, interface design and human-machine interaction.

Bob, on the other hand, knows very little of any of these problems. From his point of view, the sooner the software is out, the sooner it can start earning revenue; he sometimes literally tests in production the very same day a change that was thought of earlier in the morning. To him, lead time is all about how quickly he can transform hypotheses into in-service facts.

Meanwhile, John faces lead time of the business and contractual sort. He is not restricted by the slower development cycles of hardware, but still operates in a market with expectations on release dates: not unlike the opening night of a movie, customers expect a game to be available at a certain date, communicated well in advance and largely dictated by the marketing and finance side of the business. The same applies to post-release updates and paid-for downloadable content, though to a lesser extent, if only because the attention from customers and media is less intense. As a consequence, continuous deployment makes little sense in John's context, although continuous delivery to enable rapid test and feedback cycles – including late night gaming sessions in the office to simply try out whether a feature is fun or not – is extremely valuable.

Summary

In this chapter we have explored the variability dimension of Lead Time. Lead Time is a tricky dimension, because it can take many shapes and forms, and some of them can actually be remedied by continuous practices. In other words, it can be difficult to determine whether a particular case suffers from long lead times because it is in desperate need of better continuous practices, or whether the adoption of continuous practices needs to conform to the long lead times dictated by factors that are simply part of the game. Depending on which is the case, possible solutions include starting out small and scaling up, or investing in simulated environments to circumnavigate the challenges of a long architectural runway.

Chapter 10

Proximity to Hardware

How closely integrated the software is to its underlying hardware has significant consequences for the ability to successfully exercise continuous practices. First, let us be clear that when we speak of Proximity to Hardware, the implication is to specific, often bespoke hardware. Of course, it is entirely possible to be tightly coupled to very generic hardware as well, but in practice, the situation arises where one is dependent on highly specific equipment with particular physical interfaces – be it radio wave antennae, visual surveillance systems, mechatronic control systems or analog circuit controls.

This is because such specific equipment doesn't come with the tooling and the deep abstraction layers that have been built up over decades for more generic systems in the software engineering community, and it doesn't come with the same economies of scale. In other words, when you're developing embedded software for your in-house developed sensor, you will end up developing much of the supporting tools, such as compilers or test frameworks or even operating systems, and every unit of physical equipment is going to be costly.

Working in such a context we can identify several challenges to continuous integration directly or indirectly associated with embedded software [28]. Under the heading Proximity to Hardware we group four of those: long build times, scarce test resources, complex user scenarios and numerous technology fields. In addition, close proximity to hardware can make software deployment difficult.

Long Build Times

In our experience, the build time of large embedded systems is generally longer than what one might expect for a similarly sized system built for a more generic environment, due to two factors.

One is that they are often tightly coupled, with low support for modularization and thereby for isolation of change impact. One example of this is a rate-monotonic cyclic execution vehicular system with scheduled communication both within and between individual on-board computers. In such a system, even a small change to the internal logic of one of those computers may require building and linking of major parts of the entire system, thereby driving up the build times in the continuous integration pipeline.

The other factor is quality of tooling. When you use javac or the GNU C++ compiler, you use a tool that has been optimized over many years through contributions from large communities, and been tested and tried and critically appraised in thousands upon thousands of projects. When you're forced to build your own tools or use highly specialized tools commercially provided to a niche market of only a few players, that couldn't be farther from the truth. Which scenario is actually worse is a tough call – being in the hands of a vendor who cornered your market years ago and has zero incentive to improve their product, because they are the only game in town and they know it, is not a happy place to be. Then, what should be a quick and trivial build job can take minutes or even hours, something that will profoundly affect your ability to continuously integrate and produce new release candidates.

Scarce Test Resources

In a perfect world, tests can be infinitely parallelized such that the total time required to execute the entire test suite is exactly equal to the time required for the longest running test case. And as long as test resources are cheap and elastic enough, that is actually perfectly possible. On the other hand, when the production environment is something like an airliner or a submarine it is neither, so what does one do?

Clearly, the answer is to not test more than absolutely necessary in that expensive production environment. Although we have yet to see a case where you can completely get away from at least some testing of the complete system in the production environment, the goal is to do away with as much as you responsibly can. There are multiple strategies for dealing with this, such as testing in simulated environments and pushing tests down through the test pyramid [24] to a point where functionality can be tested on generic hardware (non-functional requirements are trickier).

A sometimes overlooked aspect of this is test resource utilization. This may not be directly related to how one sets up one's pipeline, but is more of a general reflection on how one manages and schedules one's precious hardware resources. While we're used to resource elasticity in everyday cloud platforms, all such concepts tend to fly out the window when engineers manage their bespoke hardware resources, even though they very much apply. I have seen too many cases of very expensive test environments being configured just so, to execute one particular test case, and then left to idle for 90% of the time. With just a little bit of extra concern for genericity and dynamic allocation of those test environments the value derived from those very expensive bottlenecks could be increased ten-fold.

- Daniel

Complex User Scenarios

The easiest thing to test automatically is arguably a pure software stateless input-to-output algorithm: given this input, assume this output. It gets worse when things like long-running states and complex interactions between systems enter into the picture. It gets even worse when the input and/or output is no longer software, but the state of physical reality, which must then be affected and/or measured by the test case. Worse still, measurements of physical reality are notoriously difficult to make precise and consistent, introducing a rich source of test flakiness, an issue we will have more to say on in Chapter 17. The absolute nightmare, however, is when the definition of success is what subjectively feels good to a human user – does the vehicle respond in a way that feels right when the joystick is pushed just so, or does the resistance in the clutch feel right? – situations which are all too common when working in close proximity to hardware.

When you come up against test cases like these, which are all but impossible to automate, you need to consider how to construct your automated pipeline around them. It is likely that manual testing is going to be part of your software's life cycle before it can be released or deployed, but how often do you conduct those tests, and on what versions, and which types of changes require you to re-test them? The answers to those questions come down to other contextual factors, such as regulations, safety criticality and lead time; in subsequent chapters we will look at how some of our archetypes deal with them. We will also return to various techniques for evaluating release candidates in the pipeline in Chapter 17, and how to think about structuring pipeline activities in Chapter 21.

Numerous Technology Fields

Something that might be considered a "soft" but nevertheless important factor prevalent in software projects closely tied to hardware development in general and physical interfaces in particular, is that they by definition are not pure software projects. Instead, a multitude of technology fields are involved – fields such as electrical power systems, radio wave propagation, aerodynamics, engine control – all with their own specialists with varying degrees of understanding of software development.

Unless guarded against, this diversity can easily drive divergence and silo mentality, where each field becomes more concerned with "their" part of the system, than with the system as a whole. This in turn impedes the introduction of a holistic continuous delivery pipeline, as members of the organization simply may not see the use – as long as their component works, the rest is somebody else's concern, right? Another effect of multiple technology fields is that the ratio of software developers in the development project goes down, which also detracts from the focus on software development in general and continuous practices in particular. In previous work we have found that the more non-developers there are in an organization, the less frequently those developers tend to commit new software [29] (see Figure 9). A low ratio of developers in the organization can have a number of causes, the need for experts in other disciplines than software due to close proximity to hardware and physical interfaces being one of them (with an overly bureaucratic and bloated organization being another, as we will return to in Chapter 11). We will look more closely at this phenomenon and strategies to deal with it in Part IV: Onboarding the Organization.

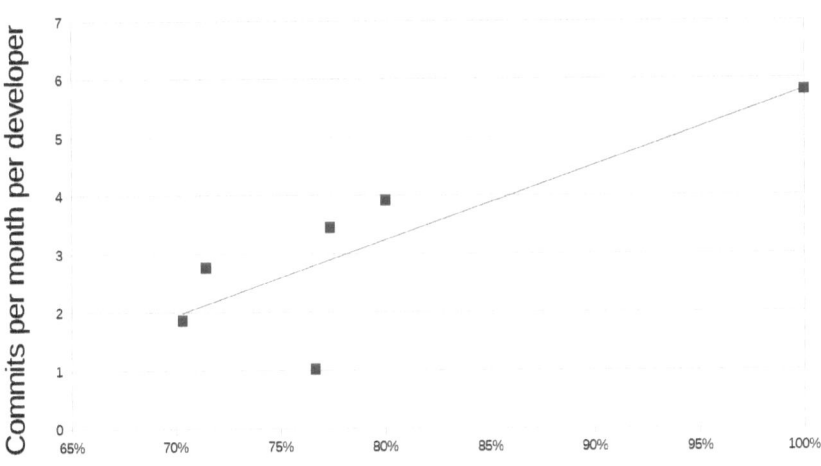

Figure 9: Correlation between percentage of developers and developer commit frequency in six studied industry cases [29].

Hardware Longevity

An often overlooked challenge to continuous deployment of embedded systems is that the longevity of such systems tends to be longer than that of generic PC hardware or cloud platforms. Consider, for instance, the car industry. Contrary to some popular perceptions, the average life expectancy of new cars is getting longer and longer: from less than seven years in 1930 to over a decade in 2013 [30], and obviously many vehicles last much longer than that. In other words, there are cars in service that were built (and had software installed in them) before continuous deployment or even continuous integration were coined as terms. Similarly, many of the cars manufactured today will still be on the streets in twenty or thirty years. This means that to the extent that a car manufacturer doubles down on continuous deployment technology today, they will need to deploy to the same hardware targets in twenty or thirty years.

This is in stark contrast to the rapid pace at which software engineering tools and frameworks are being replaced. The way we deployed software five or ten years ago already feels old, and few of the tools and environments are the same. As a thought experiment, consider a phone or a desktop computer from twenty years ago, and ask yourself how much of the software you use today on a daily basis would even run on that device.

This means that engineers working in close proximity to hardware face a difficult choice. Either they take a conservative stance on the tools and methods they employ and only upgrade infrequently, or they need to support a very long tail of (obsolete) technologies in parallel.

Tooling and Frameworks

In the world of virtualization and containerization, pushing software updates onto an in-service system over the network can be relatively easy, and there are plenty of popular tools to help you do it, both commercial and non-commercial. In embedded systems, on the other hand, actually getting the software onto the hardware can be non-trivial.

Traditionally, the embedded software is loaded onto the hardware during manufacturing and rarely, if ever, updated. This is changing, however. For instance, at the time of writing this book, most car manufacturers will update the software in your car when you hand it in for servicing, but deployment over the air is done and is picking up. Out of the box solutions for pushing software onto bespoke hardware targets are lacking, however, especially when those targets are freely roaming around the countryside, with or without an internet connection. In other words, continuous deployment of embedded software can be done, but it requires custom tooling and infrastructure that e.g. a web based Software as a Service solution gets (more or less) for free. Whether building that infrastructure is a sound investment is a strategic decision that needs to be made in each individual case.

The Archetypes

In Figure 10 you can see each of the software engineering archetypes from Chapter 5 mapped onto a scale ranging from software in close proximity to hardware, to software far removed from hardware.

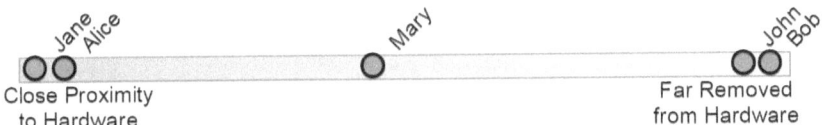

Figure 10: Proximity to Hardware dimension.

The scale in Figure 10 is highly polarized. At one end are John and Bob who care very little about the underlying hardware. In Bob's case it is a virtual cloud environment able to execute code in practically any language and style of his choice. John's software must run on the end user's own computer, of which there is a nearly infinite space of possible configurations, but all of that is abstracted away by layers upon layers of abstractions: operating systems, drivers, frameworks and APIs which – most of the time – produce the same result regardless of the hardware brand.

Jane and Alice, on the left-most extreme of the scale, suffer from all of the consequences related to proximity to hardware listed in this chapter. They build tightly coupled embedded systems using more or less custom tooling, with ensuing long build times, and test resources are scarce. Not only are they scarce in the pipeline, curtailing the test scope and driving its lead times, but gaining access to actual on-target test environments during development is also difficult. For instance, Alice, developing software for an electronic control unit in a car, rarely has access to its actual collaborators, but spends most of her time developing according to specifications. This means she only gets feedback from tests in an integrated vehicle system scope at a much later stage, sometimes months later. To make matters worse, engineers with a holistic view of the entire car – including software, hardware, physics and vehicular controls – are extremely rare. As a consequence, the default mindset for Alice and her colleagues is that of their respective isolated ECUs, ensuring that the software they develop functions according to specifications. Alice does make a conscious effort to see the bigger picture, even though she feels as though she has to do that despite the information, processes and tools available to her, rather than with their help.

Mary straddles the scale in-between the two extremes. Parts of the networking solution she develops executes on in-house bespoke hardware, which places very specific restrictions on the development environment and tooling she can use. These are the parts concerned with scheduling, emitting and receiving actual pulses over the network interface, and translating those pulses to and from packets of data. Other parts, however, at a higher abstraction level, are completely virtualized. These perform tasks such as traffic control, monitoring, authentication, authorization, analytics et cetera. They execute on generic PC hardware and are written in languages and using tooling that any developer from any part of the industry would be familiar with. In other words, depending on which part of the system Mary is working on, her practices and her tool sets change accordingly. Likewise, the various parts of the network of pipelines that builds her system operates under very different circumstances.

Summary

Even though Harvard Business Review famously asked "Does Hardware Even Matter Anymore?" [31], to the adoption of continuous practices it does matter. Or, more precisely, it matters how tightly your software is coupled to its executing hardware, how mature and optimized your tools for building and deploying are, and how readily available, cheap and scalable that hardware is.

Like several other contextual dimensions we bring up in this book, Proximity to Hardware isn't necessarily set in stone: to some extent it is a strategic decision, and we currently see a sea change where traditionally embedded software systems are being virtualized on a broad front, and important factors in that change are the difficulties of developing, building, testing and deploying embedded software.

Chapter 11

Scale

Scale is of critical importance when adopting continuous practices. The relevance of scale has long been known and was highlighted in research literature early on [32, 33], but a rarely mentioned fact is that scale impacts each continuous practice differently. In this chapter we will take a closer look at the effects of scale on continuous integration, delivery and deployment, respectively, and consider scale from our archetypes' points of view.

The Definition of Scale

Large scale can mean different things: is it the size of the software system (and if so by what metric), or is it the number of deployments, number of users, number of people involved in development, or specifically the number of software developers?

Even though several types of scale tend to correlate, the factor we have found to be of most significance in research is that of headcount: the sheer headcount of the software development effort, regardless of their roles [29]. So, with the caveat that this does not imply that other types of scale are irrelevant, the number of people involved is what we will be focusing on in this book when we discuss challenges related to scale.

Continuous Integration

At its surface, continuous integration is a simple concept. Every developer checks in their changes frequently, at least once per day, and those changes are then automatically built and tested to ensure that the product is not obviously broken. What could go wrong?

As long as the number of developers is small enough, not much. But what happens if the number of developers is larger? What if there isn't a handful, but a hundred developers? Or a thousand? That would imply at least a thousand source code changes per day. Assuming those changes are evenly distributed (which they never are) across a ten hour working day, that's roughly one change every thirty seconds. In other words, in order to build and test every change individually, you would need a turn around time of thirty seconds from the moment one developer commits her changes until that change has been evaluated and integrated with the common development branch – or rejected. Theoretically speaking, this would allow the next developer to commit her changes, which hopefully do not conflict with the recently merged ones (because most of us mere mortals will not be able to reliably determine that in a handful of seconds).

In practice, this does not happen. In particular, it doesn't happen for systems built by a thousand full-time developers – remember, the size of the organization correlates with the size and complexity of the product, and thereby with its build and test times. There are strategies for coping with these problems, of course. Build and test times can be reduced in various ways and multiple builds can be optimistically evaluated in parallel[4], but such techniques only work up to a point, not least because human decision making and analysis is still part of the development process. Instead, multiple changes will end up being batched together in every build, which causes several problems. First, the risk of failure increases with every additional change. Second, troubleshooting becomes that much harder when a failed build could be the result of any one of a number of unrelated changes, or, more likely, those changes in combination. Third, the consequences of failure are greater, since reverting all the changes since the last successful build will cause substantial rework for lots of people. Even worse, a red build

---

4   See https://docs.openstack.org/infra/zuul for one example of this.

on mainline will prevent hundreds of people from committing, creating an almighty pile-up of code waiting to be merged.

Another approach is to avoid these situations altogether and argue that such a large system needs to be broken down into components, each with its own pipeline and ideally its own life cycle. This is indeed the approach we recommend, based on numerous observed cases: do not expect very large monolithic products with lots of software developers to be continuously integrated. The critical factor here is the number of people involved in developing a single, clearly delineated source context – ideally protected by separately versioned interface definitions. This affords you a certain level of autonomy within that protected context – less people to impact and be impacted by, and thereby less coordination overhead and less rework in case of failure.

The price you pay for this modularization is a more complicated integration pattern and therefore an equally complicated network of pipelines, with the infrastructure requirements that come with it. Also, there is the overhead and lead time brought on by negotiating and managing all the interfaces that are needed to maintain the integrity of the individual components. All in all, modularity is not a silver bullet for scaling continuous integration, but rather a trade-off. Notably, this is another reason why it's rarely a good idea to start out super-modularized in a new, small project. Instead, start out with fewer pieces but actively prepare to split them when the need arises.

What happens when too many people are involved in a single continuous integration context is that they will simply begin to integrate less continuously. Studying developer behavior across multiple cases this becomes very clear. As engineers we have observed this phenomenon many times and there is plenty of anecdotal evidence to support it, but we also set out to gather quantitative data on it. Figure 11 shows one of the findings of this research: the larger the organization, the larger and less frequent the commits made by developers [29].

It is important to acknowledge that this is not because the developers are lazy, or aren't interested in integrating more frequently. On the contrary, if you scratch the surface and investigate the reasons why integration isn't as continuous as one might expect (or wish for) in these cases, developers cite a number of impediments [34]. Some recurring themes are that there simply aren't enough test resources to go around (which is exacerbated in situations where those test resources are very expensive, see Chapter 10) and that the system architecture does not support large numbers of small concurrent changes.

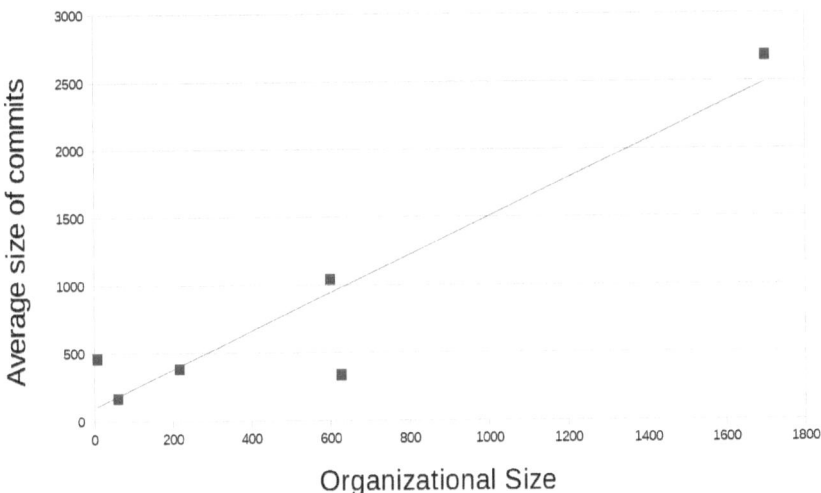

Figure 11: The relationship between average size of commits and organizational size found in research into six industry cases [29].

When we say that the architecture does not support small concurrent changes, what we mean is that it is difficult to make a small, atomic change that does not have ripple effects throughout the system. In such an architecture, even a small functional change turns into a very large change in the code base, thus forcing developers to verify a much larger scope before committing their change. Then, once that is done, since they have made such a large, sweeping change chances are that others have committed code with which they must merge, restarting the entire cycle. This is why successful continuous integration is not just about the process and the tools and the pipeline, but also about designing the integrated product in such a way that developers can collaborate effectively without disrupting one another. And once again, the solution is about modularization, affording developers a space in which they can move about and work autonomously, without constantly coordinating with too many people.

Another issue often mentioned by developers, particularly relevant to the finding shown in Figure 9 is that the more non-developers there are in an organization, the more lengthy and convoluted processes tend to get invented for checking in code. As a rule, in organizations where all or nearly all members are developers themselves, checking in code tends to be rather straight forward. The more "supporting" roles are involved, however, the more checklists, gates and reviews are required. These are of course not invented out of spite – the road to hell is, after all, paved with the best of intentions – but they are invented without awareness of the cost they incur on committing code to the common development branch. And the more that cost goes up, the more developers tend to stay away and instead commit larger, more infrequent changes.

All this being said, it is not a law of nature that developers in large organizations will commit code less frequently than developers in small organizations, because scale is not the only factor at play. It is extremely difficult to effectively scale continuous integration, however.

It's important to be forthright about the challenges large scale contexts present, not least with regards to continuous integration. At the same time, they're not insurmountable. I have encountered engineers who bemoan even attempting to adopt continuous practices in very large organizations, yet I have personally seen (and been part of) both successes and failures. Simply because you have failed in one case, that doesn't mean it can't be done, particularly if you're judicious as to which benefits you try to realize.

- Daniel

Continuous Delivery

Continuous delivery scales differently than continuous integration. In a way, if the purpose is to produce a steady stream of evaluated release candidates, large scale can be a help: given a large enough number of developers, you can have lots of release candidates every day, even if every developer only commits once a month on average.

Is a high frequency of release candidates really an end in itself, however? No, of course it isn't; it is only valuable insofar as you can get the individual change into production quickly, can respond effectively to new requirements, and can gain incremental growth in a safe and predictable manner. Arguably you miss out on all of that in a situation where you produce numerous new versions simply by virtue of having lots of developers, but where those developers themselves commit big bangs once a month.

Continuous delivery faces a different set of scaling problems than does continuous integration. The size of the organization has very little impact on the continuous delivery pipeline. Instead it is its secondary effects on the system size that matter in this case, as large organizations tend to produce large systems (seemingly regardless of whether that is warranted by the problem it addresses, but all the more related to Conway's Law [35]). A large system, in turn, implies more, longer and more resource consuming tests, which essentially comes down to a dimensioning problem. A problem which depending on other factors, such as Proximity to Hardware (see Chapter 10), may have different solutions.

The organization isn't completely irrelevant, however. It is important to understand what is going on within the pipeline, how software changes traverse it and what happened to an individual change, what didn't happen and why. When only one or a handful of engineers are involved they probably all know the ins and outs of that pipeline, or if they don't, someone who does is never far away. In a large organization of hundreds of people that simply isn't the case, which places increased demands on the clarity and precision of traceability data, as well as on visualization of it. We will return to this in greater detail in Chapter 15.

Continuous Deployment

The scale of the software development effort has very little immediate impact on continuous deployment. A large organization may develop a large system, which may result in more software to transport over the network or longer upgrade times in the production environment, but such links are very tenuous.

Archetypes

The software engineering archetypes introduced in Chapter 5 can be seen mapped onto the Scale dimension as shown in Figure 12.

Figure 12: The Scale dimension.

Mary's networking solution is split into a number of components, big and small, with Mary's being the largest – it is actively developed by approximately 500 developers. When she receives a development task it is not as an individual, but as part of a team, in the form of a feature to be added to the system. The expected time required to fully implement the feature is usually measured in months. Even so, she and her teammates would like to develop in much smaller increments, ideally committing small changes – if not daily then at least several times a week. Despite these intentions, when push comes to shove they end up developing the complete feature on their private branch – where they integrate continuously within the team – before merging with the common development branch and then delivering their feature. This is because the code on the common development branch changes so rapidly, they get stuck in a more or less endless cycle of merging. Even though the project goes to great lengths in planning to avoid functional conflicts in concurrent work, the highly coupled architecture of Mary's component means that there are still plenty of conflicts at a code level.

Consequently, by the time Mary has merged her work with the latest changes and tested that it works, several new changes have been committed, significantly impacting her feature development, forcing her to restart the cycle. Thus she feels as though she is constantly two or three commits behind the tip of the development branch, and after a few days of this she gives up and decides to make her changes in peace on her team branch, and just deal with the inescapable integration hell when her team has something of value to deliver. Sure it's painful, but it's a pain she only has to deal with once in a while, rather than on a daily basis.

An added effect of this behavior is that Mary and her teammates try to keep the footprint of their changes to the source code as small and contained as possible, purely as a survival strategy to minimize merge conflicts. A direct consequence of this is that any form of refactoring is effectively shunned, as it tends to result in large, sweeping changes across the code base. Such changes are punished mercilessly when Mary and her team try to merge their team branch back into the mainline, with predictable consequences to the level of technical debt in the product.

Jane is in a very similar situation to Mary. Ideally she would like to integrate more frequently, but like Mary and her team she feels as though she ends up spending most of her time merging and testing, and very little actually coding.

Meanwhile, Alice has mixed experiences of continuous integration in her project. Her electronic control unit (ECU) is integrated as a complete entity into the larger system. All its interactions with its collaborators are through heavily specified interfaces which can only be changed through rigorous (and regrettably slow) processes. In other words, even though she is part of a fairly sizable development operation, only a minority of it is actually made up of software developers, and she integrates only indirectly with their software except for the cases where they collaborate on the same ECU. Within that ECU Alice and her teammates are conscientious about frequently integrating their code, but on a system level the integration is anything but continuous. When the ECU is delivered for system integration Alice loses track of it completely, and has very little insight into which tests are performed by whom and why. When there is a problem she's contacted by a tester – often regarding a software version that is already weeks old – even though she feels she could be more proactive and fix problems sooner if she had better visibility of the system test process.

> In my experience, when people speak in terms of "teams delivering", as opposed to "developers committing", it's a safe bet that they haven't fully adopted a continuous integration mindset – often despite assurances to the contrary.
>
> *- Daniel*

Bob's social media platform is split into several parts – the backend, the web service and the mobile device app – each with its own pipeline and life cycle. Consequently, there are rarely more than a dozen or so people working concurrently on any one part at any given time, and Bob has rarely experienced any challenges related to scaling. In recent months the company has expanded rapidly, however, taking on a large number of new developers. Since then, during peak hours there have sometimes been too many concurrent changes coming in to let Bob perform isolated A/B tests without inadvertently being "polluted" by unrelated commits by other developers. Because of this, Bob and his colleagues have been debating whether they should construct multiple parallel instances of the web service and backend pipelines to afford bug fixes and feature experiments a fast track to deployment, directly from separate branches without first being integrated into the common development branch. This hasn't come farther than the discussion phase yet, though, and Bob is reluctant. Not only would it require significant effort to set something like that up, but he fears that the added complexity of managing all the parallel branches would cause a lot of overhead to development.

Finally, John has never really had reason to consider the scalability of their continuous integration and delivery setup. Naturally, some tests take a while to execute, but never to the point that he or any of his two co-developers felt impeded by it. And whenever there has been some trouble with the continuous integration job, the only other people affected by it (as well as the likely culprits) haven't been more than one or two desks over from where John is seated.

Summary

In this chapter we have looked into the Scale dimension. The scale of development efforts varies widely in the industry, and has significant impact on continuous practices. Particularly continuous integration simply scales very poorly, but the good news is there's something you can do about it. First, take a very close look at whether there is any way you can actually get by with a smaller project, particularly with a smaller number of people not actually developing software (and a welcome side effect of a smaller project is that it's cheaper!). Amazingly enough, once organizations reach a certain size, it's almost as if they take on a life of their own and begin to grow of their own accord. To paraphrase Oscar Wilde, the organization expands to meet the demands of the expanding organization. Second, take an equally close look at the product architecture. How well does it support concurrent development? The key properties to maximize are modularization and separation of concern, allowing developers to co-exist in the same code base without constantly getting in one another's way.

Chapter 12

Regulation

Regulations come in many shapes and forms, and covering all of them here would be impossible. Instead we will focus mainly on the software regulations for off-the-shelf (OTS) software enforced by the Food and Drug Administration (FDA) as a representative example. There are several reasons for this choice. First of all, compliance with FDA regulations is a very common requirement: it applies to any software used in a medical context, even for seemingly innocuous auxiliary use cases such as administration. Second, it is based on generally recognized software validation principles and can be applied to any software. Third, it is widely regarded as maintaining a high standard of quality and has strongly influenced the development of regulations in other industries. Finally, OTS software validation is highly relevant as the majority of software used by device manufacturers is supplied by third-party vendors, whose records may or may not be available or sufficient from a validation point of view [36]. Even in non-OTS situations similar techniques apply, depending on the particular requirements of the regulations in question. That being said, it is of course important to understand those particulars as they apply to your case; the contents of this chapter shall not be interpreted as a guarantee of successful validation, but merely as exemplification and general guidance.

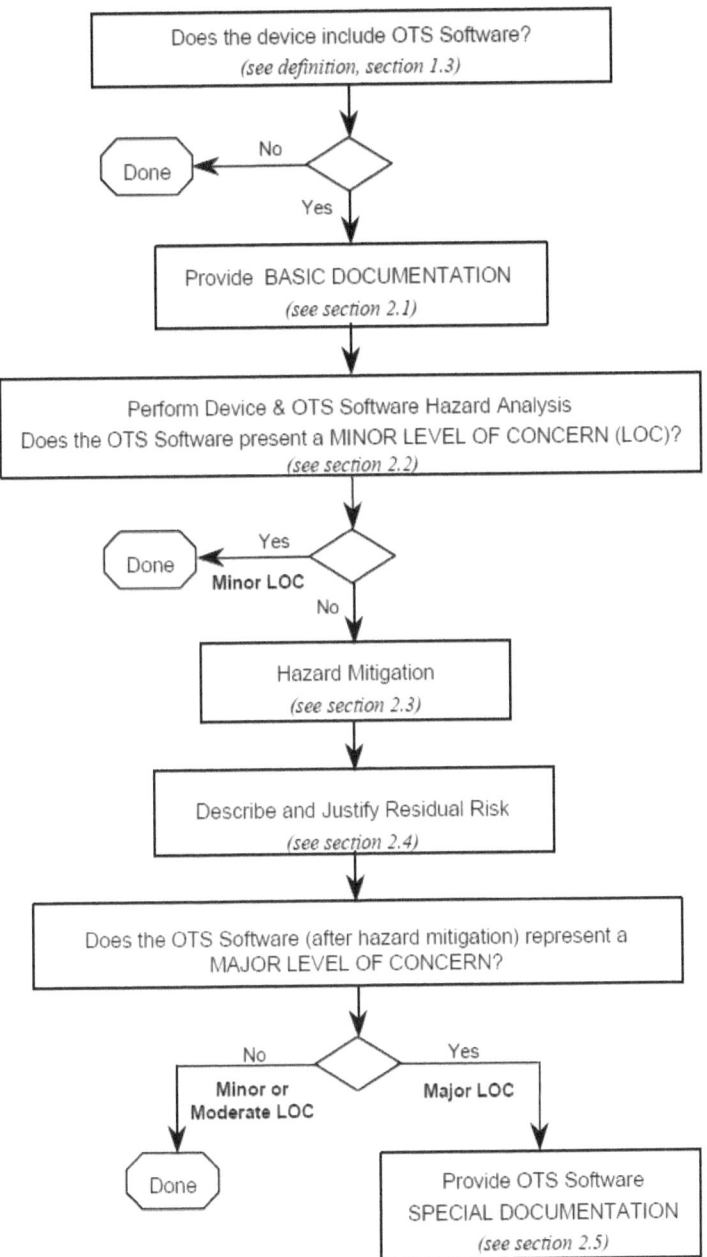

Figure 13: FDA decision schematic for off-the-shelf software, as shown in FDA's documentation [37].

Taking the Easy Way Out

FDA OTS regulations, like most regulations, exist to keep people and assets safe. In order to do that, they want you to keep track of what is what in your software, what it does, how you know it works and how you know it's safe – and they want you to be able to produce an appropriate level of documentation to that effect. To determine what appropriate means, software is classified as belonging to one of three categories depending on the level of concern for health and safety: Minor Level of Concern, Moderate Level of Concern and Major Level of Concern. The higher the level of concern, the more documentation is required to demonstrate how risks have been mitigated. The FDA helpfully provides a decision schematic to illustrate this (see Figure 13).

As Figure 13 illustrates, you can think of this process as a gauntlet with the objective of getting out as early as possible. No matter what you do, you always need to produce Basic Documentation:

- What is it, on a component by component level?

- What are the hardware and software specifications of the system it will run in?

- How will you assure appropriate actions are taken by the End User?

- What does it do?

- How do you know it works?

- How will you keep track of it?

These are all questions which should, given a modicum of rigor in the software development process, be possible to answer for any component of a software system. Some can be answered once and then rarely touched again, while others need to be answered again and again for every introduced change (particularly the "How do you know it works?" part), which is important in a continuous delivery context.

The good news is that as long as you are able to demonstrate that any failures in the software can not be expected to result in any injuries, this is all you will need. If you can't, then you have a problem: you need to perform Hazard Mitigation, which essentially means that you are

---

required to redesign the product and/or take other protective measures until that is no longer the case.

Hazard Mitigation can be arduous and costly, but in the ideal scenario it's a one-time effort: if the software can be redesigned or the dangers otherwise protected against in such a way that they do not need to be re-assessed and re-documented for every change, they do not pose a problem for continuous practices per se. If, on the other hand, following Hazard Mitigation your software poses a risk for *serious* injury, your software will be classified as Major Level of Concern. This means you will be forced to run the full gauntlet[5] and produce Special Documentation [37], which is not something you want to do if it can at all be avoided. Keeping Special Documentation up-to-date and relevant throughout the life cycle of a software is a daunting task, and one that will make continuous delivery that much more challenging.

If you do find yourself facing a Major Level of Concern, there are two comforts. One is that your competitors will face the same challenge, and if you manage to construct an effective pipeline that satisfies even the harshest regulations in your market, those regulations present a formidable barrier of entry to would-be challengers. The second is that software is malleable: by isolating and minimizing the software that truly poses safety risk, the vast majority of your system can be developed with a minimum of regulatory friction.

You Are Never Done

When speaking of regulations and providing assurances and producing Basic Documentation and Special Documentation, it is important to point out that none of this can be performed only once and then be over and done with. Most regulatory bodies, the FDA among them, may perform an audit at any time, meaning that you must always be ready to show the appropriate documentation for any version of the software released to users. In other words, assuming literal adoption of continuous delivery, it must be produced – and stored – as continuously as the software it documents. That being said, any software not intended

---

5   Survival not guaranteed.

for release, such as prototypes or proofs of concepts, is naturally exempt from that rule.

Continuous Delivery as the Solution

When we consider regulatory compliance in the context of continuous practices, it is often as a problem of two irreconcilable paradigms. Regulations conjure up images of stacks of paper, lengthy review meetings and bureaucracy – the very antithesis of continuous delivery and deployment. And this is all true, at least some of the time. Some of the time, however, continuous delivery is the solution to regulatory compliance. It is important to keep in mind that documentation doesn't necessarily mean natural text written by flesh and blood human beings; it may just as well (or better!) be structured as machine readable records generated by automated processes.

In the gauntlet of compliance, if you can escape by the Minor Level of Concern route, then all you need is Basic Documentation. And you need that for every version you release of the product, making it a de facto part of the continuous delivery scope: without this documentation in place, release is simply not an option. The good news is that this type of documentation can be automatically generated by the pipeline, assuming it receives sufficiently detailed input.

Parts of the Basic Documentation can be considered more or less static; assuring appropriate actions by end users, once done, shouldn't have to be updated for every minor change to the software. Other parts, such as demonstrating what the software consists of and how it was tested, comes down to connecting the dots in the continuous delivery pipeline: which changes went into this version of the system, why were the changes made, which tests were executed in which environments and under which circumstances, and which requirements were thereby verified? As long as you can pull out records showing that, you shouldn't have to fear any auditors knocking on your door.

To sum it up, complying with regulations requires you to run a tight ship, keeping track of what you do, why you do it and how you test it – just the things you need in an effective and transparent continuous delivery setup. In other words, a carefully planned continuous delivery pipeline will get you the traceability you need to comply with many regulations (in Chapter 15 we will go into solution mode as we return to the challenge of building traceability into the pipeline, thereby making it self-documenting). Unfortunately, the opposite does not hold; rigorous traceability practices will not enable continuous delivery, unless great care has been taken to make these practices automation friendly.

Before moving on to other types of regulation, a word of caution. We have witnessed heavily regulated software projects where this extensive focus on compliance ends up detracting from the ultimate goal of producing working software [28]. When project milestones revolve more around audit deadlines than delivering value, and employees are measured more on compliance with regulations than on delivering value to customers, introducing the concepts of continuous integration, delivery and deployment can be a tough sell, simply because they are secondary concerns. Unfortunately we have no silver bullet solution to offer in such situations – we simply wish to offer fair warning, should you find yourself facing one of these projects.

Confidentiality

Some regulations do place very specific demands on not only demonstrating safety and appropriate protective measures – they can be very opinionated on *how* the product is developed. One such case, which is primarily a concern in the defense industry, is the requirement on confidentiality. Essentially, government agencies may require that the software and/or information pertaining to the software is only exposed to authorized personnel. This poses a significant impediment to any adoption of continuous practices [28], since it means that the transparency and visualization of the end-to-end pipeline that is otherwise one of the main incentives for constructing that pipeline in the first place is suddenly out of the picture, or at the very least severely restricted. This can lead to difficulties in onboarding the organization (see Part IV: Onboarding the Organization) and requires us to design special restrictions into the infrastructure (see Part III: Building the Pipeline).

Archetypes

Figure 14 shows how the software engineering archetypes introduced in Chapter 5 can be mapped onto the Regulation dimension.

Figure 14: The Regulation dimension.

Bob and John are blissfully unaffected by any regulatory concerns. Jane, on other hand, struggles with both regulatory compliance and confidentiality. While her project is one with long lead times until anyone is expecting a finished product, government agencies are requesting documentation demonstrating compliance to regulations and standards on information security and anything related to system safety (which may sometimes seem like just about anything). As a software engineer, Jane finds herself frustrated that actually constructing a functioning vehicle appears to be a secondary concern, taking the back seat to writing documents convincing bureaucrats that they should be allowed to construct it in the first place; as a consequence she receives very little attention from management when she advocates continuous practices. That being said, although Jane and her teammates commit new versions of their component as frequently as they can, they sometimes fail in integration. Most of the time they will simply revert the change and troubleshoot the problem, figuring out together with the developers of the collaborating component whether it is the behavior of one component or the other – or both – that needs to change. When she runs up against parts of the systems where she is not authorized to access the source code, or even get the details on how exactly it is supposed to work, all that becomes easier said than done. Suddenly the informal collaboration between colleagues to solve a common problem is prohibited, because Jane is literally not allowed to see the whole picture.

Alice and Mary have it somewhat easier, in that confidentiality is not an issue. They can, at least in theory, access any part of the system to study specifications and source code, although Alice in particular finds that the processes and the mindset are not at all tailored for it. Instead, each electronic control unit (ECU) is treated as a black box, with watertight bulkheads in between, making access to source code from other parts of the system theoretically possible, but pragmatically difficult.

Both Alice and Mary are also required to produce documentation motivating every change to the system. In Alice's case, this takes the form of separate manually created documents stored in a dedicated documentation storage, which is rarely used except for audits. Mary, on the other hand, simply needs to write specific enough commit messages with appropriate references to any relevant bug report, change request or requirement. These commit messages are then used, along with other automatically generated traceability data, to create visualizations and documentation for a number of purposes, including regulatory compliance.

Summary

In this chapter we have looked at regulations in software development and the challenges they present to continuous practices, but also at the opportunities for effective solutions those practices present. Rather than attempting to address the entire field of software regulations – which would require its own book, and a much longer one at that – we have chosen to lift up FDA regulations for off-the-shelf software as a representative example. We have also seen that each of the archetypes is affected by, and also deals with, compliance to regulations in rather different ways. In subsequent parts of the book we will go further into solution mode, discussing ways of achieving the level of automated real time traceability that can enable continuous practice in spite of stiff requirements on documentation. In the next chapter, however, we will introduce our final contextual dimension: the software distribution model.

Chapter 13

Distribution Model

The fact that one's software distribution model dictates the applicability of continuous deployment is self-explanatory, yet it is often overlooked in literature on the subject. Indeed, a casual reader on contemporary software engineering literature may be forgiven for thinking Software as a Service is the only model around. It does represent a paradigm shift in the industry to be sure, but it's far from the only game in town.

In this chapter we will return to the distinction between continuous deployment and continuous release, which we introduced in Chapter 2, and take a closer look at that difference through the eyes of our software engineering archetypes. Before we do that, however, let us be upfront and honest about the fact that this is an area of shades of gray, rather than sharp boundaries between black and white. While maintaining the conceptual difference between release and deployment is useful, a number of cases occupy a middle ground – something we would technically classify as release, rather than deployment, but yet shares many of the characteristics and benefits of continuous deployment. This is particularly the case with user installed software which is pushed out to the individual user. Examples of this are the frequent upgrades of certain operating systems or mobile device apps, where it's the user who ultimately makes the decision, even though she is prompted and strongly encouraged to install the new software (or, as in some cases, not even given the choice of *whether* to install, but only *when* to install).

From a continuous practices point of view, we argue that there are four distinct distribution models, as depicted in Figure 15. Granted, this is a simplification – in reality, there are all sorts of variants and hybrids – but simplifications are also useful. One distribution model is where the software is deployed by the user, on the user's own initiative. In such cases, continuous deployment is simply not an option. Another model is where it's still the users themselves who perform the actual deployment, but producers push the software to them. Here, continuous deployment is still inapplicable, while continuous release has a place.

Continuous deployment comes into play in distribution models where the software producer performs the deployment. We identify two major variants: where the producer operates the equipment themselves, and where they deploy to the user's own equipment. To better illustrate these scenarios, we will make use of our five archetypes.

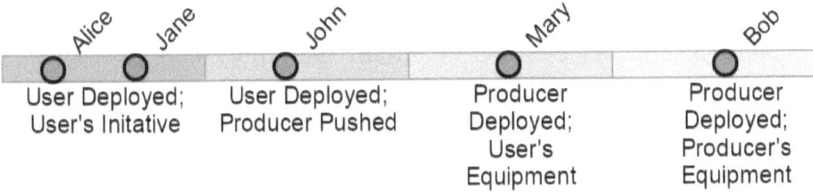

Figure 15: The Distribution Model dimension.

Archetypes

The software engineering archetypes from Chapter 5 can be seen mapped onto the Distribution Model dimension in Figure 15. Note that unlike the other dimensions introduced in previous chapters, we do not present this as a continuous scale, but rather as a series of discrete steps corresponding to the limited set of distribution models outlined above. These should not be construed as representing the entire space of possible software distribution models – there are many variants, and variants of variants – but representative examples to which we think most readers will be able to relate their own experiences and challenges. On an additional note, the broader trend in the industry from product to service business models is steadily pushing more and more cases towards the right in this dimension.

Alice's company supports the vehicles they produce through software updates for many years after they roll off the production line. There are several approaches in the industry to deploying these software updates. The cars Alice's company produces are updated by connecting a specialized support system to the vehicle, which is able to upgrade ECU software. This means that the user must make the active choice of upgrading it, or at least to turn the car in for servicing at an authorized repair shop where software upgrade is part of the service package. In other words, it's down to the user taking the initiative, and Alice and her colleagues have no way of controlling which software is in service, or to roll back a bad revision. What they can do is to request users to hand their vehicles in for servicing, or if things get really bad, recall them. Another consequence is that live testing on target becomes expensive and cumbersome: Alice has – so far – been unable to set up an automated job that remotely downloads new software onto a test vehicle to evaluate it. Instead she needs to physically be at the test plant, or remotely instruct an engineer to install the software for her, which prohibits any tests on actual vehicles as part of the continuous delivery pipeline.

That being said, other companies in the automotive industry have pioneered remote installation of software to in-service vehicles over the air. Even though Alice's company are not quite there yet themselves, they are actively pursuing such a solution – a solution which would shift them to the right in Figure 15, placing Alice next to Mary in the "Producer Deployed; User's Equipment" segment.

Jane's situation is similar to that of Alice in that her customers – that is, national armed forces – own the equipment and manage their own software maintenance procedures. Unlike Alice, however, Jane is under no pressure to change that distribution model. On the contrary, her customers are unwilling to relinquish that control, and instead tend to write requirements to the effect that the system shall function and withstand unforeseen malicious attacks for years without update – requirements which strongly impact testing practices and tend to drive down the release frequency in favor of more comprehensive testing and vulnerability analyses. So even if Jane and her colleagues may strongly encourage their customers to deploy a new version of the software, it is a very conscious and active choice by the customer whether to do so, as they are in full control of their property.

John's software, on the other hand, is deployed by the user, just like Alice's, but is actively pushed to them; in fact, users have to do very little to accept an upgrade. In these scenarios, as in the case of John's game, declining to upgrade requires more effort on behalf of the user than consenting. Indeed, the average user will diligently install every update, while power users are the ones who tend to pick and choose versions.

This model is very common for constantly connected consumer devices, and in John's case handled by a dedicated third party distribution platform. For all intents and purposes this distribution model shares many of the traits of producer deployed software on producer controlled equipment (e.g. a cloud environment), with the crucial difference that every upgrade is an inconvenience to the user, if only a minor one. In other words, John is unable to ship multiple new versions every day merely to experiment and study the effects on user behavior simply because he is unable to do it stealthily. His users would soon grow weary of the constant updates unless they brought tangible and visible value to them.

Moving further right along the Distribution Model dimension we encounter software that is deployed by the producer, even though the equipment is owned by the user. There is a wide variety of both contractual and technical solutions to such scenarios. In some cases, producers require users to allow deployment of new software versions, and in some cases the producers are operating the equipment on behalf of the user. Technical solutions also vary, e.g. depending on the connectivity of the equipment in question: a vehicle without a fixed connection and moving in and out of wireless coverage, as in Alice's case, requires different solutions than a piece of networking equipment sitting still in a rack in a data center, as in Mary's case.

Finally, Bob deploys his company's social media service himself in a cloud environment under their control. Apart from the simple fact that there are no legal or contractual restrictions on how, when or how often he may deploy in that environment, this also means that he is able to deploy both stealthily and selectively, which is a key enabler for very rapid deployment schemes, particularly for purposes of experimentation. To run A/B tests, for instance, you need to expose different users to different versions of the software, and you need to do it in a way so that they are not aware that they being experimented upon. Understanding this degree of freedom is one of the most important contextual factors dictating your continuous delivery, release and deployment strategy.

Summary

In this chapter we have looked at a number of software distribution models and how they affect continuous practices, particularly continuous deployment. In short, different distribution models afford software producers different degrees of freedom in continuously deploying their software, which in turn dictates which benefits of continuous deployment are attainable, or whether continuous deployment is even on the table to begin with. For instance, if deploying dozens of times per day is not an option for contractual reasons, then you will either have to try to renegotiate those contracts or find other ways of gathering user behavior data than through systematic fine grained A/B testing.

Part III:
Building the Pipeline

Chapter 14

Introduction

In this part of the book we will focus on building the actual pipeline: the mechanics of continuous practices, transporting and transforming sources into live software serving end users. Just like in Part IV: Onboarding the Organization, we will cut across all three main continuous practices: integration, delivery and deployment. On the other hand, concerns such as culture, collaboration, organization, communication and behavior are deliberately left out of the scope of this part of the book.

Before proceeding, we want to stress one critical fact: pipelines come in a wide variety of shapes, flavors and sizes. There is not one size that fits all. That is why we will not describe *a* pipeline, which we believe is ultimately a disservice to you as a reader. Instead we will try to help you figure out what *your* pipeline should look like and how to build it, in the spirit of teaching how to fish rather than handing out ready-made fillets.

To highlight this variety and to bring the possibilities to life we will not only break the subject down into individual success factors and discuss how they are impacted by the dimensions introduced in Part II: Understanding Your Context, but will also return to the assortment of archetypes and tell the story from their individual points of view. You will notice that some of them will care much more about certain parts of the pipeline than others, and to others some parts will be completely irrelevant.

This should not come as a surprise. To explain why, let us recall the definition of continuous delivery we use in this book: a development practice where every change is treated as a potential release candidate to be frequently and rapidly evaluated through one's continuous delivery pipeline, and that one is always able to deploy and/or release the latest working version, but may decide not to, e.g. for business reasons. This suggests that there is a high frequency of changes entering the pipeline (or one wouldn't be able to frequently evaluate new release candidates!), but depending on the scale of the software project, it does not necessarily mean that the individual developer integrates very frequently.

Similarly, at the other end of the pipeline is some software artifact ready to be deployed and/or released. What that means, precisely, differs from case to case. Are there regulatory demands to which compliance must be demonstrated? Are there specific types of tests that must be passed? Are there trade laws stipulating which algorithms may and may not be present in your software? Is there product documentation that needs to be compiled and packaged along with the product? And what is the end result? Is it a Docker image, a Java servlet, a Yocto distribution, an Android app, or something else?

Elements of Building the Pipeline

Figure 16 shows the question of how to build a transparent and reliable pipeline broken down into multiple elements. Subsequent chapters will address these elements one by one, and tease out their respective success factors.

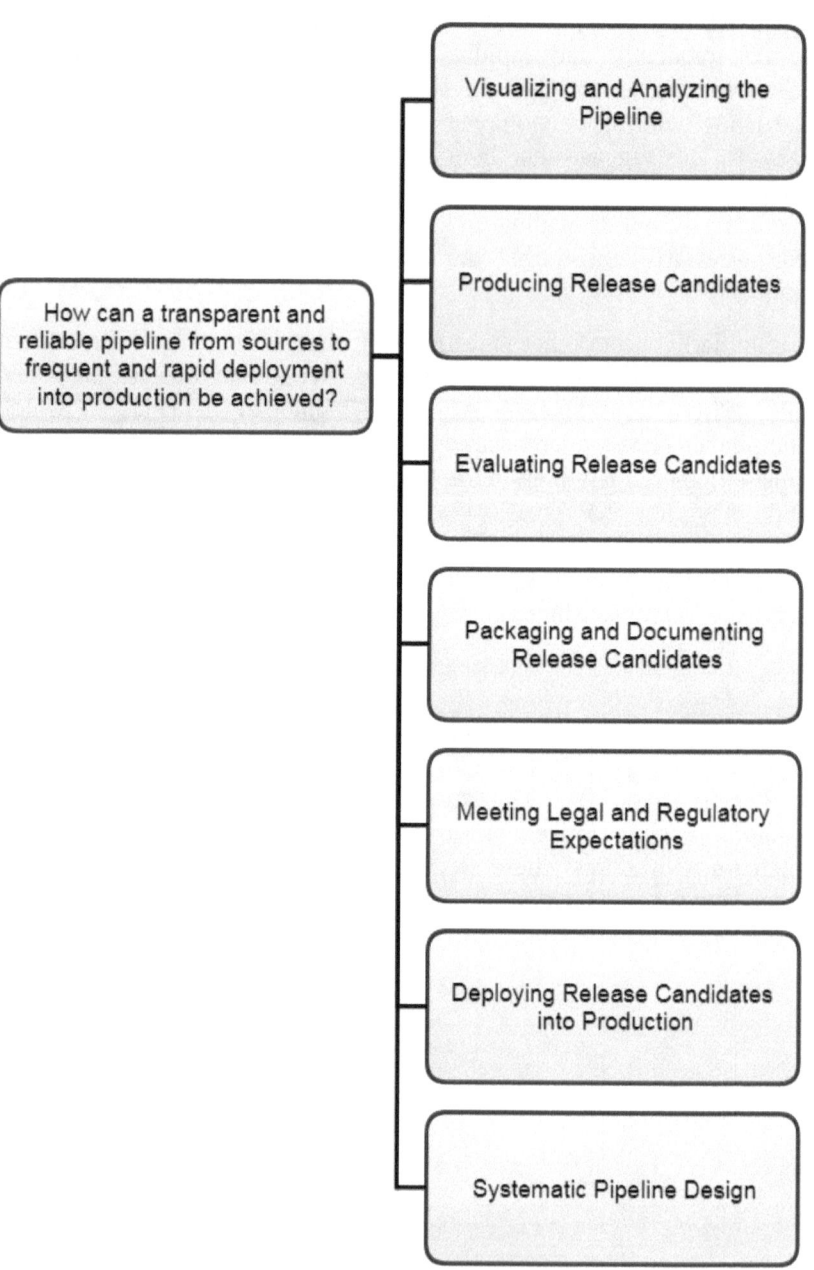

Figure 16: Elements of building the pipeline.

First of all, let us be upfront about the fact that there is never *one* way of breaking down a topic into its constituent parts, particularly not a comprehensive and thorny one like building a software pipeline from sources to deployment into production. The particular approach taken here strives to break this very expansive subject into a set of mutually exclusive yet collectively exhaustive elements [38]. By explaining these smaller elements one at a time we believe that you as a reader will be well equipped to find your answers to the challenges they pose, and consequently solve the original, larger question.

Second, allow us to preempt a potential misconception. In Chapter 6 we state that not every pipeline will necessarily include deployment to production, but in this part of the book we will primarily discuss pipelines that do just that. If this appears to be contradictory, we ask you to consider the definition of continuous deployment introduced in Chapter 2, where the practice is regarded as an additional step on top of continuous delivery, rather than an alternative. Accordingly, if continuous deployment is not relevant in your case, you can safely read on and focus on the parts that instead address continuous integration and delivery.

Chapter 15

Visualizing and Analyzing the Pipeline

The first element of building the pipeline (see Figure 16) is *Visualizing and Analyzing the Pipeline*. Visualization and analysis of the pipeline may seem like a strange place to begin when cataloging the elements of building a software pipeline. Wouldn't it make more sense to begin with its actual construction and design? Must not the overriding concern be that the pipeline does its job, and then we can worry about monitoring it? As it turns out, some of the answers to how to make the pipeline transparent hold the key to solving a string of other challenges, such as how to demonstrate compliance or keeping track of which requirements have been verified in which environments in a large, distributed and rapidly evolving enterprise context. And when you think about it, that shouldn't come as a surprise: to achieve a certain desired outcome, understanding what is going on is usually a good place to start. Consequently, in this chapter we look into five success factors relevant to the visualization and analysis of pipelines.

Collecting Data from Every Pipeline Actor in Real Time

To analyze and/or visualize the behavior and performance of a continuous integration, delivery and deployment pipeline, one must first collect data. Any non-trivial pipeline is built from multiple parts, each with its separate responsibilities, separate life-cycle and separate formats, interfaces and concepts. The usual suspects one will find (at the time of writing) include software configuration management (SCM) systems like Git[6], Subversion[7] or Mercurial[8], code review systems like Gerrit[9] or GitLab[10], continuous integration servers like Jenkins[11], Bamboo[12] or GoCD[13], artifact repositories like Artifactory[14] or Nexus[15], and test execution frameworks. As the software makes its way from the developer's workspace into production it passes through and is processed by these actors. To achieve a holistic view of what is going on with that software at any given time requires an unbroken chain of communication that encompasses all of them. As long as test verdicts are locked into the test framework, build results are only stored in the continuous integration server and code reviews are only visible in the review system, answering the simple question of "Where in the pipeline is my change right now, and how is it faring?" requires a great deal of detective work.

That detective work, unfortunately, falls upon a great number of people in different roles, often unaware of one another. Developers are obvious stakeholders: any developer who takes pride in their work will want to know what the status and impact of their software is once it is checked in and integrated. In a small scale setup this may be trivial; sometimes the entire life-cycle from source code change to deployment and in-production monitoring is captured by the one continuous integration server. In larger organizations and ecosystems of software, where a change may be built into any number of products and variants of products, it is less obvious. At the same time, many of us like talking about the need for developers taking end-to-end responsibility for the software they are developing, but taking responsibility for something that is completely opaque to you is easier said than done. Recall the

---

6   https://git-scm.com
7   https://subversion.apache.org
8   https://www.mercurial-scm.org
9   https://www.gerritcodereview.com
10 https://gitlab.com
11 https://jenkins.io
12 https://www.atlassian.com/software/bamboo
13 https://www.gocd.org
14 https://www.jfrog.com/artifactory
15 https://www.sonatype.com/nexus-repository-sonatype

developer who thought of his job as tossing software into the black hole of system integration (see Chapter 6); not even the best of us can take responsibility for what happens beyond the event horizon.

Other stakeholders include various types of managerial functions – project managers, product managers, line managers, configuration managers, track managers, test managers, release managers and so on – who may be interested in real time data on things like current feature status or test coverage, as well as statistical data such as lead time trends or fault frequency trends (leaving any discussion of the precise purpose and necessity of so many manager roles aside).

Addressing all these needs simultaneously boils down to two problems. First, multiple data sources from a vast and rapidly evolving tools landscape must be tied together and combined. Second, that must be done in real time. Questions of efficiency aside, in the olden days of one release every six or twelve months it may have been acceptable to spend a couple of weeks playing detective and digging through documents in order to figure out what precisely changed since the last time around, but with multiple releases every day that is no longer an option. The realities of continuous practices and the high frequency of changes they imply dictate that traceability data must be generated in real time, *in situ* rather than *ex post facto* [25].

We have repeatedly witnessed attempts at solving this problem by deciding on a certain set of mandatory tools and integrating them point-to-point. Variants of this approach are also published in literature from time to time and can be found as offerings by various tool vendors. There are two major flaws that invalidate this as a strategy, however. One is that the amount of tools in a non-trivial pipeline is such that the number of point-to-point integrations quickly becomes unwieldy. That is particularly the case because of the second flaw, which is that the preferred set of tools tends to vary from team to team and product to product, and also rapidly change over time. In other words, a set of blessed tools thou shalt use will quickly turn into a straitjacket forced upon the developers. What's more, two years down the line it will be an obsolete straitjacket.

One proven solution to this conundrum is to use a technology agnostic communication framework that allows real time collection of the data regardless of the tooling used. An example of this is the Eiffel protocol.

Eiffel[16] was originally developed in and specifically for a telecommunications context, addressing challenges of traceability in very-large-scale and heterogeneous systems development. Since then it has evolved, been generalized and open sourced.

A key contribution of Eiffel is that it introduces a set of information entities – source changes, software artifacts, test case executions et cetera – allowing tools to publish information on a clearly defined format as events on a message bus. In other words, whether you use Git, Subversion, Mercurial or all at once, you can have them publish events on a common format announcing changes to the source code.

As shown in Figure 17, the published events can then be picked up and acted upon by a continuous integration server, whether that is GoCD, TeamCity[17], Jenkins or something else, which can then communicate their actions back via the same message bus. More importantly, the publisher of the information doesn't even have to be aware of who – if anyone – will read the information or for what purpose, affording a clean separation of concerns. This means that those same events may on the one hand be used for driving the behavior of the pipeline (e.g. triggering a new build activity), while at the same time be collected to support visualization and analysis of the pipeline itself.

---

16 Full documentation, schemas, examples and other resources can be found at https://ericsson.github.io/eiffel. Not to be confused with the programming language of the same name.
17 https://www.jetbrains.com/teamcity

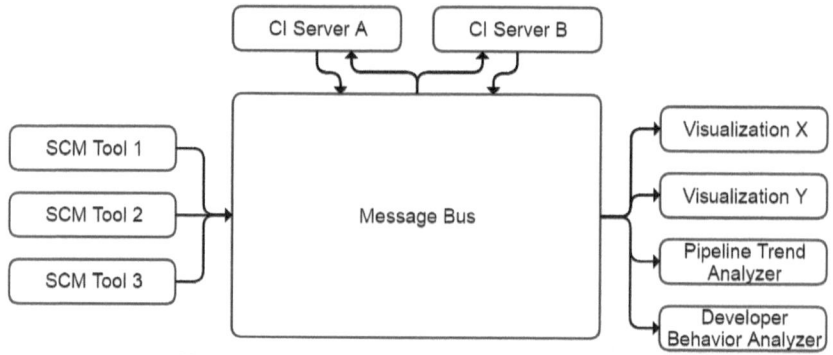

Figure 17: Eiffel message bus.

This allows data collection from every actor in the pipeline in real time, while granting developers the freedom to pick the tools that work for them, and even change their minds the following day. The only caveat is that those tools need to communicate over the agreed upon message bus on the agreed upon format; something easily achieved in most modern tools via dedicated plugins.

This is made possible by the fact that each message published over the Eiffel protocol – each *event* in the pipeline – is small and atomic, making it easy for the individual tool to produce. Instead, its expressive power comes from references. Each event contains a set of semantically expressive links to other events, providing context: why was a build activity started, what was an artifact built from, what was the previous version, where was a test case executed and what was the item under test. This way a directed acyclic graph (DAG) of events is formed (depicted in Figure 18). Traversing that graph can answer a wide range of questions, both questions of instantaneous behavior, of statistics and of trends over time.

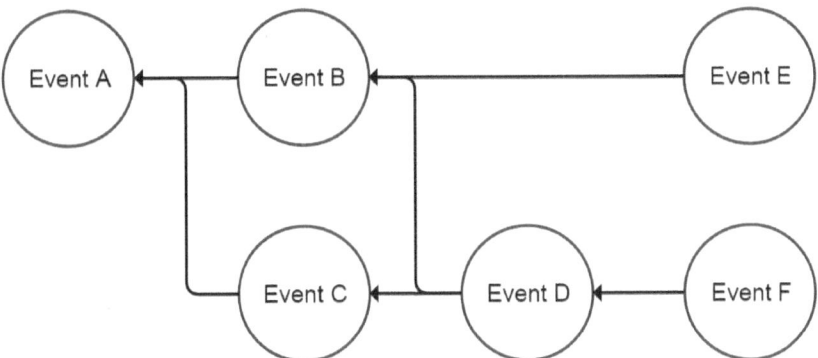

Figure 18: An example of a directed acyclic graph (DAG) of events.

We will have reason to return to the Eiffel protocol several times throughout this book and explain its properties and behaviors. This is partly because we, through experience and research, have seen it successfully solve many of the challenges that emerge in pipeline design, particularly in large scale contexts [25], and partly because comparable solutions to the challenges it addresses are lacking in the public domain.

Our archetypes (see Chapter 5) struggle with this data collection in their own ways. Mary's network solutions company has consciously worked on this capability for years, leading to a situation where Mary has access to a rich dataset describing all actions past and present in the pipeline. This serves as input to a number of visualizations and monitoring services, but Mary's team also explores the data in a more ad-hoc fashion on occasion, testing hypotheses and looking for correlations in their pipeline.

Meanwhile, in John's game development company, this is less of an issue. Most of the pipeline is managed by a single continuous integration server and the data captured by it is sufficient for his needs. Consequently he doesn't regard the evolution of tools as much of a problem, either. In the hypothetical case where he and his fellow developers decide to switch continuous integration server, he simply assumes that the new one will have equal or better data collection and visualization capabilities. Instead, the major effort would be to redefine and migrate their build and test activities, and so he fails to see the return on investment of adopting something akin to the Eiffel protocol.

Collecting Data from Across the Network of Pipelines

While the previous success factor was about collecting data from all of the actors within a pipeline, regardless of the technology or tooling they happen to be based upon, this one is about achieving that same feat across the entire network of pipelines. No matter how clear a picture you have of the changes being made to your sources and the builds produced and the tests executed in your pipeline, that's not enough if you are blind to what your external dependencies deliver to you, when they deliver and why they deliver. Conversely, to take full responsibility of the software you produce, you need a similar level of visibility into where that software goes after it leaves your hands. Who picks it up, what is it integrated into, and where is it deployed?

The challenges in achieving data collection and subsequent transparency across the entire network of pipelines are largely the same as for data collection across tools. This is because it is ultimately the same problem, but one degree worse: these other pipelines you would like to collect data from are also made out of other tools, except they are running in environments where you may have very little control or access – often in other companies or organizations altogether.

Let us consider Jane, the military vehicle developer, to illustrate the problem. A number of vehicle components – some of them pure software components, some of them physical boxes with pre-installed software – are purchased from third party suppliers and integrated into the vehicle. Jane and her coworkers have no visibility into the development methodology of these suppliers and no say in how their software pipelines are constructed. In the bad old days, as Jane remembers them, there was no common way for these suppliers to communicate their releases. Jane had no way of knowing (apart from picking up the phone and calling them) when to expect a new software delivery, and when it eventually arrived it was documented in unstructured (as in non-machine readable) text documents, describing changes made, requirements implemented, bugs fixed and tests executed in more or less prosaic form.

This meant that whenever Jane's company needed to produce their own release documentation, they were able to automate that for their own in-house software, but when it came to third party components they would have to open up those text documents, read them and manually copy the information over into their own documentation. Similarly, when an in-service incident would require them to analyze the life-cycles and statements of verification of all the implicated software, that also needed to be manually collated.

In the new and slightly better days, Jane's company has defined a structured and machine readable delivery documentation format, requiring all its suppliers to conform to it. Like Mary's company, they have adopted Eiffel for their own internal pipelines and now expect Eiffel events to be used by their suppliers as well. This allows structured documentation of all third party deliveries, allowing the expansion of their traceability graphs outside of in-house development, all the way into those third party pipelines.

As always in Jane's business, confidentiality is an important concern, however. Regulations are rather lax for some parts of the software system, while bordering on draconian for others (see Chapter 12); the implementation of the delivery interface varies accordingly from case to case.

In completely unregulated cases, suppliers may opt to publish their Eiffel events in real time to an open repository of events, exposed to the Internet. Since events reference other events not via location (e.g. based on URLs) but via Universally Unique Identifiers (UUIDs) it is perfectly fine for any events produced internally in Jane's pipeline to reference events produced and stored externally by a third party, as long as any visualization or analysis service reading the events is aware of that external location. This type of setup is depicted in Figure 19.

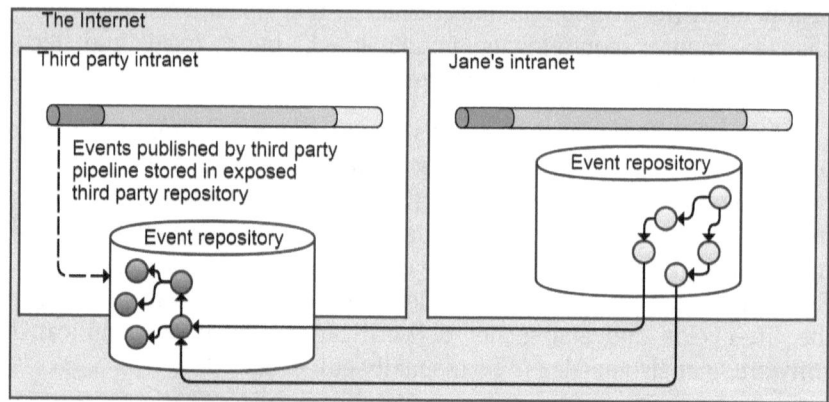

Figure 19: Third party exposed event repository.

Sensitive software components, on the other hand, may not be thus exposed, and neither may meta-data describing it. For those cases, as well as for third party suppliers who are not willing or able to produce events in real time, Jane's company exposes a secure web service where suppliers may put their events, which are then stored in a repository inside Jane's protected intranet (as shown in Figure 20). Naturally, the third party supplier in this setup may or may not choose to also store the events internally for their own intents and purposes. Likewise, Jane's company may or may not feed their own events back to the supplier in a similar fashion, in order to allow them to take proactive measures based on how their software fares in Jane's pipeline.

As described in Chapter 12, Jane has one serious concern that the other archetypes do not: access to any information pertaining certain software components is restricted by law, and may not even be shared within the company. On its face, this would appear to prohibit the use of Eiffel events published on message buses and persistently stored in intranet repositories. Jane and her coworkers have solved this by using multiple repositories, however.

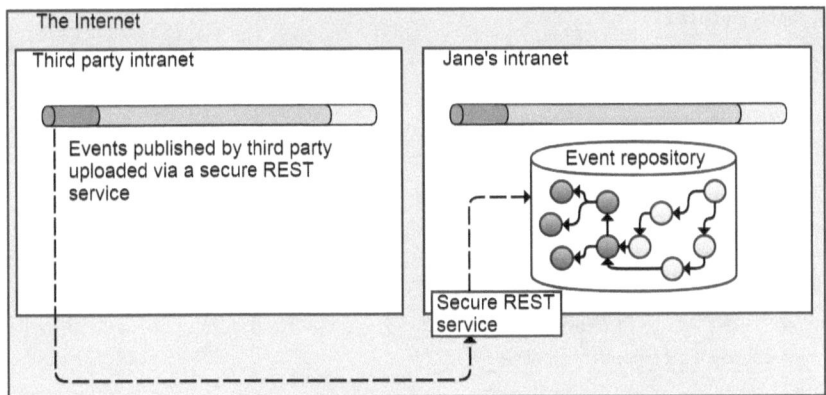

Figure 20: Third party publishing events via a secure web service interface.

Any events containing sensitive information that may not be internally published are stored in separate, protected repositories. Again, since Eiffel events reference one another using UUIDs rather than locations, non-sensitive events may still reference sensitive ones and thereby complete the traceability graph, as shown in Figure 21. For instance, this means that Jane (who is not trusted with access to this sensitive software) will see that a new version of the system was built from a composition containing some sources she can see, and some sources she can't. From her point of view, the system has integrated *something*, but when she searches the repositories she has access to, she gets no hits on the UUID of this something. Jane's trusted colleague, on the other hand, who has access to the confidential repository, can follow that trace link to learn about the particular source revision integrated, who made it, why it was made, which issues it addressed et cetera.

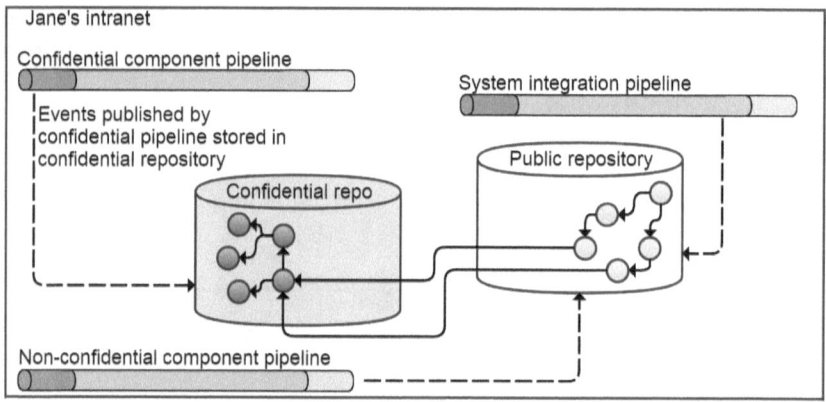

Figure 21: Confidential event repository.

Not all of Jane's suppliers will be able to produce the same level of detail in the documentation of their deliveries, something the delivery interface must allow for. In other words, the format for documenting these software deliveries must be extensible so that the level of detail can increase in a backwards compatible manner. This is why one of the guiding principles of the Eiffel protocol is "What you communicate is volitional; how you communicate it is not". In other words, it is perfectly fine to only use a small subset of its vocabulary, but the parts that are used need to be unambiguously defined, agreed upon and conformed to.

Aggregating and Analyzing the Pipeline Data in Real Time

Even if one is able to extract all the information from the actors in the pipeline, that in itself does little to help any stakeholder unless the data is aggregated and composed into a coherent view. A product owner would much rather be presented with a report on which product versions include their new prioritized feature, and which of its requirements have so far been successfully verified and what the trend of that is, rather than having to piece that information together manually from test reports, build results and commit messages. Similarly, developers are much more helped by a complete progress report on their personal source change's real time progress through reviews, builds, integrations and tests, than by having to monitor each of those aspects separately.

So far in this chapter we have been promoting the practice of using events to document pipeline performance and behavior in real time, with the Eiffel protocol as an example of this strategy. Eiffel based setups, as all event-driven architectures, have an important-to-understand characteristic, however: there is no representation of the state of the system apart from what can be derived from the history of events. For readers unaccustomed to event-driven architectures, the implications of this can sometimes take some getting used to.

This is far from a unique problem, and there are well established solutions in the industry. The practice of using individual events from individual actors as the single source of truth is generally known as event sourcing, and is often used together with the Command and Query Responsibility Segregation (CQRS) pattern. There are plenty of great sources on event sourcing and CQRS, both online and in printed form, not least in the context of cloud and microservice style architectures.

In the CQRS pattern, the method of issuing commands (i.e. write operations) is segregated from the method(s) of issuing queries (i.e. read operations). When applied to an event-driven architecture, this means that data is written by publishing events, while data is read from other sources which provide specific, often highly denormalized, views of those events. This architectural pattern goes hand in hand with the concept of bounded contexts [39], which recognizes that trying to impose a single unified information model on a large and complicated system is really hard, and probably not a good idea. Instead, in bounded contexts, different information models are applied to separate parts of the system and displayed to separate stakeholders. A simple example of how this works is shown in Figure 22.

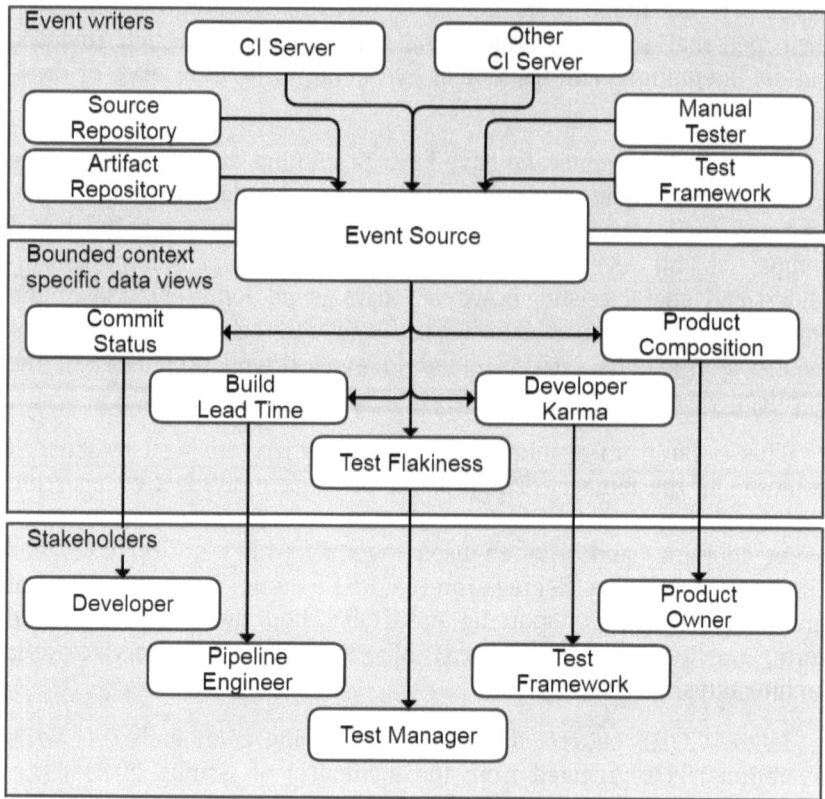

Figure 22: An example of event sourcing and Command and Query Responsibility Segregation (CQRS) in a software production system.

In essence, we advocate a mindset where one's software pipeline is designed and treated as any other software application – it just happens to be an application that builds other applications – and that the same patterns we apply to our products should also be applied to the pipelines. This goes both ways, however. Just as we would never recommend diving into the deep-end with distributed microservice cloud architectures for a very trivial application, we would urge readers to keep simple pipelines simple. If the entire pipeline is managed by a single continuous integration server and there are only a few stakeholders, then the internal reporting and analysis capabilities of that server may be perfectly sufficient.

A look at our archetypes illustrates this. John, the games developer operating in a small team uses the Jenkins continuous integration server out of the box and is perfectly happy with that. It provides an overview of its configured build and test activities and their inter-dependencies. Its logs can pinpoint the single source repository from which each version of the game was built – all of which is exactly what John needs. The return on investment into more sophisticated data aggregation and analysis tools would be questionable.

Mary, on the other hand, has other needs. Multiple organizations, each of which many times the size of John's, contribute to the development of her overall solution, using dozens of schedulers, environment managers, test frameworks, source repositories, artifact repositories et cetera. Each organization hosts a number of stakeholders in various roles, requiring their particular views of the data from the continuous integration and delivery pipeline. Besides, traceability requirements are stricter than in John's case: when a critical in-service incident requires Mary to produce documentation on the exact contents and testing procedures for the implicated software, saying that it was produced in another organization or tested using a separate tool is never an excuse for incomplete data.

What Eiffel does for Mary and her colleagues is to tie all those tools and organizations together into a single data source from which a large number of views can be rendered, depending on the bounded context in question. To exemplify, Mary herself wants to see the status of her recent commits, whether they have been successfully tested or deployed into production. As another example, the pipeline itself relies on what Mary thinks of as a developer karma view, presenting the likelihood of changes made by individual developers to cause faults, to help determine which tests to execute as part of the pipeline. A third example would be an overview of test flakiness and how it trends over time, or a report on test environment utilization, availability and queue times. The list can be made much longer – the point is that once a comprehensive and coherent data source on pipeline behavior and performance is available, the list of perspectives onto that data source is nearly endless.

So far we have talked about collecting, storing and analyzing data collected from the software production system; in the next section we will consider how that data can be rendered visually.

Visualizing the Pipeline Data

While collecting and aggregating the data produced by a continuous integration and delivery pipeline is critical, it isn't sufficient for getting its full value. This boils down to the very simple fact that human beings are much more able to quickly digest and comprehend visual, rather than textual, information. This is particularly the case for numbers, trends and numerical comparisons: few of us are gifted with the ability of making intuitive sense of humongous arrays of numbers, but compiled into a histogram those same numbers can deliver a powerful message in seconds.

There is no single solution for how to best visualize pipeline data. Instead, it is very much a generic information visualization problem, and not only are there many excellent sources on the topic – The Functional Art by Alberto Cairo [40], Information Dashboard Design by Stephen Few [41] and Visual Thinking for Design by Colin Ware [42] to mention a few – there are also several data visualization and business intelligence software packages out there, such as Tableau[18], Qlik Sense[19] or Microsoft Power BI[20] as well as numerous visualization software libraries for those who prefer to roll their own specialized solutions.

Before you get started building your dashboards and trend graphs we would offer a word of caution, though: no visualization will be better than the quality of its underlying data source. This is why we have spent the majority of this chapter on how to build that data source: in real time, across the many tools and actors of the pipeline, and across the many pipelines of the software production system.

Most modern information visualization tools are very mature in their ability to consume event-sourced data on the format we have introduced in this chapter, e.g. based on the Eiffel protocol. In other words, by following our recommendations on data collection in previous sections you will already be well on your way towards powerful visualizations. This is particularly the case because you will likely end up with many different visualizations – more than you would originally anticipate.

---

18 https://www.tableau.com
19 http://www.qlik.com/us/products/qlik-sense
20 https://powerbi.microsoft.com

Then a high quality comprehensive data source, minimizing the effort of setting up new visualization variants, is invaluable.

It is also important to consider the type of visualization most suitable to the stakeholder's needs. One of the first questions to answer is whether the data view that is requested is of a real time nature, or a statistical nature. To exemplify, test managers in Mary's organization have long requested better visualizations of test failures and test flakiness. This could mean a great many different things, however, and not all of them are necessarily what these test managers had in mind. For instance, is it a real time view of tests failing at any given time (e.g. right now), or is it identification of frequently failing tests, or trend graphs of test failure rates over the last few months? Or perhaps all of the above? Simply put, as with any software development, it is important to try to understand the end user and their requirement, and to be ready for the fact that they themselves probably don't understand them very well.

Finally, there is one not-so-generic type of visualization that frequently comes up in the context of software production systems: visualizations of the actual anatomy of the pipeline(s) involved. These answer questions such as what happens when, why and in which order. What triggers that code analysis job, and why didn't it trigger for my change? When is this component integrated into that product variant? Are these test activities executed in parallel or in sequence? That ability to graphically answer such questions and provide an overview of how software flows from sources to target environments is extremely empowering – in essence, it is the antidote to the "black hole syndrome".

When constructing such graphical representations of pipelines (and networks of pipelines) a watershed decision is whether to statically define the anatomy or to dynamically derive it from the data. A static model of the pipeline anatomy is arguably easier to create from scratch, but one that is dynamically derived has two powerful advantages.

First, a dynamic representation can be applied out-of-the-box to any pipeline with a minimum of configuration. The second advantage is that a static and manually defined model will only show you the anatomy you *think* you have, or more precisely, the anatomy you thought you had when you created that model. As soon as you change the configuration of a build job, that model will be invalidated, and so you have to remember to update your visualization as well. In contrast, a dynamic solution will change with the software production system it visualizes, and it will show you what is actually going on rather than confirm your original assumptions. An example of such a dynamically derived anatomy based on Eiffel data is shown in Figure 23.

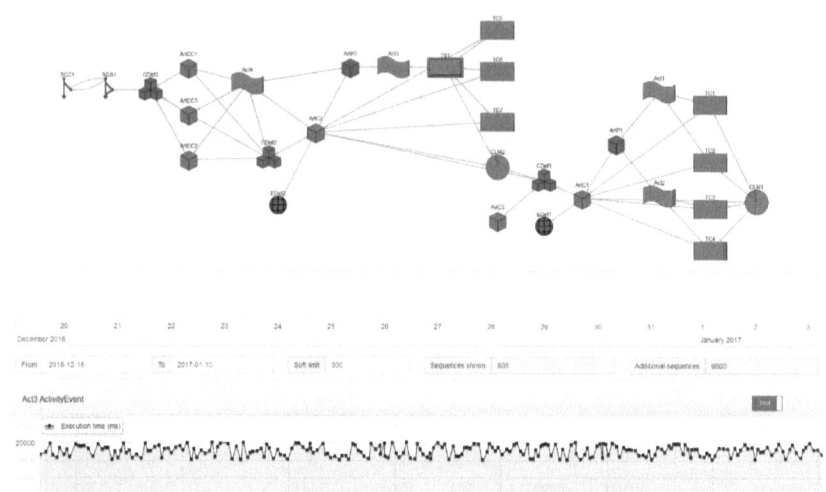

Figure 23: Screenshot of Eiffel Vici dynamic pipeline visualization.

I have seen more pipeline anatomy visualizations than I can count, and they have all been variations on a central theme: icons representing various activities in the pipeline, and connecting edges representing some form of consuming and/or causal relationships between them. Some are rudimentary, and some are impressive in their expressiveness and attention to detail. Nearly all of them rely on statically defined models of the pipelines they visualize, however: these are the activities we know we have and that should be executed, and here is the data source for each such activity, respectively. The problem is that every pipeline is slightly different, and so these solutions can never be replicated in other cases without extensive re-configuration. And so the wheel ends up being reinvented again, and again.

- Daniel

Integrating with the Enterprise Landscape

A continuous delivery pipeline is not something that exists in isolation. If you are like most software development outfits you will have bug trackers, requirement management systems, test management tools, planning tools and more – and if you're truly blessed you'll have more than one of each! That's why it is important for the information produced by the pipeline to integrate with the requirements, bug reports, backlog items and other artifacts stored in these other tools and databases, by referencing them. It is important to understand not just that *a* test case was successfully executed, but *which one,* and not just that *a* requirement has been implemented, but *which one.* Conversely, it must be possible to trace those references in either direction: both figuring out which bugs were fixed by a given change, and which changes address a given bug.

In other words, the pipeline traceability data solution needs to not only handle the artifacts produced in the pipeline, but also relate to artifacts created and managed outside of it. There are several ways to think about this problem, and several potential solutions.

One approach is that of Open Services for Lifecycle Collaboration[21] (OSLC) which publishes specifications for several types of engineering artifacts or *resources*: requirements, defects, tasks et cetera. The aim is to provide a form of *lingua franca* for documenting these items, regardless of the particular tool managing them. The upside is a high degree of flexibility and interoperability between integrated systems, e.g. allowing your requirement management tool to easily display related defects from any bug reporting tool, or as the case may be in a pipeline, for reports from your test framework to include the executed test cases in a generic format. The downside is that rich yet generic specifications are extremely difficult to arrive at, and the end result can be rather watered down. This is particularly the case as new tools emerge advocating new ways of working and new interpretations of what a task or a user story or a requirement even means.

The Eiffel protocol takes a different approach. Rather than attempting to represent or redefine the actual items managed by other tools in the enterprise landscape, Eiffel strictly limits itself to representing events. In a sense, if the test cases, requirements, defects and so on stored in various databases are the nouns of the software production system, then Eiffel events are the verbs that animate them. Rather than attempting to define them they are merely referenced – typically via Universal Resource Identifiers (URIs) – as indicated by the dashed edges in Figure 24.

The nomenclature and underlying concepts of Eiffel events and event graphs may seem opaque to some readers at first glance. If you would like a more in-depth explanation of the protocol, along with tutorials and examples, please visit the project on GitHub[22]. Otherwise, we encourage you to not get stuck worrying about the details of Figure 24 and similar examples further on in this book. Instead, regard them as representative instances of the concept of graph based automated traceability in continuous integration and delivery.

---

21 https://open-services.net
22 http://ericsson.github.io/eiffel

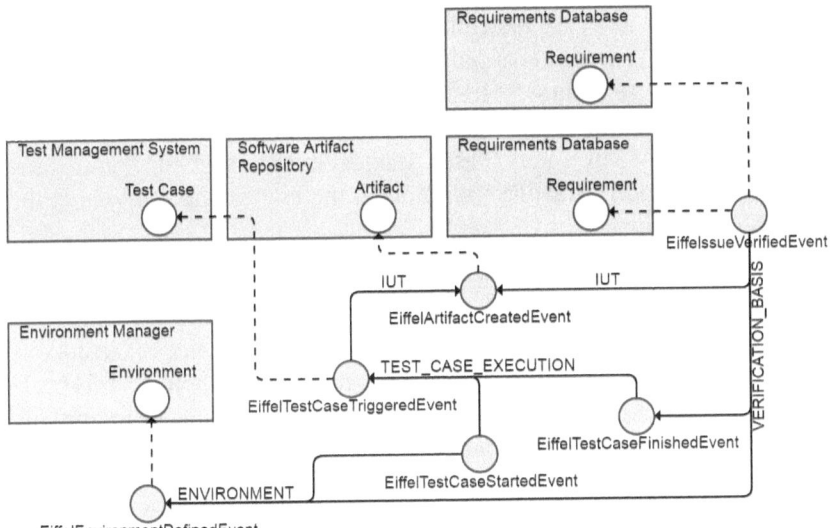

Figure 24: Eiffel events referencing artifacts managed by other tools.

An example of this pattern can be found in Alice's organization. For historical reasons, they use two separate systems for functional and non-functional requirements, respectively. These maintain very distinct data models, and despite several attempts over the years they have never been successfully merged into a single database. This has long been considered a problem, but now the decision has been made that any further attempts to consolidate the two systems simply would not be worth the effort: they have instead decided to embrace the situation and the benefits of highly tailored tools and information models for the two types of requirements.

Both functional and non-functional requirements need to be verified in the pipeline, however, and so the test framework needs to report which requirements are verified by which test case execution, regardless of where they are stored. This is accomplished by emitting Eiffel events, as shown in Figure 24, where event-to-event references are shown as solid edges and references to Eiffel external artifacts are shown as dashed edges. The EiffelTestCaseTriggeredEvent, EiffelTestCaseStartedEvent and EiffelTestCaseFinishedEvent in the figure report the test case execution itself, which is then followed up by an EiffelIssueVerifiedEvent pointing to the functional and/or non-functional requirement(s) verified by that execution, but without replicating them. Similarly, the EiffelTestCaseTriggeredEvent points at the test case in the test management system, and the EiffelEnvironmentDefinedEvent points at the environment in which the test case was executed.

Using this pattern, Alice and her colleagues are able to connect items under test, environments and test cases to both functional and non-functional requirements. Crucially, they are able to do this regardless of which database they happen to be stored in, through their life-cycle events, rather than by changing their intrinsic data models or by making point-to-point integrations between the various tools.

Summary

In this chapter we have argued for the importance of and presented solutions for securing the transparency and traceability of one's software production system, by ensuring that data can be collected across the many pipelines of that system, as well as across the many tools and actors that make up those pipelines. Collecting the data in and of itself is not enough, however: to deliver value to the engineers in the organization it needs to be visualized and presented on a format that fits the individual stakeholder's needs. Depending on the scale of the organization and the complexity of the pipelines involved, these needs may be addressed by built-in capabilities in e.g. one's continuous integration server, or may require specialized solutions such as the Eiffel protocol.

In the next chapter we will look into the actual raison d'être of any software pipeline: producing release candidates.

Chapter 16

Producing Release Candidates

In this chapter, we address the challenge of producing release candidates and list its success factors, while returning to the archetypes from Chapter 5 as illustrative examples.

In our experience, when asked what they find most challenging about continuous integration and delivery, most engineers tend to say something about test automation. Indeed, automating one's testing, achieving sufficient confidence in release candidates to automatically release and/or deploy them is certainly a daunting challenge – particularly in the case of complex safety critical systems. This is something we will look closely at in Chapter 17, but constructing those release candidates in the first place is no trivial task, either. In this chapter we will bring up several success factors that we have identified through experience and research.

Integration Time Modularity

The integration time modularity success factor particularly applies to large scale software projects. As we described in Chapter 11, there's a correlation between the number of people collaborating on any single piece of software and their behavior: the more people, the more infrequently the individual developer tends to commit her changes. Intuitively and anecdotally, it is reasonable to expect the same to also apply to the size of the actual software, although we don't have quantitative data to back up such a claim (partly because consistent measurement of software size in a way that makes cross-product and cross-domain comparisons meaningful is surprisingly challenging).

In other words, unless a large software system can be broken down into smaller pieces – pieces within which engineers are able to operate more or less autonomously – integration should not be expected to be all that continuous. Apart from just making things go faster, a proven solution to the problem is a modular architecture [33], and various strategies for continuous integration of software modules have been proposed in literature [32, 43].

It's important to be clear on the fact that there are several types of modularity. A product can be highly modular in the sense that its functionality is realized by multiple collaborating and communicating parts of executing software, yet be built from a single monolithic code base. Conversely, a single-process monolithic runtime system may be built from any number of independent sources, all with their separate life-cycles. We refer to this as runtime modularity and integration time modularity, respectively. Purely from the perspective of producing release candidates, integration time modularity is critically important, while runtime modularity is irrelevant. From a deployment perspective, on the other hand, the opposite is true (see Chapter 20).

Taking a holistic view they are of course both important. One way of thinking about software modularity is in terms of empowerment and autonomy. Something you create together with a small group of teammates is something you can take personal responsibility for, whereas a system where you are only one of thousands of engineers is not something you have any way of taking ownership of or responsibility for, regardless of slogans about end-to-end responsibility and holistic mindsets. And the sooner your personal work is merged with that of thousands, the sooner you are forced to relinquish ownership of it. In very simple terms, there are three typical situations, as shown in Figure 25.

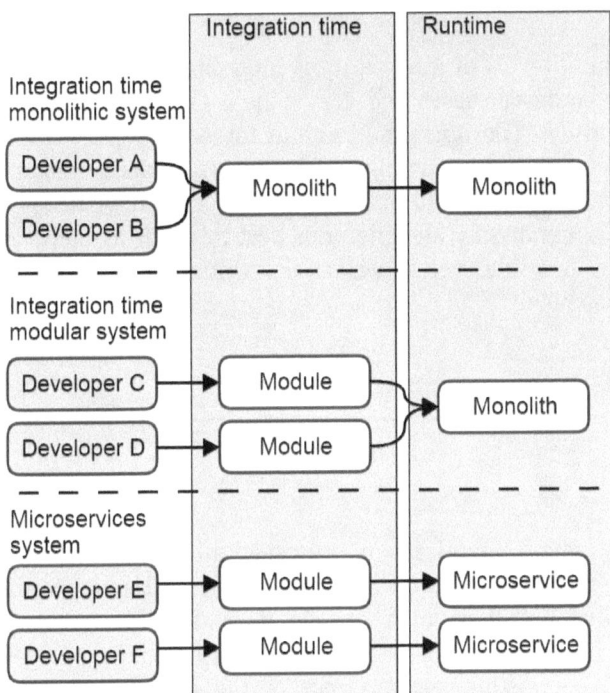

Figure 25: Three levels of modularity.

In an integration time monolith, developers A and B integrate the moment they commit sources, which means that from that point onwards in the software life-cycle they are interdependent. In an integration time modular system, on the other hand, developers C and D can build and test their respective modules independently. This means that the sources of one module can be updated without impacting parallel source changes to another module (assuming a conducive architectural split between the two). As they are integrated into a coherent, monolithic system, however, this independence and autonomy ends: neither Developer C nor Developer D can claim to "own" the larger system in runtime, and so can not take responsibility for it in its entirety.

> Describing levels of modularity is incredibly difficult – there will always be corner cases and gray zones. The fact of the matter is that software designs and architectures vary so widely, that finding precise yet generally applicable concepts and language to describe them is near impossible. Daniel and I have debated these examples endlessly and tried our best to cover as many real life cases as possible, yet a perfect description of reality is always hard to achieve.
>
> *- Torvald*

Finally, where modularity is preserved all the way into deployment (e.g. in a microservice style architecture), it becomes possible to take responsibility for their own service throughout its entire life-cycle, including its in-service performance and functionality. Of course, that microservice constitutes but a part of the complete solution, which neither Developers E and F still do not "own." That being said, they can claim ownership of a clearly identifiable part of it, which is a huge step up from the other two scenarios.

A different perspective on modularity is a purely mechanistic one, and is ultimately about congestion and fragility. To illustrate the point, consider the following back-of-the-envelope calculation. Assume a large software system which takes ten minutes to fully compile, package and test any source code change to the utmost confidence (needless to say, ten minutes is rather an optimistic figure, but stay with us for the sake of argument). This means that during a typical working day of about ten hours, 60 new release candidates can be sequentially created and evaluated.

As long as the number of developers committing source code changes is low – let's say a team of five – this is not much of an issue. If they commit once per day or several times per day, chances are the pipeline will be idle and ready to immediately act on those commits. In a worst case scenario, a change may be queued up for 10 or 15 minutes before being built and tested. Now consider the same system, but instead of five developers there are five hundred. If all of them were to continuously integrate, committing at least once per day, there would be more than 500 commits to process, but only time to build 60 release candidates. Essentially, there are two ways to handle this: optimistic parallelization and batching.

In optimistic parallelization one assumes that the latest commit was okay, even though it has not yet been tested, and so for every new commit one triggers a new build and test cycle. When a commit fails to pass, it and all subsequent commits are reverted. In batching, on the other hand, one simply runs the build and test cycle sequentially and as quickly as possible, every new run picking up the latest available commit and thereby building the entire delta that has accrued since the previous run in a single batch.

Neither of these approaches is ideal. Parallelization drives resource utilization and thereby cost, while failing to address the problem of one bad commit invalidating everything added on top of it. Batching, at the same time, suffers from fragility: the more changes that are batched, the lower the chance of the entire batch not failing the build and test activities of the pipeline. To continue the back-of-the-envelope calculation above, if one assumes that the chance of any one commit passing through the pipeline successfully is 95%, then a batch of eight commits (the average batch size in our example) would only have a 66% chance of passing through – and that is assuming zero interference between the batched commits, which is a rare occurrence.

So far we have only viewed this from the pipeline's point of view, however. From the developer's point of view, there is also the problem of having to stay up to date with and rebase onto more than 500 changes per day. In interviews with developers in large software development projects we find that this by itself effectively puts a soft cap on the pace of integrations. It's not that developers wouldn't like to continuously integrate; rather they find that when the sheer volume of incoming changes is so high, they tend to get stuck endlessly merging everybody else's changes rather than implementing their own. Consequently they retreat into a feature branch, finish their work, and then take the pain of merging when they're done. The ceaseless merging becomes too much like death by a thousand cuts, whereas a big bang merge at the end of development may be painful, but at least it only hurts once.

The only solution, in our experience, that adequately addresses the underlying problem is to simply avoid the situation altogether: to the extent that the software system requires such a large organization that collaborating on a single source base becomes problematic, break it apart into as autonomous a set of modules as possible, owned by teams who take full responsibility for them. In other words, a one-to-many relationship between modules and teams should be avoided, while one-to-one or many-to-one relationships are preferred.

This raises two questions, however. First, what is the right team size? How many engineers and/or developers are too many? Jeff Bezos' two pizza rule is frequently cited: a team shouldn't be larger than what two pizzas can feed. In our experience, this is as good a rule of thumb as any.

Second, how does one ensure the autonomy of those teams? Apart from organizational and managerial aspects of the problem, the key is to enable asynchronous evolution of software across modules. This, in turn, requires strict enforcement of interfaces with life-cycles separate from their implementations. The concept is identical to that of interface separation to enable continuous deployment in the target environment, explored in greater depth in Chapter 20, but applied on a source code level rather than on runtime services.

Just as in the runtime deployment case, the keyword is asynchronicity. This reason is that, practically by definition, it is impossible for a development team to act autonomously if they need to coordinate their changes with a large organization in order to not break dependencies between modules. A knee-jerk reaction among many software architects is then to require developers to never break backwards compatibility in their interfaces, but this can also turn into a straitjacket, where one bends over backwards and accrues large amounts of technical debt just to stay compliant with an obsolete interface.

A more successful pattern is to allow modules to break backwards compatibility, but when doing so also maintaining their old interfaces in parallel for a limited period of time. This provides their dependents a window of opportunity where they can migrate to the new interface. This does require a certain amount of communication – the module changing its interface must broadcast that information to its dependents

---

– but very little coordination. This is key, because nothing kills both autonomy and responsiveness as effectively as synchronization meetings and development coordination spreadsheets.

On a side note, we find that this all comes down to the question of the manufacturability – or perhaps the developability – of the software. In most engineering disciplines, manufacturability is an important concern: how can the product be designed to facilitate manufacturing and to reduce costs? In software engineering, however, this question is rarely raised. An obvious reason for this is that software is immaterial and therefore doesn't require manufacturing the way a physical product does, but we argue that the concept as such – with a slightly adjusted meaning – is valid, and deserves more attention. In software engineering the question is not how to reduce manufacturing costs, but how to design a software product so as to facilitate its development, integration and testing. In that sense, we find that integration time modularity is a critical success factor.

Integration time modularity and, in a more general sense, manufacturability is a non-issue for some of our archetypes, either because their products are not large enough for it to be relevant, or because they are highly runtime modular. John exemplifies the former situation – the code base of his game isn't larger than he can make sweeping and consistent changes to the entirety of the game in single, atomic commits – while Alice's car is an example of the latter, but with an important caveat. The electronic control units of her vehicle system could have been the embodiment of runtime modularity: until they are hooked up in the target environment, they exist as perfectly isolated entities, with their own isolated pipelines. Communication between the units is controlled by a central signal database, however, forcing any interface change to be synchronized not just between the affected electronic control units, but across the entire development project (see Chapter 20).

One of the products in Mary's network equipment portfolio, on the other hand, is built into a single monolithic entity from dozens of modules, large and small, most of which produce multiple versions per day. In other words, the pace of integration is much too high for any manual intervention. Instead, the pipeline constantly rebuilds new versions of the product, swapping out old modules for new ones as they are published.

Archiving in a Definitive Media Library

The Information Technology Infrastructure Library (ITIL) is a set of detailed practices for IT service management. ITIL has achieved a fairly poor reputation in certain parts of the industry, largely because they're just not Agile (with upper case A), or not regarded as being sufficiently agile (with lower case a), while others will argue the opposite.

Whichever side of the argument you come down on with regards to to its compatibility with agile practices, ITIL's goal is commendable. It merely strives to standardize good practices and procedures, providing a baseline of professionalism that allows organizations to measure their performance and demonstrate compliance with regulatory standards. Whatever one's opinions on ITIL as a whole, much of it is based on what we would label as common sense – as elusive as that may be.

One item of common sense, in particular, is the concept of a Definitive Media Library (DML). According to ITIL, a Definitive Media Library is a repository of the organization's definitive, authorized versions of software media. In a nutshell, this means that ITIL believes you shouldn't scatter your software artifacts all over the place, but maintain a protected storage where you can find any artifact you're looking for.

All of which is perfectly reasonable; it is merely an example of the concept of a single source of truth. To exemplify, when the QA people in John's company pick up a new version of the game to test, they don't go looking for a suitable version on John's laptop, the continuous integration server or some random Network Attached Storage (NAS) folder. Instead, they pick up the latest version published to the blessed artifact repository – their Definitive Media Library – the same repository from which releases are shipped.

Many organizations apply this principle without thinking of it in terms of a Definitive Media Library or even having heard of ITIL, and several excellent software repository tools can serve as excellent DMLs[23]. That being said, using a Definitive Media Library is not just a question of tooling, but of practice.

---

23 See e.g. Artifactory, https://www.jfrog.com/artifactory.

Using a single repository as the point of access to and archiving of software (preferably in its ultimate deployment format, see Chapter 18) leads to several benefits. First, it provides a guarantee that if software exists, it is accessible to those who should have access to it, and not to those who shouldn't. This is also a prerequisite for sharing and reuse of common assets within the organization: if you know where to look, it's much easier to find what you're looking for.

> One large organization I worked with struggled with the fact that the wheel would get reinvented over and over again. Instead of being developed once or twice and then reused, generic functionality like protocol serialization and deserialization would get implemented ten or twenty times in as many products. One major reason for this waste was the lack of a Definitive Media Library – there was simply no straightforward way of first finding relevant software and then managing your dependency to it. It is ironic that in many companies, it is much easier to find an external open source library that does the job than something developed internally.
>
> *- Daniel*

Another benefit of having a Definitive Media Library is that it allows safe management of dependencies to third party software. If your organization is anything like most we have worked with, chances are your developers tend to pull in the dependencies they need from the Internet without much consideration of licenses, copyright permissions and trade law. And while that may be fine in an experimentation and prototyping phase, when it comes to in-production commercial software – particularly software exported across national borders – uncontrolled import of third party software can expose you to some very unpleasant and expensive surprises of the kind lawyers make their living from.

A reasonable compromise between legal compliance and developer creativity is to allow freedom with responsibility in developer workspaces, but to lock down the continuous integration and delivery pipeline to prevent it from pulling in dependencies from anywhere but the Definitive Media Library and to ensure that anything that gets stored in the DML is okay to use. That way any release candidate is guaranteed to include only approved software, internally or externally developed.

As an example of this practice, during development of one of her system's graphical user interfaces, Mary finds an open source Javascript graph rendering library that fits her needs perfectly. She plays around with it and decides it's the right tool for the job, and so she uploads it to her company's third party software library. The upload fails, however: the automated static code analysis finds several files licensed under the GNU General Public License (GPL), which company policy prohibits from inclusion in commercially distributed software. In other words, since Mary's continuous integration and delivery pipeline can only fetch software from the Definitive Media Library, this highly useful but problematic software will never make it into any release candidate. Bad news for Mary, but on the other hand, without this check her failure to manually inspect the applicable licenses would have exposed her company's intellectual property (personally held beliefs regarding the moral and philosophical aspects of software copyright and licensing aside).

Bob also makes heavy use of a Definitive Media Library, around which the network of pipelines producing their social media software revolves. Figure 26 shows the pipeline producing one of the microservices making up their backend, along with a pipeline producing one of its library dependencies. As the figure illustrates, the release candidates of the library and the microservice, respectively, are produced and archived early on in the pipeline. They are then reused for multiple purposes (evaluation in the continuous delivery pipeline and downstream integration, respectively). Dotted edges represent transport of the library dependency, and solid edges represent transport of the resulting microservice.

To make sense of Figure 26 it's important to understand that consuming relationships in a network of pipelines are not necessarily causal or temporal relationships [44]. We will return to this issue and methods of reasoning around these distinct types of relationships in Chapter 21. For now, suffice to say that even though both the library continuous delivery pipeline and the microservice continuous integration pipelines consume the same input from the same source, that does not imply that they respond to the same triggers or execute in parallel. On the contrary, as exemplified in Bob's case, a library release candidate is produced in the continuous integration pipeline, stored in the DML, evaluated through continuous delivery and – assuming success – stamped as being good enough for downstream integration. This causes the microservice continuous integration pipeline to pick up the exact same artifact and build it into a new version of the microservice, which is also stored in the DML, from where it is fetched by the microservice continuous delivery and deployment pipeline.

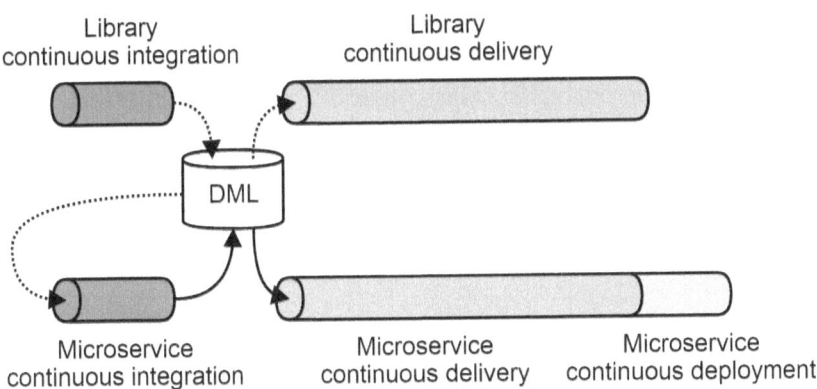

Figure 26: Multiple pipelines writing to and reading from a Definitive Media Library.

Meta-Data as Source

Transforming sources into release candidates requires all sorts of meta-data, apart from the sources themselves: meta-data such as dependencies, build tools to use, deployment instructions, runtime configurations, various types of documentation and pipeline promotion policies, as well as test case sources. A common, but unfortunate,

---

practice is to spread this data wide across any number of auxiliary tools and databases.

I have worked on several products where I have grappled with the fact that even though the source code was conscientiously maintained in SCM systems, everything else needed to actually make use of it was scattered to the four winds. The ad-hoc build system was maintained separately and regarded as a product in its own right, the dependency information was stored in a dedicated property database, documentation was stored in multiple repositories without any direct connection to particular source code versions, and automated tests depended on scripts strewn across a number of NAS disks. Unsurprisingly, the average developer had no idea how to actually build their own software, and while reproducibility was ostensibly a strict requirement, is was something everyone quietly prayed would never actually be necessary.

- Daniel

Needless to say, we regard this as extremely bad practice. This is not least because of the damage it does to reproducibility. If, for instance, the software is built according to scripts and recipes stored in the pipeline's build activity configuration rather than as part of the source, this means there are no guarantees that the current version of those scripts are actually compatible with any given version of the sources: if you need to go back two years in time to rebuild a particular version, you would also need to find the exact pipeline activity configuration that built it. While not impossible, this is rarely out-of-the-box functionality. Similarly, where a particular build activity depends on multiple source repositories and/or built artifacts (e.g. integrating multiple modules), how they all hang together should never be part of the build activity configuration.

Even though we in Chapter 15 explained the importance of traceability, traceability alone will not help you. To understand why, think of your software product as an intricate Lego set. Having designed a stunningly beautiful Lego set, you make careful drawings of every single brick you used and how you fit them together, and then store the pieces in labeled boxes so you won't lose them. As your design evolves you produce multiple sets of drawings and update the contents of the boxes as you go along. A few years down the line you decide to rebuild your grand creation, and thanks to your disciplined labeling and storage system you can easily gather all the individual pieces you used. To your dismay, you realize that you didn't actually put the instructions in the boxes with the pieces, but in a binder in your bookshelf. Since then you have moved house twice, and those instructions can now be just about anywhere, and even if you find them, only trial and error will tell you which version of the drawings goes with the contents of the boxes.

Unfortunately, we come across such practices time and time again: intricate build and deployment scripts are implemented e.g. as part of Jenkins job configurations rather than as sources in their own right, and immediately all version control and configuration management considerations go out the window. To counter-act this, we offer two simple rules of thumb: pipeline activity configurations should be made as stupid as possible, preferably invoking a single shell command, and they should always map to one and only source repository, containing the necessary information to build, package, document and configure whatever the output of that pipeline is.

To exemplify this, let us take a look at the pipeline producing one of the microservices in Bob's social media backend. It pulls in three separate libraries to build them into the deployable service. It would be perfectly possible to do this by having the pipeline activity trigger on any update in any one of these dependencies, thereby always including the latest available set of libraries, but Bob and his team have chosen to introduce a separate repository specifically to identify these libraries, thereby isolating any knowledge of their existence from the pipeline itself.

The rationale for this setup comes from the same architectural principles Bob applies to the commercial software he develops. A vital aspect of software architecture is managing the state of a system: maintaining state in as few places as possible, and only in the right places. This is because stateless software is simply much easier to deal with, in so many ways. A stateless service, for instance, is easily scalable, easily disposable and easily restarted in case of trouble. Once state is introduced, however, things get trickier. The same applies to pipelines – remember, we insist on regarding a continuous integration and delivery pipeline as any other software system – and the same architectural principles apply. Consequently, the ideal pipeline is completely stateless and only acts on the input it is given, and the best place to store that input is in a single source code repository where it is properly version controlled as atomic, coherent commits. In other words, the pipeline should be clever, flexible and powerful, yes, but it should *know* nothing.

This is why Bob's team follows a strict rule of one-to-one mapping between pipelines and source repositories: every pipeline stems from one and only one repository, and all the configuration determining its behavior is found in that repository. This allows the pipeline configuration to be extremely simple – it spawns an environment (e.g. from a container image, see Chapter 19), checks out the sources and invokes a command. Any additional magic on top of that is strictly forbidden.

This makes reproducibility very simple: every built version of the software points back to one and only one revision of a single source code repository, which contains an unambiguous declaration of all dependencies included as well as the environment in which it should be built, clearly identifying e.g. compilers and environment variables. In many cases, the repositories Bob and his colleagues use to configure their pipelines contain no actual code apart from build scripts, configuration and dependency declarations: they only serve to stitch the system together.

A common misconception is that this practice implies manual updates of these repositories for every new version to be built. To trigger a build of Bob's microservice, wouldn't someone need to update that repository every time a new version of one of the library dependencies is published? The answer is yes, but there is no reason for that someone to be a human being. Rather, it's a matter of separation of concerns between two automated processes. As shown in Figure 27, when a new version of any of the libraries is published by their respective pipelines, a dedicated job updates the source code repository at the head of the microservice pipeline with the new dependency information. This in turn triggers a new build of the microservice, even though that pipeline knows nothing about the reasons for that change.

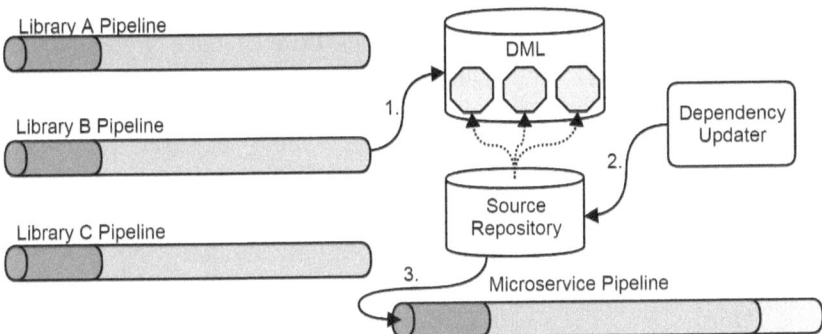

Figure 27: Separation of concerns between dependency monitoring and pipeline execution.

In Figure 27, the first step is the Library B Pipeline publishing a new version to the Definitive Media Library (DML). Second, the Dependency Updater triggers on this and commits a new version to the Source Repository, identifying the new version of Library B (represented by dotted edges). Third, this commit triggers the execution of the Microservice Pipeline, including the updated library version.

The same principle applies to configuration data, environment specifications, deployment topologies and so on. One exception, however, is the version of what is built from the sources – in other words, the version of what comes out of the Microservice Pipeline in Figure 27 should not be defined in Source Repository. We are well aware that in some circles this is a controversial statement, so let us elaborate the point.

First of all, we must keep in mind that the version of the source code and its derivative – that which is built from the source – are two different things. The former is best identified via the SCM system itself, i.e. via a Git hash or tag, a Subversion revision or similar. The derivative needs a separate versioning scheme, however, ideally on a format that carries some information regarding type of change and backwards compatibility (e.g. Semantic Versioning[24]). Common practice is to store this information in the source code and step the version every time a new release candidate is created. Indeed, this is prescribed by various popular build tools.

This practice works well in cases where there aren't too many developers involved, not too many incoming changes, and the generation of new release candidates from those changes is predictable. Essentially, when it's just you making changes it's easy enough to update the version according to the changes you make. If others are making unrelated parallel changes with which you need to merge, however, deciding which version to put in the source isn't trivial, particularly when you don't know which source revision is actually going to end up being built into a release candidate in the end (e.g. due to batching of multiple changes, as described previously in this chapter).

Some try to work around this problem by introducing fluid versions which may be published multiple times, representing work in progress, and then – when a source revision has tested to a certain level of confidence – branch it off, change the version number to a fixed one and then rebuild the release candidate from that and re-test it. We regard such practices as unnecessary complications made superfluous by changing approach to the underlying problem. Just as the source code is best versioned by the SCM system, its derivative is best versioned by the DML, rather than by the source. Every time the pipeline builds a new release candidate it can itself derive its correct version and upload it as such to the DML. The key to doing that is using commit messages to declare the type of change made.

Writing clear, informative commit messages is a highly respected skill in the software engineering community, and its importance widely acknowledged. Commit messages are not just for human readers, however. They can also inform automated agents, such as pipeline build activities, as to how to treat the commit. When developers, as part of their commit messages, declare whether the change they made is a patch, a minor change or a major change (assuming Semantic

---

24 http://semver.org

Versioning), that is all the information the pipeline needs to determine the correct version of the new release candidate.

Let us consider the software in Alice's electronic control unit as an example. The latest software version was built into version 1.5.3. Based on that commit, Alice makes a commit tagged as representing a minor change (i.e. backwards compatible functional change) while her teammate makes a commit tagged as being a patch (i.e. a backwards compatible bug fix). The pipeline picks up the latest commit and determines that the delta since the latest release candidate is one minor change and one patch, and consequently the new release candidate version is 1.6.0. This type of analysis of commits in the pipeline has other uses as well, such as analysis of commit author and/or code changes in order to dynamically determine which tests to execute, something we will return to in Chapter 17.

Before moving on to the next success factor, we would like to issue one more word of advice on this topic. Semantic Versioning and similar versioning schemes do two things at once: they identify a linear sequence of incrementally increasing software versions, and they carry semantic information as to the relationships between those versions. This works well enough as long as that linearity holds true, but when it no longer doesn't, the system breaks down. The ensuing problem of how to version variants and maintenance branches and how to represent their internal compatibility relationships can be a deep, dark rabbit hole that is best stayed away from. One could argue that one ought to maintain but a single development track and thus avoid the problem altogether, but as we have noted before, quoting scripture to the suffering is rarely helpful. In our experience, few developers maintain multiple branches and variants because they enjoy it – rather they are forced into it by prevailing circumstances (as we will return to in Managing Variability further on in this chapter). In this situation there are essentially two options. Either one gives up the semantics (or at least changes the semantics to something other than representing compatibility relationships) or one gives up on linearity. One source of inspiration here is how some SCM systems (e.g. Git) deal with the problem by representing version history not as linear sequences, but as directed acyclic graphs (DAGs).

Job as a Service

The age old developer excuse "But it works on my laptop!" in the face of in-service software failure is often derided as shirking from responsibility – after all, the developer's job is to produce software that works in the production environment. Before we can expect that level of responsibility from developers, however, we have to give them the tools they need to shoulder it. Transparency and traceability, as we discussed in Chapter 15, is one prerequisite. Another is the ability to (quickly and painlessly) test software changes in the target environment. If all the developer has access to is their laptop, then that is all they can be expected to take responsibility for.

This problem very much applies to continuous integration and delivery pipelines as well. Particularly large systems in close proximity to hardware (see Chapter 11 and Chapter 10, respectively) tend to include non-trivial test environment setups in their pipelines. These environments are used to test complex scenarios which can not be tested on a developer's laptop.

One example of this is Alice's continuous integration and delivery pipeline. As software is promoted through the pipeline, it is tested in various constellations of partial vehicle systems (including components such as windshield wipers, lights, brakes, steering, powertrain et cetera) and ultimately in more or less complete vehicles. Until recently, the prescribed process was for Alice to book these environments for a period of time and configure them for her tests. This is highly valuable, and she still does this on occasion, but it doesn't tell her whether her changes will actually work in the pipeline or not. Also, the process of booking, settings up and tearing down such environments introduces a great deal of overhead leading to low effective utilization of these scarce and valuable resources.

Today, all the pipeline activities are split into two parts: triggers and jobs, with the latter being exposed as services behind network APIs. The pipeline itself is just another (privileged) user of those job services, which means that Alice can execute the exact same tests that are executed in the pipeline, but as part of her software design and experimentation process, without committing to the product mainline.

The same applies to build jobs. Rather than producing a "black" build of the software locally and trying that out, she can get her change built by the actual pipeline job, in the same environment, exactly as it would have been had she committed her software. In other words, she can create complete release candidates from any local branch of the code with the push of a button.

This is achieved by a separation of concerns between a pipeline activity's trigger and its function, i.e. the actual job. The trigger is strictly a pipeline concern – it is the configuration that controls what gets executed when and why. The job, on the other hand, is available as a service which can be called by the pipeline or from the developer's workspace.

The problem with most continuous integration servers is that they jumble up these two separate concerns: the job to execute and the conditions under which to execute it are blended into a single activity configuration. Separation of the two enables a cleaner pipeline architecture and reuse of the jobs: reuse both within the pipeline, having the same job execute under multiple conditions, but also reuse by developers and other stakeholders.

As depicted in Figure 28, instead of building her software locally, Alice first calls the build service to compile her sources into a binary. The build job then stores the resulting artifact in the Definitive Media Library and finally returns a report, including a reference to the artifact, to Alice. Now ready to test her freshly built artifact, Alice invokes the test job's API, including the reference to her artifact. The test job consequently fetches the artifact from the DML and, having completed its tests, returns the result to Alice. This allows her to get away from any concerns regarding consistency and reliability of build and test environments: without worrying about whether her development environment is correctly configured and up to date, she gets a correctly built binary served to her, identical to an actual release candidate. It is important to note that while in Figure 28 it is Alice who invokes these build and test jobs, the pipeline itself would follow the exact same process. The point of this setup is that it enables developers to "play pipeline" and manually emulate selected parts of the software production system.

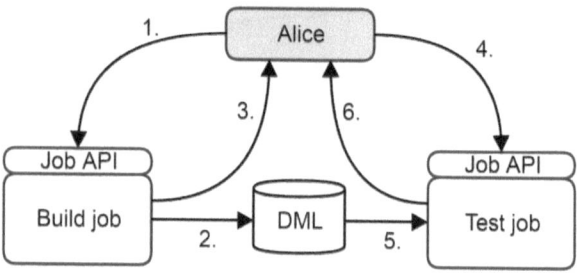

Figure 28: Build and test jobs as services.

What's more, assuming the type of self-documenting pipeline we introduced in Chapter 15, Alice automatically gets full traceability of her own private release candidate in the process. In other words, to the extent her company considers that to be good practice, Alice's private release candidate could actually be deployed to production with the same life cycle documentation as anything that passed through the canonical pipeline. Naturally, she will also want to sometimes build her own binaries, particularly when experimenting with build parameters and environment variables. The availability of the pipeline's jobs as a service allows her to avoid lots of unnecessary errors caused by environment discrepancies.

Managing Variability

Just about every software developer would love to be able to produce a single variant of their product, which all customers would use. For some that is reality, while for others it is but a distant dream. The reasons for this go back to the power balance between producer and customer (see Chapter 8) as well as the distribution model (see Chapter 13). It matters whether the software is a mass-market product where customers take it or leave it, or whether it is more of a partnership oriented relationship where the customer may require tailored solutions. It also matters whether the producer can deploy it to their own environment or the customers install it on their own devices where they can fiddle with it and integrate it with any number of other products.

Pious wishes aside, much of the software industry is stuck maintaining as many variants of their products as they have customers. A traditional way of dealing with this is to either create these variants at integration time (essentially maintaining one pipeline for every variant) or even worse, in development by cloning and owning the software for every customer solution. Both approaches create enormous amounts of overhead and waste – particularly the latter, as any functionality must be reimplemented multiple times, tested and verified multiple times, and even so there are no guarantees it will work the same in each variant.

Mary's networking solution is constantly challenged by this problem. Three major customers, A, B, and C, have very different wishes and requirements on functionality. While Customer A desires Feature X, Customer B only wants Feature Y. Customer C, on the other hand, would really like both Features X and Y, but hasn't paid for either, and Mary's company doesn't want to give them away for free. What Mary and her colleagues could do would be to clone the source code and develop it on separate tracks, as shown in Figure 29, where individual source code revisions on each separate track is represented as a circle.

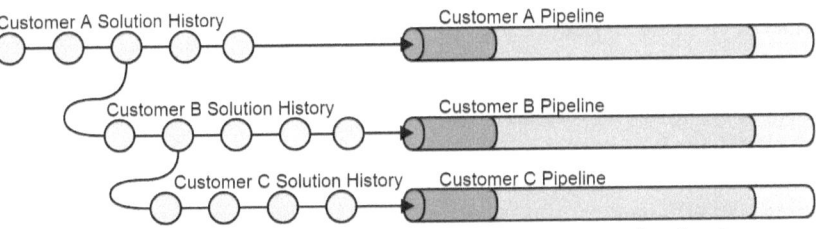

Figure 29: Software variability based on source code cloning.

They could also split the product into parts with Features X and Y isolated in dedicated modules, which are then included or not included in the build for each customer, as shown in Figure 30. Another strategy would be to supply Features X and Y as plugins to be added at deployment, and yet another to implement feature flags for activation and deactivation of particular features, e.g. based on a licensing scheme. This allows Mary to develop any given feature once and only once for all customers, whereupon who uses it and who doesn't becomes a later concern. This practice comes with the added benefit of greater flexibility, where licenses can be enabled and disabled in runtime without even re-deploying the software. For instance, Customer C can be provided temporary trial licenses and possibly enticed into purchasing the extra features for their system.

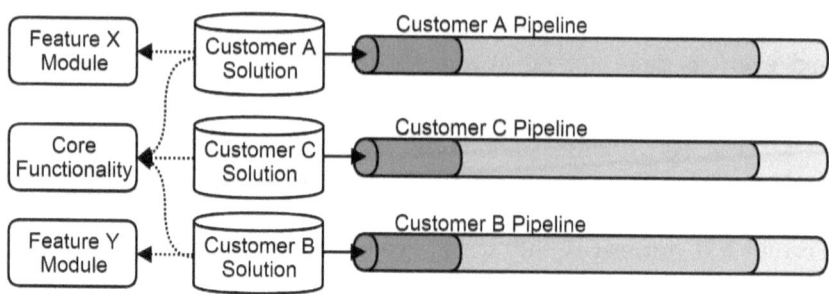

Figure 30: Software variability based on modularity.

Which strategy is optimal in the given case depends on several factors. The distribution model is one, but also the proximity to hardware (see Chapter 10); for instance, in certain situations the need to minimize hardware resource utilization may override all other concerns and drive the product towards cloning just to be able to optimize each individual customer solution.

Regardless of strategy the variability problem doesn't quite disappear, however, at least not from a verification point of view. Particularly in safety critical contexts (see Chapter 7), each unique combination of license activations may be regarded as a variant to be verified, whereupon the demands on the testing resources of the pipeline will literally increase exponentially, unless sufficient functional isolation between the variants can be demonstrated. There are strategies to get around this, which we will investigate in Chapter 19, but it may be worthwhile for the business side of Mary's company to perform a cost-benefit analysis of complying with these wishes before choosing either strategy. It is quite conceivable that such an analysis would reveal that sticking to a single variant containing all the features at a lower price, but also developed at a lower cost, would be more profitable – even if it meant losing Customer B, who absolutely do not want Feature X, in the process.

Summary

In this chapter we have identified success factors for effectively producing release candidates. Careful consideration of the architecture both of the pipeline and of the software product itself can greatly impact one's ability to rapidly and consistently produce new release candidates. In the next chapter we will look into techniques for evaluating those release candidates.

Chapter 17

Evaluating Release Candidates

An obvious core feature of an effective pipeline is its ability to ensure that a release candidate lives up to expectations and does not introduce any (critical) faults into the production environment. At least, that is, where one regards testing as necessary prior to deployment and/or release. As always, it's important to understand one's context to know what one can get away with. In this chapter we will introduce the success factors we have identified in order to frequently and rapidly evaluate release candidates, thereby allowing data driven release and deployment decisions.

Before diving into those success factors, let us mention one factor which is *not* on that list: automating all testing. Assuming the scale of the software system is non-trivial, the sum of the test cases would put a huge strain on the pipeline, as they require significant time and resources to burn through for every change. Meanwhile, and at the end of the day most of them tend to find very little in terms of actual faults. A common phenomenon we have witnessed multiple times in organizations adopting continuous practices is a huge effort to get rid of all their manual testing and – by extension – testers. This is typically achieved by having those same testers, who are rarely experienced developers, write test scripts mimicking the rote regression tests they would perform manually. One result of this is inevitably a huge pile of poorly written, copy-pasted and unmaintainable code. Another result is that once the manual test cases have been automated all the testers are laid off or reshuffled in the organization, meaning that not only did the manual test cases go away, but the testing discipline and mindset went with them. These factors explain why we consider the "automate all testing" approach to building tests into one's pipeline to be an anti-pattern. Instead, in this chapter we will discuss what we find to be more effective approaches to the problem.

> From time to time people will tell me how they want to execute "all the test cases" on unit, component and system level before new software is integrated. The problem with that is that the test resources would then become a huge bottleneck, severely limiting the number of changes to the mainline and disincentivizing frequent commits by the developers. Rather than preventing bad code from being committed, in reality you end up with very little code being committed at all.
>
> *- Torvald*

Identifying Automated and Manual Test Activities

Automation is key to evaluating release candidates with sufficient speed and frequency, but as already pointed out, simply automating whatever one might previously have done manually is rarely conducive. One reason for this is that manual and automated testing have different strengths and weaknesses.

A skilled human tester, even when running rote scripted regression tests, will keep an eye out for unexpected behaviors, even outside of the explicit scope of the test – something automated test scripts will never do. At least, that is, unless we assume sophisticated artificial intelligence, but then we have practically by definition moved outside the domain of scripted regression testing. Automated tests, on the other hand, have other strengths, such as a much greater capacity to explore parameter permutation spaces, boundary conditions and perform fault injection at a large scale. Simply translating manual test plans into automated test suites tends to result in the worst of both worlds.

The other reason is that not all tests must necessarily be on the critical path of the pipeline. Here we use the term critical path, borrowed from project management theory, to denote the longest series of sequential activities on the path to the pipeline's ultimate output (see Chapter 21 for more on reasoning around and managing the critical path). In other words, in the typical project you will find a set of tests that *must* pass to guarantee core functional and non-functional requirements. These are things that must under no circumstances slip into production; things that can not be easily recovered from. The size of this set varies from case to case. At one extreme end of the spectrum one will find evangelists declaring that it should be literally zero: just get the code into production and see if it works, and if it doesn't, fix it. This may be a viable strategy in certain contexts, even though it is easy to suspect that its proponents have limited experience of safety critical systems engineering. At the other end of the same spectrum you will find extreme demands on reliability and resilience – requirements such as being immune to all unforeseen malicious attacks for several years after being deployed – implying extensive testing before deploying or releasing. In the end, it comes down to looking critically at your test scope: which tests, and not least which types of tests, are truly required for you to be able to release and/or deploy? This needs to be considered with a skeptical and conservative mindset, because it's always easy to add tests, but it can be very scary to remove them. We will return to this in Chapter 21, but for now let us conclude that not all testing one might conduct needs to be done for every version of the product, and that even in a continuous delivery and deployment scenario not all testing needs to be automated.

> It's important to not allow the quest for automation to turn into disregard for testing as a discipline. What you don't want is to have to delay a software release until your testers have caught up with their test plan, but that's not the same as not doing manual testing. The value of having people come into the office 40 hours a week doing nothing but try to find new ways to break your system should not be underestimated.
>
> *- Daniel*

This means it is essential to consider which test activities should be automated and which should be manual. Manual tests are actually a highly valuable complement to automated activities as long as they are not allowed to turn into bottlenecks. One example of this is regular exploratory testing (e.g. daily or weekly) of the latest release candidate to pass some suitable level of confidence in the pipeline; not for the purpose of evaluating that release candidate's suitability for release and/or deployment, but purely for feedback purposes, as shown in Figure 31.

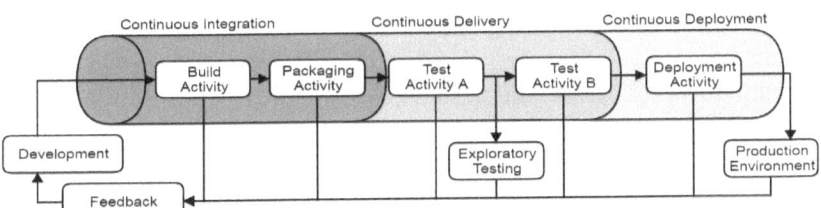

Figure 31: Exploratory testing outside the critical path of the pipeline.

While feedback is an important part of the value of an automated pipeline, different types of activities in that pipeline will answer different types of questions. As shown in the figure, developers (and other stakeholders) receive feedback from all of the activities in the pipeline, as well as from the production environment. They also receive valuable feedback from the exploratory testing, however, even though the outcome of that testing has no influence over whether a particular release candidate gets deployed or not – particularly since that release candidate is likely deployed long before the exploratory testing even begins.

This type of testing as a complement to an automated pipeline has several benefits, such as effectively identifying system level characteristics and faults, and making cost-effective use of scarce and valuable test environments. The close connection to the automated activities also means that the time of the testers is not wasted on trivial faults identifiable by less expensive testing and that they have a clear picture of the development status and open bug reports on the particular version they are currently exploring [45]. The most value from exploratory testing is obtained when new functions or systems are to be tested. The method is of course applicable to regression testing as well, but will provide more limited value.

One example of this way of working is the web frontend of Bob's social media platform. New versions are automatically deployed very frequently, not least in order to carry out A/B testing, and Bob and his colleagues are confident that nothing catastrophic will slip through the automated tests. Once a week, though, they will all log in on the public service as users and try their best to break it or subvert it in any way they can think of – particularly the parts they themselves have not developed. A couple of times they managed to compromise the system to the extent that some of the in-production services required redeployment, but most findings simply make their way to the backlogs of whichever teams seem most suited to deal with them.

John's game development studio serves as a counter-example. Due to their distribution model and their relatively low frequency of releases, any release candidate must pass through manual evaluation by the QA department before being considered for distribution, as shown in Figure 32. Consequently, as opposed to Figure 31, this manual testing can be thought of as part of the pipeline's critical path, rather than off to the side of it (with the caveat that such a manual process on the critical path will slow it down to the point where "continuous" becomes a bit of a stretch). On the other hand, it is closely tied to the automated activities in the sense described above in that the QA department would never dream of picking up any version not produced by the pipeline and stored in the Definitive Media Library, to ensure full traceability and that trivial regression faults have presumably been weeded out.

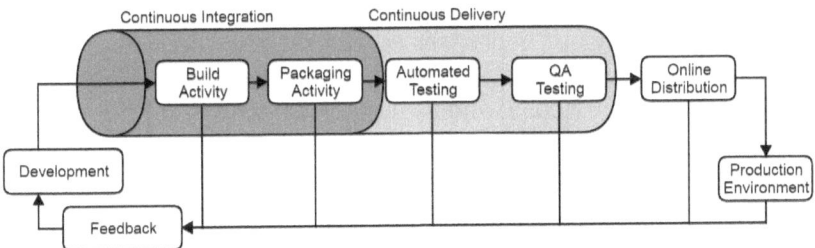

Figure 32: QA testing on the critical path of the pipeline.

Automated Test Case Development

The success factor of automated test case development follows naturally on the previous one: having determined which tests should be automated and where in the pipeline they belong, those (automated) tests need to be implemented. This can be easier said than done, however. Implementation of the test scripts together with the supporting tooling and frameworks to execute them requires every bit as much engineering skill as the implementation of the software they are testing.

Software testing in general and test automation in particular is a vast and deep research field, but from years of industry experience we find that the gulf between academic research and industry practice is equally vast. The cause and nature of this divide between theory and practice can be (and is being) debated. Where some researchers would regard the day-to-day challenges of test automation in the industry as solved problems – in theory – we in this section take a more pragmatic stance grounded in experiences from the trenches. This is because the difficulties we find there have much less to do with the bleeding edge of theoretical research than they do with people and attitudes.

We find that effective test development requires three core competences: software development skills, testing skills and thorough insight into the system being tested. Unfortunately, engineers tasked with writing automated test suites frequently lack one, two or all three.

When test case developers lack general software development skills, the result is an unmaintainable heap of test scripts with strange and fascinating cobwebs of dependencies and runtime inefficiencies. One tell-tale sign is test cases that make a call to the system, sleep for an arbitrary number of seconds and then check the state to see if it matches expectations (which, apart from being the most common cause of test flakiness [46], will drive execution times like nothing else when executing a few thousand such test cases) or long setup and tear-down procedures copy-pasted from test case to test case. This is the expected result when an organization turns an existing group of testers into automated test case developers.

The opposite situation, where those developers lack testing skills, is equally bad. This will result in test cases that may be skillfully implemented with a clean architecture and a maintainable code base, but naively constructed. In such cases one expects to find test that upon scrutiny turn out to not truly test what they claim to test, as well as a lack of e.g. boundary value analysis or testing of exception handling and faulty input. In short, developers not trained in testing tend to not reflect on the validity of their test cases, and easily fall into the trap of verifying their own assumptions regarding the system by creating "happy path" or "sunshine" test cases – as opposed to "sad path" test cases. The end result is a false sense of good test coverage and confidence.

Finally, even when test case developers are skilled developers and trained testers, unless they understand the system under test they will struggle to create effective and worthwhile test cases. This is because of the simple fact that only an engineer knowledgeable about the system and its behavior and functionality can determine what is straining out gnats and what is swallowing camels. Not least, it is vital for the test case developer to have a keen understanding of how the test environment and/or simulator works, in order to create both effective and efficient test cases.

We have seen examples of all three scenarios outlined above in industry projects: testers reclassified as test case developers, and failing; developers tasked with developing all the system's test cases without any additional training, and failing; skilled testers and developers being brought in from the outside to write test cases for a system they are unfamiliar with, and failing. The root cause of all three is a general disregard for testing skills and expertise – the unspoken yet erroneous belief that testing is a less qualified and therefore less prestigious discipline than development, and that test case development is so much simpler that the same rigors applied to the engineering of the item under test are unnecessary.

To conclude, let us consider one of our archetypes. Mary has witnessed the effects of this attitude at close hand. Her pipeline is bogged down by tests created by highly skilled testers who have been reassigned from testing to test automation. They have consequently produced a monstrosity of a test suite that literally takes hours to execute, and that nobody dares refactor out of fear of breaking its fragile and inscrutable inner workings.

Avoiding Test Flakiness

A nearly ubiquitous problem with automated test cases is what is generally known as test flakiness: non-deterministic behavior in test case executions. A typical automated test case is assumed to either pass or fail, and to consistently pass or fail as long as the software doesn't change. This assumption is crucial – without it, the outcome of the test case execution has limited value. A flaky test, however, breaks that assumption, as it may intermittently fail even though the item under test remains unchanged, seemingly at random.

The presence of flaky tests in a pipeline causes damage is multiple ways. First of all, unreliable tests tend to be ignored by developers – failures are simply assumed to "not be real". This ends up eroding the overall confidence in the automated tests and negates the value of having them in the first place. Second, insofar as engineers are correct in assuming that flaky test failures are indeed false positives, this will stop perfectly good release candidates from reaching the end of the pipeline (assuming these are gatekeeping tests). This causes frustration, delays and inefficiencies at multiple levels of the organization. Third, insofar as engineers are *not* correct in assuming that these are false positives, the flakiness of the offending test case will mask a very real fault, albeit one that the particular test case fails to reliably reproduce. Besides, there's a broken windows phenomenon at play here: when a test suite fails now and again anyway, chances are nobody will care much if another test begins failing.

These problems are exacerbated by the fact that flaky test cases are notoriously hard to troubleshoot, practically by definition. As the failure only occurs *sometimes*, reproducing the failure and locating the root cause can be a very frustrating and time consuming process. This goes a long way to explain why flaky tests are often left unattended. It is common practice to quite simply ignore them or re-run them [46].

More drastically, some will advocate removing flaky tests altogether. There is good reason for doing so, but it's not without danger. Flaky tests do provide questionable value: a verdict you don't trust is a verdict you could do without. Besides, as already mentioned, they're great at generating what one might think of as "negative work": re-runs, administration, follow-ups, difficult troubleshooting, escalations, delays et cetera. In light of all that, simply throwing them away is certainly an appealing option. The problem is that without first analyzing the flaky test case, it's impossible to know whether the flakiness lies in the test case or in the product. If it's the former, good riddance. If it's the latter, that might be something you want to fix.

Consequently, when faced with flaky tests in the pipeline, we regard the following as a balanced approach to the problem. First, consider whether the tested behavior of the system is actually critical. In other words, would it be really bad if there truly was some intermittent failure mode in the product itself? If not, whether fixing the test is worth the time and effort is questionable, and it's probably safe to remove the test. Second, if the test behavior really is critical, start by searching for common causes of test flakiness in the test environment or test case implementation (more on this below) and refactor them until no more sources of flakiness can be found. If refactoring proves impossible, or no sources of flakiness can be found in the test environment or test case, it's time to roll up one's sleeves and start troubleshooting in the product itself.

The good news is there is a fairly small set of usual suspects to look for when investigating test flakiness. By far the most common cause is asynchronous waiting, already touched upon in this chapter. Asynchronous waiting is when the test case makes an asynchronous call to a remote resource or to another thread, waits some arbitrary stretch of time, and then assumes that some criteria have been fulfilled. Using one of the archetypes to exemplify, when Bob writes a test case for a user authorization function, he *could* launch a user account database object, wait for two seconds and then query it, simply assuming it will be online and available by then. This introduces flakiness, however: sometimes two seconds will be enough, and sometimes it will not. A safer option would be to properly wait for the asynchronous call to complete before continuing.

Other common causes of test flakiness include other concurrency related issues and test order dependencies, where test cases fail if they are not executed in a particular order. For a more in-depth analysis of test flakiness and its causes, see the excellent overview provided by Luo et al. [46].

To summarize, even though test flakiness is as harmful as it is common, it can be avoided through a good understanding of common causes of non-deterministic behavior. To the extent that flaky test cases cannot be avoided or refactored, however, discarding them altogether may well prove preferable to keeping them around.

Requirement Verification

Pure implementation concerns aside, we would like to point out the importance of test case meta data management. Not every software product is strictly defined by requirements, or will even bother with requirements at all, but for those who do (typically related to safety criticality as described in Chapter 7) verification of those requirements must be considered.

Let us keep in mind that testing and verification are two separate concepts: one can test without necessarily verifying anything, but one can also test in order to verify. To complicate matters further, there are many interpretations of verification, particularly as opposed to validation. In this book we use the broad definition of verification, which includes both static and dynamic verification for the purposes of assuring that software satisfies all expressed requirements. In products that require formal verification of requirements, that verification must be performed before release and/or deployment of any given version of the product. This means that by definition these verification activities must end up must end up on the continuous delivery pipeline's path (critical or otherwise) towards a fully evaluated release candidate. Unfortunately, it is not uncommon to see cases where continuous delivery is ostensibly practiced, but only as an R&D internal phenomenon, with formal verification being performed by a separate department. Even though any release candidate is extensively tested in the pipeline and valuable feedback to the developers is generated, it is not actually verified. Instead, the release candidates – all done and ready to go from R&D's point of view – are handed over to the verification department where a couple of weeks or months of lead time is added before the product can be released, despite the fact that much of what is then verified has already been tested previously.

This problem of wasted effort and added lead times comes down to two root causes. One is a fairly obvious organizational one, and the other a more subtle technical one. The organizational problem is one of silos: on its way to the customer the software gets thrown over the fence from one department to another, with little or no insight as to what is going on on the other side, consequent overlap of efforts and resulting waste. With a bit more transparency, or even assigning the verification responsibility to the R&D department in the first place, this could be avoided. Granted, there is a point to having an independent party perform verification – indeed, it is sometimes prescribed by regulations – but the cons of such a silo setup need to understood and outweighed by the pros.

The technical root cause is one of data management and traceability. The many tests executed in the pipeline could very well be used to formally verify requirements, if only they were explicitly linked and their execution transparently reported. One way of achieving that is by using the Eiffel based traceability techniques introduced in Chapter 15. Additionally, an obvious prerequisite is the quality and realism of the test environments utilized by the pipeline.

To exemplify this practice, let us consider the automated requirement verification of Alice's car. Any car model comes with a vast database of requirements covering every aspect of the car – requirements that need to be verified for any given released version of the complete system. Some of these requirements can be verified in pure software, some in a partial vehicle, and some only in a complete vehicle. Which is the case for any one requirement can be difficult to determine upfront, as this depends on the architecture and separation of concerns within the system. In other words, the successful execution of any test case anywhere in the network of pipelines – manual or automated – may or may not serve as verification of one or more requirements on the car as a whole.

To utilize this fact and not have to re-test what has already been tested earlier, every test case, regardless of its scope or which level of system completeness it operates on, can be explicitly linked to requirements which can be considered verified if the test case passes. Coupled with Eiffel based traceability throughout the pipeline, this means that any given version of the vehicle system can be analyzed to determine all the modules that were integrated into it, all the test cases that have been executed for those modules, the environments in which those test cases were executed, the outcome of those executions, and consequently which requirements have been successfully verified – regardless of who happened to perform the test where and how (although that information can also be collected, if necessary, for accountability reasons).

A simplified illustration of this pattern is shown in Figure 33. The creation of a new system version is represented by the rightmost EiffelArtifactCreatedEvent. By tracing its COMPOSITION link via EiffelCompositionDefinedEvent and its ELEMENT links, all the parts built into that system can be retrieved, in the figure represented by the leftmost EiffelArtifactCreatedEvent. Additionally, there are two EiffelIssueVerifiedEvents claiming verification of one each of the two requirements in the Requirements Database, but they do this for separate artifacts, identified by IUT (Item Under Test) links. Analysis of the traceability graph, however, reveals that both requirements have been verified either at the complete system level or for one of its elements. To complete the graph with further information, such as the basis for the verification, additional events and links are required; these have been omitted for readability and simplicity. For a more complete view, please see Figure 24 on page 125.

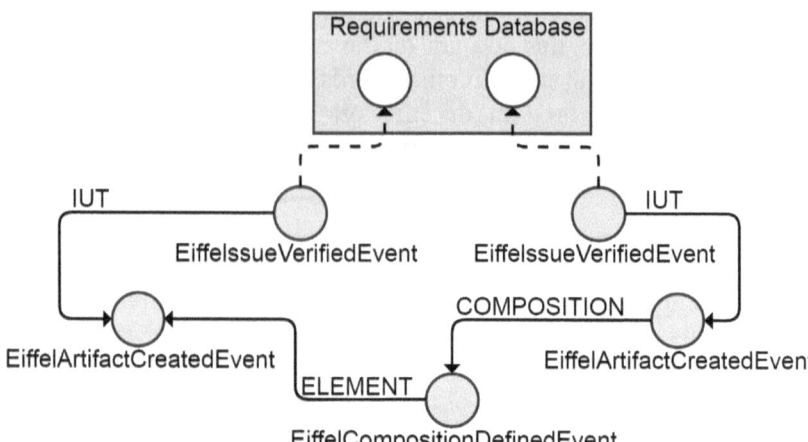

Figure 33: Requirement verification distributed across Alice's network of pipelines.

Dynamic Test Case Selection

It is easy to end up at a point where the number of automated test cases inserted into the pipeline just keeps growing indefinitely. No test cases are ever removed, and new ones are being added all the time, with the consequence that the pipeline becomes ever slower, and/or ever more costly, depending on the ability to scale horizontally by adding more hardware in the given case. This is particularly painful in cases where the test equipment needed to execute those test cases is not virtual machines in the cloud, but actual cars, airplanes, robots or other expensive mechatronic systems. Then the ability to dynamically select which test cases to execute at any given time to maximize the derived value and confidence in the product is essential. Selection can be done using a number of methods: based on which tests fail frequently, failed recently, fail uniquely, fail for this particular type of change, fail for changes made by this particular developer, and so on. Typically you'll want to be able to mix and match these methods and formulate test selection strategies that make use of all of them.

In one project I was involved in it was discovered that the scope of one of the test activities in the pipeline had remained completely unchanged through three years of active development of the product. It had more or less been forgotten about and left there, and like any other ancient piece of code, over time people grew afraid of changing it. At the end of the day, though, I would seriously question the value of executing those tests at all.

- Daniel

As with test automation in general, there exists a substantial body of research on test selection techniques, but industry adoption of those techniques is lagging behind. While acknowledging this divide we again take the pragmatic point of view rooted in industry practice and experience. This is because what tends to keep practitioners from effectively selecting test cases is not the design of the selection algorithms, but that they lack the basic prerequisites to make any informed decisions in the first place – prerequisites that are sometimes overlooked in academic research. We argue that these prerequisites are test case homogeneity, test case atomicity and traceability.

By test case homogeneity we mean the property of test cases to be similarly managed, stored, documented and executed in a similar and compatible fashion. This is important as it allows the construction of a complete and informative inventory from which those test cases can be selected, and makes execution of those test cases feasible. Too often, test cases are fragmented across multiple databases, test management systems, information models and test execution frameworks. This fragmentation makes it difficult, though not impossible, to effectively select an arbitrary collection of tests and then execute them as part of a coherent suite. If, on the other hand, all tests are documented on a shared structured format, available in the same database and can be dispatched to the same execution framework, that becomes rather a straightforward task.

The second prerequisite is atomicity. By atomicity we mean the property of test cases behaving as independent entities, which can be executed in isolation without assumptions as to any particular state resulting from the execution of some other set of tests. It is common to find test cases implemented as lengthy, static suites which must be executed as a whole, as they are riddled with implicit (and unintentional) assumptions on the sequence of test cases. Needless to say, in such a situation it is impossible to extract any one test case from the suite and execute it by its own. Instead, it is in fact the entire suite that constitutes the smallest executable entity, and on which any dynamic selection scheme must operate. This is certainly possible, but the value of such dynamic selection greatly diminishes when its granularity is thus reduced. In simple terms, if one has a database of 1,000 individual atomic test cases, dynamically selecting the most valuable ones to execute at any given time is extremely helpful. If, instead, one can only choose between either a suite of the first 500 test cases or a suite of the remaining 500 test cases, that is a much less meaningful choice.

Third, dynamic test case selection requires traceability. In particular, access to adequate and reliable information about two related entities is necessary: the item under test and any historical test case executions and results. Traceability of the item under test implies its delta since the previous version, who changed what and why it was changed. This information can support selection based on developer karma [47] (i.e. the amount and the types of errors historically introduced by individual developers) or based on which test cases tend to fail for changes in specific parts of the software. Traceability of historical test case execution and results, on the other hand, allows selection based on a wide array of factors which may be relevant. To exemplify, one may wish to prioritize tests based on historical execution times (and therefore cost), or select test cases that have not been executed in a long time, test cases that failed recently or test cases that tend to fail uniquely. By failing uniquely, we intend the property of not failing as part of a group: if a dozen test cases tend to fail or pass as a group, then executing all twelve generates little more information than executing a single one, which is important from a test case prioritization point of view.

Clearly, one also needs access to relevant information about the test case itself in order to execute it. This is, strictly speaking, not a question of traceability, but rather of data quality in a wider sense, as well as data homogeneity. Simply put, if one can't learn about available test cases on a shared, structured format, then choosing between them in any meaningful way is going to be tricky.

> Dynamic test case selection is truly a great alternative to managing test cases by hand, but just as one shouldn't get carried away trying to automate every single test activity, it's important not to overlook the need for skilled engineers designing, monitoring, evaluating and tuning the test activities – whether the test cases are dynamically selected or not.
>
> *- Torvald*

Let's conclude by taking a look at one of our archetypes. In their drive to keep pipeline lead times as low as possible, Bob and his teammates have set a strict time budget for each of their pipeline test activities. The pipeline then optimizes for maximum value within that time budget, as dictated by the weighing of multiple parameters defined and continuously tweaked by the developers. For instance, time since latest execution is given a strong positive weight, while time since latest failure is given an even stronger negative weight, resulting in test suites that first of all check whether any faults discovered in the previous version have been fixed, and second ensures a steady rotation of the entire body of test cases.

Dynamic Environment Selection

Dynamic environment selection can be thought of the other side of the coin of dynamically selecting test cases. In some contexts this is either non-applicable or trivial. If there is one and only one type of environment, as in many Software as a Service contexts, then that is where you test. And if the possible variants of production environments are all similar enough – such as virtual machines with different amounts of CPU, memory and storage available to them, then mapping test cases to those environments is fairly straight forward. Many products exist in a domain with near infinite environment variability, however, where testing every requirement in every potential configuration is simply out of the question. In such cases one is forced to make the most of a bad situation, and then it's simply not good enough for a test case to require one particular unique snowflake of an environment. Conversely, this clearly also implies that test environments must be designed to support test cases being transferred from one environment to another, and to have their relevant qualities described in such a way that enables selection.

The first reason why this is important is that dynamic selection and scheduling of test case execution becomes an impossible problem if each test case needs its own particular environment. The second reason is that it prevents execution of the same test case on many different environments over time, a practice which helps increase test coverage of environment variants.

To achieve effective environment selection it is not sufficient to only let test cases dictate their needs, however. There is a second source of environment requirements to consider: the needs and/or preferences of the test case execution at that particular point in time. To exemplify, John's computer game runs on a nearly infinite range of desktop PC configurations (see Chapter 10). Most of the differences are covered in enough abstractions that they can be safely ignored, but the brand of graphics processing unit (GPU) is important enough that John and his teammates feel the need to run certain test cases on several specific variants to ensure there are no performance issues on any one type of GPU. Here it is not the test cases themselves that requires a certain environment – they are designed to be completely agnostic as to the GPU they execute on – but the Test Case Selector (see Figure 34) that injects the requirement for a specific brand into each execution.

As depicted in Figure 34, John and his teammates achieve this not by creating multiple test cases, but by letting their pipeline order multiple executions – what they refer to as Test Execution Recipes – from each test case. These Test Execution Recipes are transient entities dispatched to the Test Execution Framework and then forgotten. Apart from any environment dependencies statically associated with the test case itself, they add additional environment requirements. In this case, they dictate the GPU brand. The result in this example is two test cases, designed for low end and high end GPUs, respectively, spawning a total of six test case executions and thereby achieving a high degree of configuration coverage.

This example is clearly a simplified one, and whether the effort of setting up this system paid off for John, as opposed to simply duplicating the test cases and explicitly linking them to individual environments, is questionable. The larger the variability space, the greater the benefit of dynamic environment selection, though. We come across cases where these parameter spaces are in the thousands – in such scenarios this technique can be extremely potent.

Open Ended Testing

So far in this chapter we have discussed various aspects of test cases: how to implement them, how to schedule them, and how to maximize their value. Test cases are ubiquitous; they are what we would call the bread and butter of testing in the software industry. The first thought that comes into the mind of most software engineers at the mention of testing is test cases. The danger is that if all you have (or know of) is a hammer, then every problem will look like a nail. There are other approaches to testing, however, which have their place in a pipeline.

What test cases do well is determine whether or not a specific aspect of a system behaves as expected under a specific set of circumstances.

Due to this binary nature, they are well suited at verifying requirements. Their weakness is that they are not necessarily very good at finding faults, as they rely on the ability of engineers to explicitly phrase requirements and/or anticipate the possibility of a certain failure mode.

There are other, complementary approaches to testing that circumvent this flaw – techniques we loosely group under the label "open ended", as opposed to the deterministic nature of test case execution. Open ended testing techniques are things you typically do not use as gatekeeper activities in the pipeline, determining whether a particular release candidate is good enough to pass into production. Instead, they are best suited to providing feedback and supporting the evolution and stabilization of a software solution over time.

One example of what we consider as open ended testing is exploratory testing, touched upon earlier in this chapter. Exploratory testing was coined as a term by Kaner [48] and expanded upon as a teachable discipline by Kaner, Bach and Pettichord in their book "Lessons Learned in Software Testing" [49]. Exploratory testing is a form of testing that emphasizes the freedom and the responsibility of the individual tester (or testers) to continuously evolve and adapt their testing techniques as they explore and learn about the system under test. Different setups exist for planning, execution and reporting exploratory testing. Testing can be organized as charters [50, 51] or tours [50, 52] which are conducted as sessions [50, 51] or threads [50]. In research we have seen how exploratory testing can be successfully incorporated in a continuous integration and delivery pipeline [45]. We see great value in complementing automated testing with exploratory testing (as described on page 151), each mitigating the weaknesses of the other by addressing unique concerns. Whereas automated test activities in the pipeline are able to rapidly provide feedback to developers and to verify requirements, exploratory testing is well suited to provide more in-depth insights about the system under test.

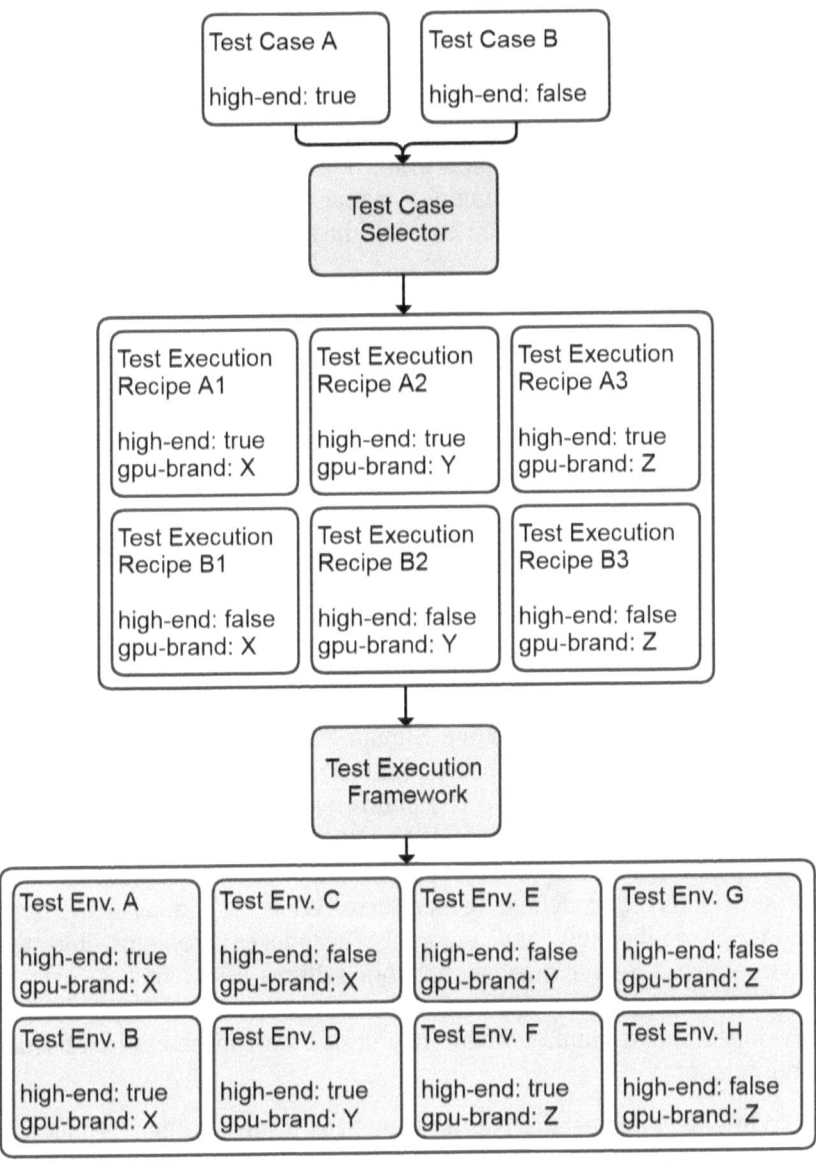

Figure 34: Test execution recipes dynamically scheduled onto matching environments.

> An added benefit of manual test activities such as exploratory testing is the opportunity for engineers working on separate parts of the product to learn from each other while testing together. This helps them gain a better and more holistic understanding of the product they are developing – something that can never be achieved in quite the same way if all the testing is automated.
>
> *- Torvald*

Another form of open ended testing is various types of fault injection. The idea behind fault injection is to deliberately introduce faults into the execution path of a system in order to investigates its ability to cope. Of course, this can be done in a traditional and static automated test case, but can also be done in a more dynamic fashion to dramatically increase test coverage.

One flavor of this is chaos testing, which has been popularized by Netflix through its open source Simian Army set of tools (of which Chaos Monkey is arguably the best known) designed to wreak havoc on the system environment [53]. The philosophy is that when disasters are infrequent enough developers will be tempted to hope for the best and not design to withstand them, but when disasters strike constantly they are simply forced to defend against them. What the Simian Army does is that it deliberately and randomly introduces problems into the environment – server outages, network failures et cetera – to expose weaknesses so that they can be fixed sooner rather than later, and force developers into a mindset where they design for robustness in a hostile environment.

While the engineers at Netflix use chaos testing in their production environment and thereby ensure that their service is robust enough to withstand actual crises, this practice works best in situations where one has perfect control over that environment, as in a Software as a Service context. For other distribution models, chaos testing as a dedicated test activity in a protected environment can serve a similar purpose.

Granted, it does take some of the edge off of chaos testing to only practice it in a safe setting, and it will not catch faults due to unforeseen differences between the environments, but it will still provide valuable feedback to the developers.

Another variant on fault injection is Lineage Driven Fault Injection (LDFI) [54]. It stems from the recognition that while chaos testing is valuable, its randomness means that rare error conditions (e.g. caused by complex combinations of failures) are unlikely to be caught. Moreover, it can never leave any guarantees as to the absence of potential failure modes. This is why LDFI does not randomly inject faults, but instead reasons backwards from a known correct outcome in order to detect failure modes that could have prevented that outcome. At the time of writing, LDFI is still a novel approach and we have so far witnessed few industry implementations – none of them integrated into a continuous integration and delivery pipeline – although we see great potential for such a practice.

That being said, many more strategies for fault injection exist; here we have presented one very popular and one very promising. The critical point we wish to communicate is that testing is more than the execution of test cases, and serves more purposes than verifying requirements. Particularly for finding faults we strongly encourage readers to consider adopting what we label as open ended testing strategies in the pipeline, as complements to more traditional test activities. Exploratory testing and chaos testing are already used routinely by large software companies, and additional open ended testing techniques can already be seen on the horizon.

Summary

In this chapter we have looked into strategies for evaluating release candidates in a continuous integration and delivery pipeline. We have not dived deep into test case development and test automation, which are substantial fields of research in their own right. Instead, we have discussed how to manage and select test cases, how to think about test environments and how to apply multiple testing paradigms to achieve separate purposes.

Chapter 18

Packaging and Documenting Release Candidates

As the scope of continuous delivery is to be able to deploy and/or release at any time, simply testing the software to see if it meets expectations isn't enough: it needs to be made available on the format in which it is to be installed, with all assets that go along with it. This might be the Java servlet to be dropped into your servlet container, your RPM package, your ISO image, your Windows Installer, your Docker image, or whatever format that happens to be. There are multiple factors that go into securing that. Some of them are about documentation handling. This is not always applicable – some software products have very little in terms of actual documentation. If you feel that the parts of this chapter that center on documents and other textual information are not applicable to your particular situation, then feel free to skip them.

One topic that will not be addressed in this chapter is containerization. It is an important aspect of release candidate packaging, both in the specific technical sense of operating system level virtualization and in the more general sense of keeping one's release candidates and all parts and dependencies contained as atomic entities. That being said, it is predominantly important because of the way it enables effective deployment practices. We will return to this in depth in Chapter 20, particularly on page 203 and onwards. Of course, a similar argument could be made for the success factors that *are* included in this chapter: treating every source as any source, building the ultimate deployment format as early as possible and compiling documentation for every change. We feel that these are more general topics, however, and we hope that readers will agree with our choice to group them together in this chapter.

Treating Every Source as Any Source

Whether it is because those responsible for documentation often do not share a development background, or for other arcane reasons, it is not uncommon to see documentation for a product be treated completely differently from the source code of that product. In the truly nightmarish cases, product documentation is a collection of office documents on somebody's laptop or private network drive, which effectively prevents any successful implementation of continuous delivery practices.

A serious cause for concern in such practice is that the dependencies between source code and documentation must be explicit and unambiguous, and preferably treated as any other dependency in the software. If it is ever a judgment call which version of the documentation applies to which version of the product, continuous delivery is by definition not feasible. What's more, there is something seriously wrong with the configuration management of the software.

Note that documentation is only one case in point, although a very common issue in industry projects. The same applies to all types of auxiliary resources, media and any other kind of data that goes into the product. Ideally, they should all be treated and configuration managed the same way as the source code. Hence the name of the success factor: treating every source as any source.

Even in cases where storing one's assets along with the source code in a common repository is not feasible, those assets should be uniquely and unambiguously identifiable from the source code. In other words, they should be treated just like any other dependency in the way outlined in Chapter 16, holding to the principle of one-to-one relationships between source code repositories and pipelines. As long as there is one and only one repository that serves as the canonical definition of what is to be produced, that can in turn reference additional software to be pulled in without compromising traceability and reproducibility.

As an example, consider John's game development. Although we have previously noted that the entire source code resides in a single repository, some types of content are an exception to that. Smaller media files, such as 2D graphics and short audio clips, are stored in the source code repository, but very large ones, including a number of movie sequences, are not (see Figure 35). This is because their sheer size slows down version control operations, and because their binary format doesn't lend itself to diffing and merging, anyway.

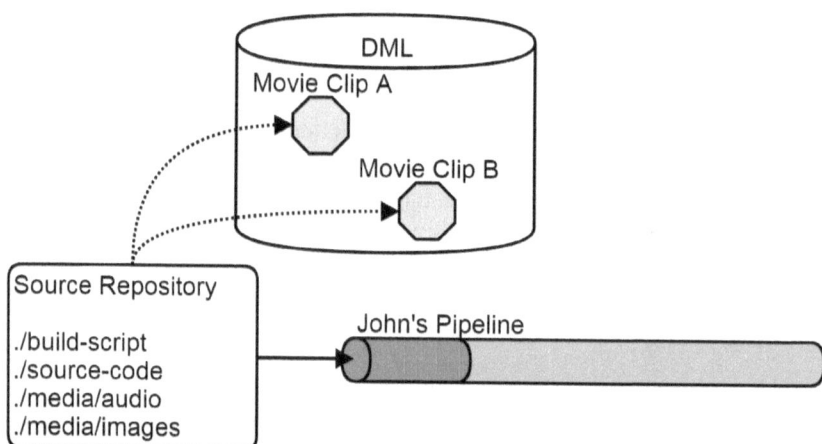

Figure 35: A single source code repository explicitly referencing external assets in a Definitive Media Library (DML).

The consequence is that in order to have a new piece of media included in the final product, a content creator cannot just produce the media, but must update the source code repository, thereby creating a new version of the game which includes the addition. There is no magic knowledge or intelligence anywhere in the pipeline that pulls in anything that is not explicitly stated in the one blessed repository.

In contrast, consider the alternative shown in Figure 36. Here, the Source Repository has no special status: it is merely one of multiple inputs to the pipeline and any release candidate produced is not the direct result of any particular version the be found in the Source Repository, but of a transient composition of assets collected from several independent locations. This makes the behavior of the pipeline difficult to predict, as multiple versions of the product may be built from the same source code version, with different characteristics. It also makes it harder to trace a given product version back to the correct set of sources in case of an incident, and thereby also hampers reproducibility. Despite these problems, we unfortunately find similar practices to be wide-spread in the industry, although mostly not so much by deliberate design as by happenstance and oversight.

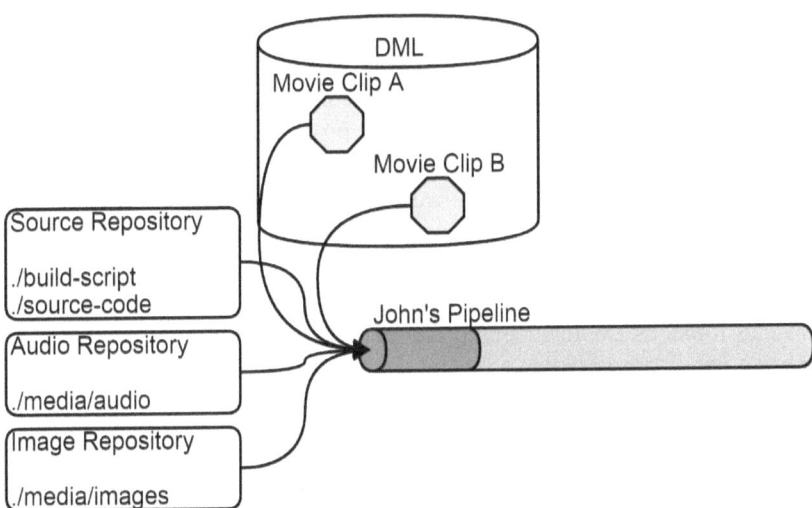

Figure 36: Multiple inputs to a single pipeline.

In conclusion, the point is to treat all assets as source code if possible, and if not, to explicitly reference them from the source code in keeping with the principle of one-to-one mapping of source code repositories to pipelines.

Allow us to close on a final remark not related to continuous practices per se, but on version control in general. When storing assets other than source code in source code repositories, consider doing it on formats amenable to version control wherever feasible. Documentation is a prime candidate for this. While some documentation and product information writers are very fond of their WYSIWYG[25] word processors, the binary formats they produce make effective version control challenging indeed. Plain text based formats, such as LaTeX, make parallel work incredibly easier while driving home the point that these documents really are sources like any other source.

Building the Actual Release Candidate

It is surprisingly common to see continuous integration and delivery pipelines that actually don't go quite all the way, but stop just shy of the goal (and, to be pedantic, therefore do not fulfill the scope of continuous delivery). Rather than building that ISO image – or whatever the end product happens to be – automatically for every change, such pipelines are content to generate all their contents. Building the final image is viewed as "just a quick" manual action before actually deploying and/or releasing. As an example, consider the production of release candidates for John's game development project, shown in Figure 35. In the anti-pattern we just described, the process instead looks as depicted in Figure 37: rather than building the actual release candidate upfront, only the source code is built and tested. The full game, including media assets, is manually packaged on its deployment format later on, for select versions of the software.

---

25 What You See Is What You Get.

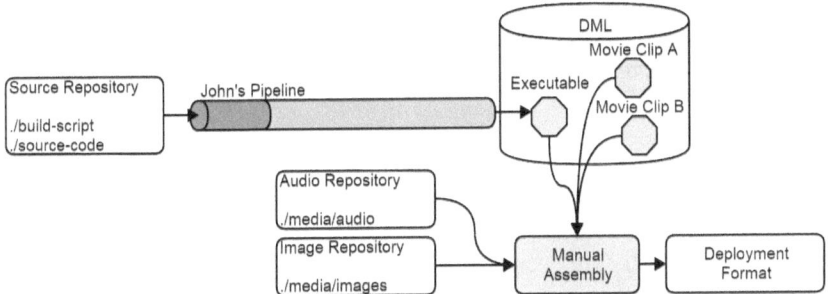

Figure 37: Assembly of the ultimate deployment format delayed until the very end.

Taking that small final step is important for several reasons, though. One is consistency: any manual action, even if it is quick and seemingly innocuous, is a risk. It may produce different results from one time to the next, and if the person who knows how to do it is unavailable tomorrow you may find yourself unable to deploy a critical bugfix. Another is trust in the tests: if the continuous delivery pipeline actually doesn't build what gets deployed at the end of the day, chances are that what you are testing isn't, either, whether it's automated regression tests as part of the pipeline or exploratory manual tests or sandbox experimentation by developers. In other words, it's difficult to argue that what the customer ends up with truly has been verified.

To illustrate the point with a simile, imagine a pharmaceutical product distributed as a capsule. Even though the active ingredient has been thoroughly evaluated in experiments and trials, it has not been tested in its distributed form as a capsule. After all, encapsulation is standard practice, and what could possibly go wrong? Quite a lot, when you think about it: the active ingredient may interact with the binders and fillers in an unanticipated fashion, the capsule may dissolve too slowly or too quickly, releasing the active ingredient at the wrong site in the digestive tract, et cetera. Such practices clearly would not inspire trust in the pharmaceutical case, and neither should they in software engineering.

Not building the actual release candidate, but an intermediate form, can also result in all kinds of unexpected complications in handling, labeling, distribution and not least in traceability. Generally speaking, the process of connecting the dots back from in-service software to its original sources tends to be as manual as the process of creating it.

I once worked with configuration managers from a project who had a serious problem on their hands. Their pipeline produced a steady stream of builds, some of which were later cherry-picked for release – though not necessarily in consecutive order – whereupon a deployable package containing documentation, configuration and other meta-data was created. Both builds and releases were versioned, and by corporate standards given alphanumerically increasing version numbers. The problem was this: any one software version could only be deployed on top of an older version, but consecutively versioned releases didn't necessarily contain consecutive software versions. Proposed solutions to the problem were impressive in their resourcefulness, such as reserving certain character positions in the release version number to signify software compatibility information, or requesting special treatment from the corporate deployment machinery. All because what the pipeline produced wasn't the actual release candidate, but merely an intermediate artifact.

- Daniel

To avoid these issues altogether, we strongly recommend the practice of building the release candidate early on in the pipeline and archiving it in a Definitive Media Library (see Chapter 16). This release candidate can then be reused in test and verification activities – at the very least in a significant portion of those activities – in order to evaluate it as a complete entity.

Admittedly, this practice can increase resource utilization. In John's case, for instance, the creation, archiving and testing of more versions of the complete game places increased demands on storage and network capacity. But then again, so do continuous integration, delivery and deployment in the first place: a business whose overriding goal is cost saving on storage and bandwidth shouldn't be adopting continuous practices to begin with.

Furthermore, we would like to make a point out of the fact that we consider this a success factor as applied to the individual pipeline. From a network of pipelines point of view (see Chapter 6), each pipeline has its own output and its own format of that output. In other words, it should not be taken to mean that a release candidate of the entire system should necessarily be built as early as possible and then all testing shall be performed on a system level. On the contrary, as we have already touched upon, it is desirable to push testing down to lower (and cheaper) levels of system completeness as far as applicable. In other words, pushing as much of the heavy lifting as possible toward the left in the network of pipelines (see Figure 4 on page 43). Within the individual pipeline of that network, on the other hand, it's good practice to construct the actual release candidate – the output of the pipeline – upfront and then archive and evaluate that, rather than some intermediate form.

Compiling Documentation for Every Change

You aren't done until you're done, and if your product comes with documentation then you aren't done unless that documentation is as natural a part of the release and/or deployment as the product itself. This naturally follows on the previous success factors outlined in this chapter.

The key verb here is compile, as actual authoring of documentation is another issue entirely. Automated authoring may be both valuable and feasible in certain cases, but generally speaking and from a continuous delivery point of view the important thing is to compile it from its sources, whether those sources were hand written or automatically generated. In some cases this is straight forward, but particularly in large-scale distributed systems, where every component is responsible for its own part of the documentation, the sheer logistics of putting it all together should not be underestimated.

It is worth pointing out that documentation also includes verification results. This calls for automated documentation and collation of the outcome of automated test case executions, bringing us back to the need for adequate traceability (see Chapter 15).

Alice's car is accompanied not just by documentation for the end user, but also by documentation for service personnel as well as documentation describing standards compliance, risk classifications and risk mitigation measures. These are authored per electronic control unit (ECU) and then, for any given composition of ECUs in any given car, compiled into coherent system level documents.

Until recently, these document fragments were authored and stored separately from the source code and then manually assembled and connected to a particular version of the system. This implied a significant manual effort for every new version of the car, but more importantly led to some ambiguity as to whether the documentation matched the actual running software version in every regard, since there were no explicit links between documentation version and source code version.

Today all these document fragments are stored alongside the source code in the repositories of their respective ECUs. Moreover, they are tagged with meta-data as to their nature and place in the larger system documentation structure, e.g. as comprising the text body of a particular chapter or section. This makes it easy for an automated activity integrating the complete system to pick up the document fragments that go along with all of the constituent parts and piece them together into a consistent artifact.

There are, however, types of documentation that are not as easy to fit into a continuous delivery context, and that may require exemption from the general rule. One example is reports from manual test activities (see Chapter 17), which are not feasible to conduct for every change. Other examples include documents required by regulations, such as formal component specifications, system hazard analyses or maintenance descriptions. We will discuss these types of problems further in Chapter 19.

Summary

In this chapter we have brought up success factors related to the actual construction of the release candidate. For the most part, this comes down to handling of assets other than the actual source code and its derivatives – assets which are too often omitted from the scope of continuous practices. It is crucial to go the full nine yards and bring all the items that make up one's ultimate output into the pipeline, however; otherwise it is impossible to live up to the tenets of continuous practices or reap their full benefits.

Chapter 19

Meeting Legal and Regulatory Expectations

In this chapter we approach the subject of legal and regulatory expectations. As we have noted previously, a catalog of all the standards, regulations and legal issues at play in the software industry isn't feasible. Instead we will list some of the typical challenges encountered and success factors for navigating them.

The success factors we identify can be split into two main categories. In the first we permit ourselves to keep beating the dead horse of traceability: setting up a pipeline, or network of pipelines, such that it allows you to produce the documentation required to demonstrate your development and test practices at the level required by whichever standards and regulations you may be the subject of.

The second category has to do with the accumulation of mileage – literal or otherwise. Some standards and regulations require that any software deployed into production has first been demonstrated as safe during production-like trials for a certain number of hours, or as the case may be for vehicles, for a certain distance traveled. This may seem like a complete showstopper for continuous practices, but we will look into strategies for overcoming such requirements without abandoning the concept of continuous releases and/or deployments.

A Self-Documenting Pipeline

A common theme in industry regulations in general – and software is no exception – is the requirement on producers to document the production process. Depending on the aims of the regulatory body this documentation might be expected to show which individuals have contributed what to the product, where the software has been developed, stored and which national borders it has crossed, which requirements have been implemented where, as well as which requirements have been verified when, how and under which circumstances.

As noted in Chapter 12, all of this can conceivably be kept track of manually. Experience, however, tells us that this is either very slow, unreliable or expensive (in other words, strictly ruled by the Iron Triangle of project management [55]), or more likely, all three at once. This doesn't rhyme well with the idea of continuous practices, particularly because humans simply don't operate quickly enough, and when we try to force them to, cost and quality suffer accordingly. In other words, the solution to the particular constraints placed on traceability by continuous practices is the automated real time generation of all trace links required to answer any questions pertaining to the history and life-cycle of the produced software, as demanded by any applicable regulations [25].

There are several ways of achieving this. We have witnessed point-to-point integrations where actors in the pipeline report their activities to a central database, but for the reasons we presented in Chapter 15 we strongly recommend event based systems in general, and an Eiffel based solution in particular.

Apart from the software already available out-of-the-box and the fact that it has been created from lessons learned the hard way by others, Eiffel is specifically designed to allow cherry-picking of the traceability data most relevant in the particular case. This means that – with the caveat that there are of course other benefits to be had from a richly documented pipeline – a minimalistic subset of the Eiffel protocol can be adopted to address the particular needs at hand.

To illustrate this point, consider the regulatory demands on Alice's car, as opposed to those on Jane's military vehicle. Alice is expected to demonstrate exactly how each software item has been tested in order to ensure its safety according to its Automotive Safety Integrity Level (ASIL) classification. Consequently, she and her colleagues have focused on reporting test activities by using the events and trace links depicted in Figure 24 on page 125.

In contrast, Jane's company needs to document which individuals made which changes to which part of every version of the software. For that reason, they have chosen to first adopt Eiffel events that represent the composition and source code changes of the product, as shown in Figure 38.

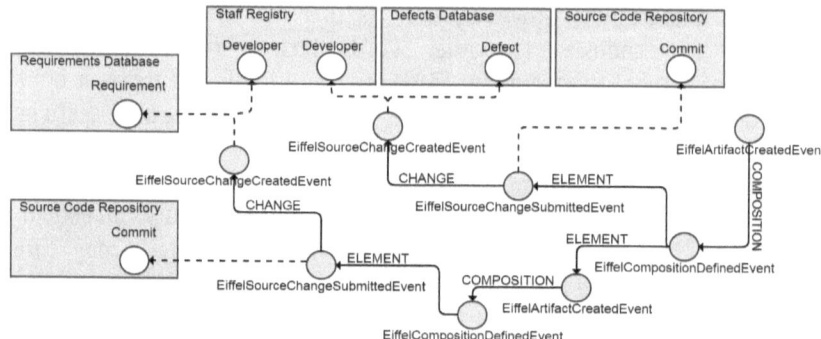

Figure 38: Eiffel events used by Jane to document changes made by individual developers.

In this example, the release candidate represented by the rightmost EiffelArtifactCreatedEvent can be traced via its COMPOSITION and ELEMENT links to individual source changes. These source changes, in turn, are represented by events identifying what was changed by whom and for what reason.

A company I once came into contact with struggled with an interesting traceability problem, which illustrates the importance of keeping your records in order not only to comply with regulations, but also for financial and legal purposes. Their products made extensive licensed use of software supplied by third parties, which required them to pay fees according to customer utilization of the features enabled by that software. The problem was that they didn't keep very good track of which customer used which version of their products, and so they couldn't tell exactly who used this licensed software and who didn't. As a result, they practically had to assume that everybody used everything, and ended up suffering considerable financial losses from over-paying their suppliers just to be on the safe side – a strong incentive if any to implement a self-documenting pipeline that reaches all the way from individual sources and into production.

- Daniel

On a final note, Eiffel's ability to cherry-pick parts of the protocol particularly applies in situations where regulations come into direct conflict with automation. Indeed, to establish a completely self-documenting pipeline may even be impossible where regulated processes define roles appointed to individuals responsible for declaring compliance with requirements, or providing an analysis of a certain aspect of the system (e.g. security threats). If these are absolute non-negotiable rules, it follows that such activities cannot be completely automated. Therefore it is important that the protocol does not enforce documentation in a specific way that assumes a certain type of process. That being said, however, Eiffel events are also designed to represent manual as well as automated activities and decisions: a declaration of compliance may be represented as an event, whether it follows manual analysis or automated evaluation.

Some will argue that the standards they are required to comply with demand various activities which simply cannot be automated, thus impeding continuous integration and delivery. I find that more often than not it isn't necessarily compliance itself that is the impediment, but the habitual processes devised once upon a time to achieve that compliance. In other words, the first step towards automation is to separate regulations from processes, and to question whether the latter are truly necessary, or if there are alternatives.

- Torvald

Separation of Intent from Action

The intent to carry out an action is not the same as carrying it out. This should be obvious enough, but surprisingly often the two become conflated in software development, particularly when adequate traceability of actual outcomes is lacking.

For instance, Mary will occasionally run into project managers showing burn-down charts of tests planned and estimated testing progress, and using those plans in lieu of actual records of the test executions. One situation where this becomes problematic is where Mary needs to troubleshoot a fault and study historical test case executions in order to carry out a fault slip-through analysis. Then she needs the actual record of which test was executed where, how and when, not that it was planned to be executed in a certain week.

The difference is illustrated clearly by the dynamic test case selection practice outlined in Chapter 17, on page 162 and onward. The Test Execution Recipes described there are a representation of intent: storing them as proof of test execution is inadequate, as they can never prove that the intent was truly acted upon. What's more, they lack sufficient level of detail: while they contain requirements on the execution environment (e.g. the brand of GPU) they can not identify the actual environment that was eventually used – an environment which may well contain other significant factors not anticipated, but nevertheless affecting the outcome (e.g. the amount of available RAM).

In other words, for purposes of traceability, reproducibility and regulatory compliance it is critical to maintain a conceptual clarity as to which information artifacts truly represent actions taken and outcomes, as opposed to merely representing plans and intent.

Returning to the example of John the game developer, when a user submits a support request reporting graphics rendering issues, the first step in troubleshooting for John is to check whether the game has actually been tested in an environment resembling that of this particular user. If all he had to go by was the information in the test activity configurations, he would only be able to conclude that tests matching the user's particular brand of low-end GPU had indeed been scheduled for testing. Since the actual test execution environments are stored along with the test outcomes, however, he is able to find additional details. For instance, although that was not part of the test configuration or the test plan, he can deduce that none of the environments where it was executed run the same operating system version as the user, giving him a starting point for troubleshooting the issue.

Environments as Containers

Going back once more to the problem of identifying the environment in which a build activity or a test execution was carried out, we would like to highlight the importance of containerization.

Too often we see cases where a product's source code is meticulously archived and managed for decades to comply with regulations and directives, even though the tools, frameworks and libraries used to build and test that source code are curiously overlooked and aren't version controlled at all. Instead they are, by definition, whatever happens to be installed on the used machine at any given point in time. As a result, on those thankfully rare occasions when one actually has to go back ten or twenty years in time to reproduce a legacy product, the source code may be identifiable and retrievable, but that isn't overly helpful when the machines originally used to build it aren't even around anymore. Particularly since simulators and other test environments tend to be much more volatile than one might expect: they are software products themselves, requiring configuration management and documentation to the same extent as the item under test.

This has always been a hairy problem, but the recent evolution of containerization technology and the tooling to support it does make life considerably easier. By encapsulating and archiving one's environment – whether it's for compilation, testing, or some other purpose – as a container image it's possible to get around this problem. As long as there is an available machine capable of spinning up a container from that image (which is far more likely twenty years into the future, than having a machine on hand precisely matching your environment specifications) the steps to create and verify a new release candidate can be reproduced. Naturally, this container image should be identified in the source code repository, in line with the principles put down in Chapter 18.

Admittedly, a container will never be a guarantee of perfect reproducibility. To be picky, the exact circumstances of a historical build can never be reproduced, just as a test case execution can never be perfectly reproduced, because absolute isolation of that environment is – theoretically speaking – simply not possible. There will always be factors which are different from one iteration to the next of any activity we ever undertake: everything from the CPU clock of the compiling machine to the phase of the moon will differ, and may theoretically affect execution. The line has to be drawn somewhere, though, and we find that for the vast majority of software projects a container image serves as a both convenient and satisfactory level of isolation.

Similarly, container images do not always suffice. For instance, when the environment is a complete physical network or a vehicle, as in the case of Mary or Jane, that is clearly not within a container's ability to capture. That being said, even those of our archetypes who work on such products can find ample use for environments as container images in their pipelines, wherever they are not addressing the full target environment.

As an example, let us consider Alice's use of Eiffel events to document test executions once more. In Figure 24 on page 125 every test execution (represented by an EiffelTestCaseStartedEvent) references an EiffelEnvironmentDefinedEvent via an ENVIRONMENT link. This event, in turn, references an external Environment object in some Environment Manager – the nature of which is uninteresting from Eiffel's point of view, but crucial to Alice's ability to analyze test executions and results.

The Environment Manager could be nothing more than a list of machines which may or may not stay the same over time. It could also be a Docker Registry[26], with the Environment object being a specific image within that registry. This allows Alice to easily fetch the exact image used for any historical test execution or software build and perfectly – or as perfectly as can be expected – reproduce it on her laptop.

Accumulating In-Service Mileage

Our final success factor in this chapter is different from the others, in that it does not concern traceability at all, but rather the ability to accumulate a certain in-service mileage required by applicable standards and regulations. We use the term mileage both literally and metaphorically: some certifications will require you to rack up a certain number of hours or a certain number of traveled kilometers without incident to be certified. This poses an interesting challenge to continuous practices, which may at first glance appear insoluble: how does one accumulate thousands of hours in-service time for every release candidate, when new release candidates are produced multiple times a week or even multiple times a day?

In many cases simulations can provide the answer, where the system can be tested with models of the hardware (bespoke or otherwise), mechanical systems and physical environments, such as temperature, humidity, weather effects, light conditions et cetera. Extensive testing in such a simulated environment can then be complemented as necessary with real-world testing, primarily for the purpose of validating the simulation itself. In some cases the simulation may even be executed at

---

26 https://docs.docker.com/registry

more than real-time speed, making it possible to earn that mileage (or those hours) even faster.

Assuming that a time accelerated simulated environment is not satisfactory, the only solution is parallelism: either testing multiple release candidates in parallel for extended periods of time, or testing the same release candidate for a shorter period of time but distributed over multiple instances. The problem with the former is that even though it helps the frequency of release candidates, it does nothing for their lead time: a requirement on 10,000 incident-free hours will still take 10,000 hours to satisfy. An even greater problem with both approaches, however, is how to achieve those large numbers of deployments. Taking Alice's car manufacturing company as an example, how can they get access to hundreds or preferably thousands of cars constantly running their latest software to accumulate that incident-free mileage?

Keeping their own fleet of test vehicles and drivers would be prohibitively expensive, but one conceivable option would be to rely on friendly users. For safety critical products, such as automotive vehicles, this is problematic, though. In effect, it would imply using customers as guinea pigs by deploying unceritifed software to their vehicles in order to later be able to certify it – a deeply questionable policy, both from an ethical and from a legal stand-point.

A better solution, although technologically demanding, is one adopted by some companies to circumvent this particular problem. Keeping with the example of cars, in this approach, two versions of the software can be deployed in parallel to any vehicle: one certified, and one uncertified but under evaluation. Both versions are running at the same time and receiving the exact same input from the vehicle's controls and sensors, but only the output from the older, certified version acts upon the physical system. The output from the newer, uncertified software is instead closely monitored, logged and compared to that of the certified one, as shown in Figure 39.

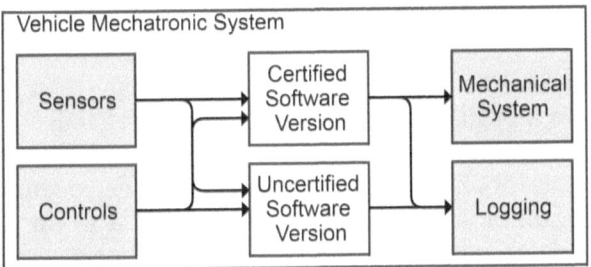

Figure 39: Parallel deployment of certified and uncertified software versions in Alice's car.

In this approach the new, uncertified software can be shown to behave correctly under in-service circumstances while not posing any safety risk to customers. Meanwhile the behavior of the two software versions is compared and any unintentional discrepancies in behavior can be detected and analyzed to inform further development and corrections.

This practice does away with the need for extensive in-house testing environments and/or friendly users for the purpose of certification, and can in theory be parallelized up to the size of the customer base: assuming 10,000 customers, the requirement on 10,000 incident-free hours can in theory be satisfied in a single hour.

The downside of this approach is an increased demand on hardware: everything with software in it must literally be duplicated. From the many embedded systems projects we have been involved in ourselves we know that this can be a very real problem (see Chapter 10). That being said, this once again leads us to conclude that one should not only regard one's contextual circumstances as limits which must be adapted to, but also consider how one might adapt those circumstances to better serve one's business needs. This holds not least for dependencies on expensive, bespoke hardware systems, and is indeed a critical factor driving the industry-wide shift towards increasingly generic and virtualized hardware. If your reliance on bespoke hardware is preventing you from continuously deploying, then that is as good a reason as any for pursuing options for losing that dependency.

Summary

This chapter has focused on common legal and regulatory challenges. To a great extent these come down to effective traceability practices, which we have cause to return to on multiple occasions throughout this book, but we have also considered strategies for demonstrating in-service safety and robustness in a world where new release candidates are produced in much shorter time spans than those required for their certification.

In the next chapter we will consider how to deploy those release candidates in the first place, and the challenges, opportunities and implications of truly continuous deployment.

Chapter 20

Deploying Release Candidates into Production

In this chapter we will address the question of how release candidates, produced by a continuous integration and delivery pipeline, can be frequently and rapidly deployed into production, and what the implications of doing that are. As in previous chapters, we will describe a number of success factors while revisiting the archetypes from Part II: Understanding Your Context.

Clearly, the steps performed and the tools used to move software from the virtual shelf onto the target production hardware and executing it differ depending on what that target is (see Chapter 10), and also depending on your distribution model (see Chapter 13). That being said, in this chapter we hope to provide some universal techniques and concepts that will speed up the process while avoiding a few stumbling blocks. We will look into six success factors for deployment of release candidates into production: rapid deployment, runtime modularity, deployables as container images, low risk deployment, tuning the frequency and calling home.

This is clearly not an exhaustive list of factors that will affect your ability to deploy frequently. As we noted in the Preface, we will try to stay away from the obvious – or what ought to be obvious – such as whether remote automated deployment of software is even technically possible to begin with.

> I came into contact with a fairly large industry project that had made great progress on the continuous delivery front, and were now pursuing an aggressive continuous deployment agenda. Having loudly proclaimed their ambitions, they were eventually stymied by the simple fact that they had no way of establishing a reliable network connection to their products in the field. Oops.
>
> *- Daniel*

Rapid Deployment

Rapid deployment as a success factor may seem self-evident, but the time interval required to bring the in-service software from one version to the next is of such critical importance that it bears repeating: deployments cannot be frequent unless they are also rapid. Fortunately, this is strictly a question of technology, and those tend to be dramatically easier to resolve than questions of process, organization and human behavior. While customers may have opinions about the style and frequency of deployments, in our experience few ever complain about them being too quick.

One reason why rapid deployment is so critical is that it is key to bringing down mean time to recovery (MTTR) of a software system, to the point where focusing on speedy recovery becomes more important than pushing up mean time to failure (MTTF). This comes with the caveat that the safety criticality of the system may skew those calculations (see Chapter 7). To exemplify, while optimizing for mean time to recovery is fine for Bob's social media platform and much of the functionality in Mary's networking solution, the situation is very different in the case of Alice's car and Jane's military fighting vehicle.

There, even if recovery time could be pushed down to mere seconds, those might be seconds in which lives are lost.

To many engineers this line of reasoning is counter-intuitive; it is almost as if avoiding downtime at all costs is bred into their DNA. A very simple back-of-the-envelope calculation illustrates why that instinct can lead them astray, however. Let us consider two hypothetical software services, A and B. A has a mean time to failure of just three days, while B fails on average once every two years. Failure is by definition not a good thing, but rather than at all costs avoiding it, A has invested in automated detection of failure and spins up a new instance, fully recovering in 20 seconds. B on the other hand, when it does crash, crashes hard. With calling in standby engineers on off hours and troubleshooting accounted for, recovery is expected to take four hours, give or take. As it turns out, the availability of A with its more frequent but much shorter outages is actually significantly higher than that of B (with four nines versus three). Additionally, one may presume that this comes at lower cost, as pushing mean time to failure of software to levels where it is measured in years and decades is very, very challenging. As Peter Alvaro et al. succinctly put it, "failure is always an option; in large-scale data management systems it is practically a certainty" [54]. Granted, which is preferable comes down to business considerations: what are the consequences of failure, and which failure pattern is least harmful? To exemplify, in an asynchronous system, many small outages can go more or less unnoticed, whereas a single large one can have a huge impact.

When speaking of rapid deployments, some will say that rolling back is outdated; instead, the best practice is to always "roll forward" (sometimes called "failing forward"). Unfortunately, exactly how to achieve this is rarely described in detail, and different interpretations exist. One interpretation is that even though a failed deployment is rolled back to the latest working version, you shouldn't try to patch it, but simply try again with the next release candidate, which will hopefully contain a fix. This is a wholly reasonable approach, and a logical consequence of maintaining a single continuously integrated software mainline.

A more radical interpretation is that the actual deployment of the service should not be rolled back to the latest working version, but rather wait until the problem has been fixed in source and a new release candidate has been produced and can be deployed. This practice is intended to force developers into a responsive mindset where they immediately react to and address any problems in production. This is a highly problematic approach, however. First of all, it puts a human in the loop, who must evaluate and respond to the problem before it can be fixed. Humans make mistakes, they need to eat and sleep, and most of them want the occasional time off. Besides, even if the developer commits a correction in seconds, it still needs to be built and tested (presumably) before being deployed. In summary, we remain skeptical about this approach and have not seen it implemented effectively in cases we have worked on. Instead, we share the view of James Hamilton [56] that "reverting to the previous version is a rip cord that should always be available on any deployment".

In contrast, we sometimes encounter the sentiment that you should never roll back, because rolling back is disaster recovery, and deployments shouldn't be disastrous. We would argue that is akin to saying that you should never wear seat belts because car crashes are bad. Forgoing disaster recovery is to invite disaster; hopefully that seat belt will never be needed, but if and when it is you will be thankful you put it on.

On a final note, it is important to note that the rapidity of deployment is not necessarily about how quickly an entire system can be upgraded, but rather how quickly any given part of it can be upgraded, preferably without injury to the functionality or performance of that overall system. This requires runtime modularity – our next success factor.

Runtime Modularity

In Chapter 16 we mentioned integration time modularity, as opposed to runtime modularity, in order to better produce release candidates – in essence as an approach to scaling continuous integration. A system's runtime modularity, on the other hand, describes its in-service deployment topology. Regardless of how it was built, whether the system runs as a single-host and single-process service, or as numerous services on multiple hosts (virtual or physical) in multiple physical locations, dictates the options for deployment and consequently the ability to continuously deploy.

At the time of writing, there is a lot of buzz surrounding microservice style architectures. As outlined in Sam Newman's excellent book on the subject [57], microservices have a lot going for them, but they aren't silver bullets. Other benefits and drawbacks aside, however, from our point perhaps their most significant feature is their ability to facilitate continuous deployment.

The root problem is the fact that upgrading running software without restarting (and thus stopping the service) is very challenging. Even when achieved, such hot swapping tends to be restricted. After all, if one's software runs in a framework that allows hot swapping it, any update of that framework without downtime would require another layer of a similar style framework, leading to something of a Russian doll scenario. In comparison, stopping the service, replacing the software and booting it back up again is just beautiful in its simplicity. The unfortunate side effect is that during the interval between stopping and (hopefully successfully) restarting the service, it will be down.

Things would be looking up if there was a way to stop and start software without affecting the service. This is where microservices come into the picture. First, a solution consisting of numerous small services allows graceful degradation of service when individual parts malfunction (or are intentionally taken offline), rather than being all-or-nothing. That can work out nicely for non-critical parts of the system, but it doesn't help when the software that goes offline is absolutely critical to the behavior of the overall solution.

This is where a second principle of microservice architectures comes into play: the paradigm of cattle over pets. While we often find it to be overlooked or misconstrued, it is critical to the ability of zero downtime continuous deployment. To understand the significance of cattle over pets, one must first of all grasp the distinction between functional granularity and instance multiplicity (see Figure 40).

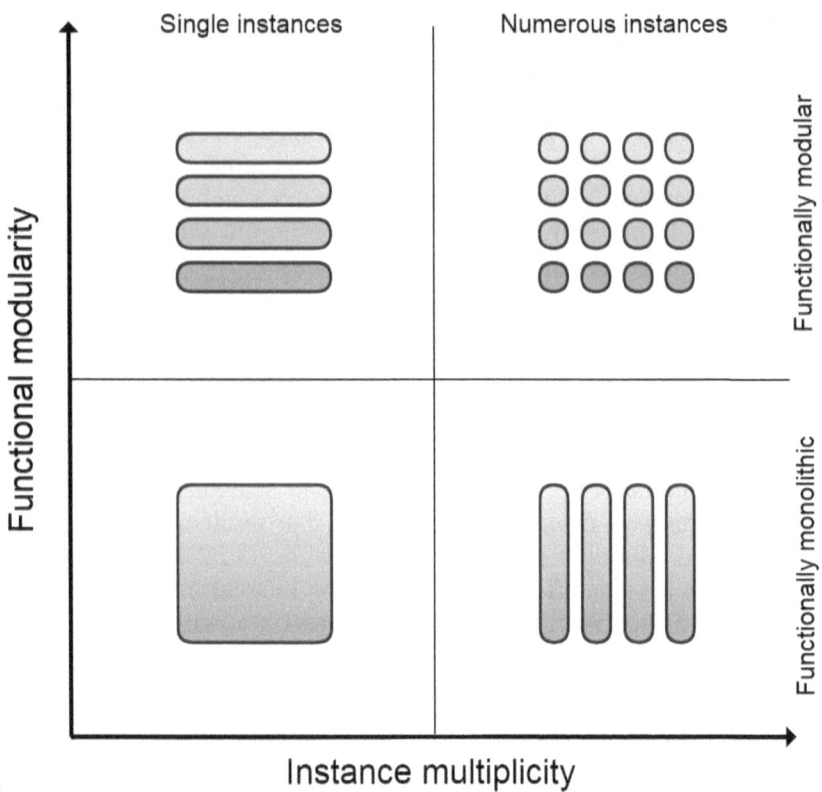

Figure 40: Functional modularity versus instance multiplicity.

In a functionally modular system, separate functions are served by separate services, while the number of instances providing that service may be either one or many. Conversely, in a system with instance multiplicity, each functional service (of which there may be one or many) is provided by multiple instances. Accordingly, any system can be mapped into one of the quadrants shown in Figure 40, and each of those quadrants comes with its own set of conditions for continuous deployment.

It is important to understand the distinction between a physical instance of a service, and the functional service provided by one or more such instances. I have several times gotten stuck in conversations over how certain services must be pets, and that cattle over pets only applies to stateless services, only to realize that this confusion of concepts was at fault: thinking of functional services in terms of cattle or pets makes little sense. But treating a set of instances as cattle does not mean that their functionality is unimportant – quite the opposite! The more critical the service, the more reason to treat the individual instances that make it up as cattle.

- Daniel

In the lower left quadrant we find traditionally monolithic systems. In the lower right quadrant, however, are *functionally monolithic* systems served by multiple instances – typically a clustered service. These are usually set up for load balancing and high availability, but also provide the option of zero downtime deployments by updating one instance at a time, or through blue/green deployments [58].

In the upper left quadrant the system is split into multiple small services, but each service is provided by a single instance (typically a single physical or virtual host). This allows for finer granularity in software deployments and graceful degradation if non-critical parts of the system fail, but it does not come with the high availability, load balancing and zero downtime benefits of multiple instances.

The upper right quadrant, finally, combines these two aspects. The system is split into a large number of services, and the services are provided by multiple instances. In other words, those instances can be treated as cattle, rather than as pets. If any one individual in a herd of cattle dies it lowers production slightly, but it's not something you fret over; you simply replace it. Pets, on the other hand, are loved and treasured. If your pet gets sick you take it to the vet and do whatever you can to save it. When you try to save a misbehaving server to avoid downtime you're treating it as a pet; when you kill it and start up a new one because it's not a big deal, then you're treating it as cattle.

Naturally, to deploy with zero downtime to multiple instances of a service requires multiple versions to co-exist in parallel – co-exist not just with one another, but also with dependencies and dependents. The aim is asynchronicity – the ability to change parts of the system without having to synchronize those changes, and the key to achieving that is interface management. There are multiple patterns available to choose from: message bus based communication, API gateways or point-to-point service discovery and interface negotiation. The underlying principle is the same, however, namely to allow collaborators to communicate across versions to provide a window of opportunity to update.

Figure 41 shows one example of how this can be implemented in an asynchronous message bus setup. In the first state of the system, there are two instances providing the service used by the client. Both instances subscribe to the same queue, and requests can end up in either instance (in this scenario load balancing is achieved by giving the request to the first instance that grabs it). In the second state, one of the instances has been updated and now supports the new version of the API, and only the newer version. It no longer subscribes to *v1* requests, but only *v2* requests. Consequently, in this state the client's requests will only be picked up by the first instance, which still supports *v1*. This situation lasts until all clients have switched to *v2*, as in the third state shown in the figure. Once that has happened, all the service instances can switch over to *v2*, as depicted in the fourth state.

The point of this pattern is to minimize synchronization between components – and thereby between people – and allow asynchronous zero downtime evolution of the system. The interim state of multiple parallel API versions (i.e. states two and three in the figure) may last for seconds, years or anything in between. A common approach is to allow clients a window of opportunity to migrate. In other words, when the service updates its API to *v2*, it clearly states that *v1* is deprecated and that clients have a day, a week, a month or a year to update. This way the responsibility to update is placed on the client component, but with a reasonable time frame within which it can prioritize its own backlog.

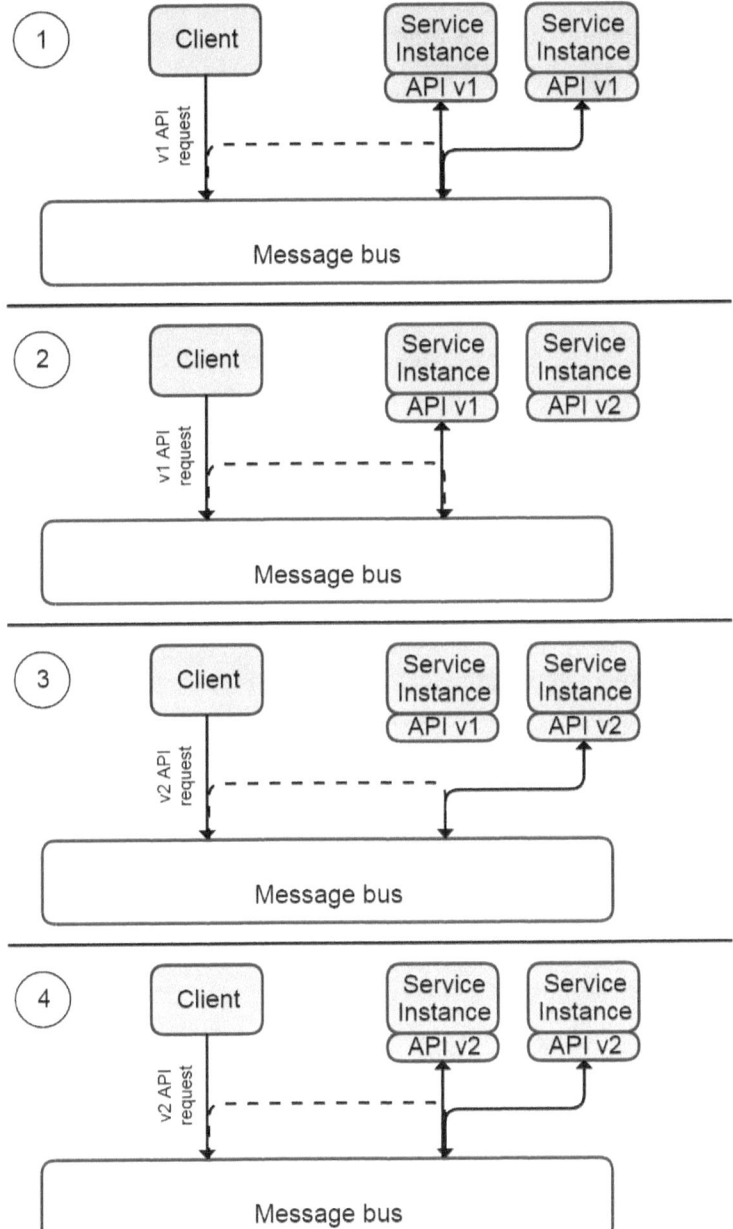

Figure 41: Asynchronous migration of service APIs.

An opposite pattern (indeed, what we regard as an anti-pattern) in ostensibly modular runtime architectures is that of the central signal database. This is, for instance, common in the automotive industry. Here, all inter-component signals are defined in a central database, accessed by each part of the system to learn how to communicate with its collaborators. This means that any API change between any two components of the system must be centrally managed, approved and synchronized, effectively precluding small, granular updates of individual services and thereby impeding continuous deployment as a practice.

A pain point in microservice architectures has long been that of persistent data storage. While a stateless service can easily be scaled horizontally into any number of instances (as exemplified in Figure 41), that is easier said than done for their stateful counterparts. In recent years, however, out-of-the-box containerized multiple-instance database solutions have become more common[27].

An often asked question is what a good number of services to break a system's functionality into is. For good reasons, many will tell you to start out monolithic and then break that monolith apart as it evolves and its architecture and characteristics emerge. This is sound advice and we happily repeat it, with one minor adjustment: start out with a small number, but larger than one – ideally two. The saying that in computing the only meaningful numbers are zero, one and many applies here: by starting out with more than one you force yourself to build a pipeline and a product architecture designed for multiple services from the outset. If not, then one day you will face not only the challenge of refactoring your software to split away the first microservice, but at the same time rethinking your continuous integration, delivery and deployment pipeline.

Finally, depending on one's deployment and distribution model, this concept of runtime modularity is more or less applicable. In no case is this clearer than in Bob's social media platform. The service backend and web frontend are highly modularized, with each service instance running in its own container (see the following section), while the mobile device app is packaged as a single entity. The third party distribution system then takes responsibility for the actual transport and

---

27 See https://crate.io for one example of this.

deployment onto the device, calculating the delta from one version to the next and downloading the required files.

Deployables as Container Images

Isolation is a key concept in frictionless software deployment, and consequently in continuous deployment. Isolation means preventing services from interfering with one another, but also isolating them from the underlying infrastructure, preventing obscure and hard-to-track-down environment dependencies. If you have ever worked in operations and cursed developers for shipping you software that "works on their machines" but won't run in production, you understand the importance of isolation. Even if you haven't, perhaps you have followed a tutorial on some new tool and painstakingly followed the instructions on installing its dependencies, setting its environment variables and editing its configuration files, only to get stuck half-way through because it turns out those settings are invalid on your particular Linux distribution. Again, lack of isolation.

The idea of isolating runtime environments and restricting their access has been around for a long time, and is usually referred to as *containerization* (although the concept predates the term; in older UNIX-style systems such environments went by the name *jails* [59]).

Containerization is often mistaken for virtualization, but there is a crucial difference. Containers do not virtualize hardware, but interface directly with the underlying operating system. As such, they come with far less overhead, scale better, require less storage and are much faster to create and deploy.

The current state of a container can be represented, stored and distributed as an *image*. While a container is the runtime environment created from such an image, the image is the object that is built distributed and deployed, rather than the container itself. Packaging the deployables as container images is a huge enabler of continuous deployment, because it effectively removes the deployment-time hassle of setting up and configuring the deployment environment. Instead, it turns it into a build-time effort: the environment with all its configuration and dependencies is created as part of the build process, rather than every time the software is deployed.

To exemplify, let us imagine that you deploy a web service as a Tomcat servlet. In a traditional scenario, deployment would involve installing the Tomcat server along with Java and any dependencies on the exact operating system supported by your web service. Then Tomcat would be configured just so, your web service servlet installed, and finally the web service would be launched. In the best case scenario all those steps are automated[28] (although alarmingly often documented as manual steps on some wiki), but even so they take a long time to execute and do not address the question of isolation at all. Distributing the web service as a pre-baked container image bypasses all those steps in deployment and can bring the time to stop, update and launch a service from minutes to seconds. The importance of this shift from deploying "raw" software to deploying containers can hardly be overestimated; it cuts down lead times, enhances reproducibility and ensures consistency between deployments.

Of our archetypes from Chapter 5, Bob the social media platform developer is positioned to make the most of containerization. The service backend as well as the web frontend are completely containerized and deployed on commercial cloud hosting services, complete with sophisticated container management tools to improve deployment and supervision of the system. The deployment format of the mobile device app, however, is strictly dictated by the online distribution platform, just like it is for John's game. Meanwhile, the other three archetypes struggle with containerization, since much of what they develop is embedded software on platforms that do not support it.

At the time of writing, the most popular containerization tool is Docker, although alternatives do exist. It is important to point out that it's not Docker that provides the actual containerization – that is a feature of the underlying operating system – but the means to easily construct, distribute, use and manage containers and images. For getting started containerizing your software using Docker, we warmly recommend Jeff Nickoloff's book on the subject [59].

---

28 E.g. using Puppet, https://puppet.com

Low Risk Deployment

A critical success factor for rapid and frequent deployment of software is the ability to do it at low risk. You never want to be stranded with an offline service, a corrupt database, users screaming at your customer support and no way out. When deploying, you always want a dependable fallback strategy in case things don't work out as planned; if you hold your breath and break out in sweat whenever you roll out a new version of your software, you're doing it wrong.

There are several patterns for reducing the risk at deployment, and we'll be discussing two of them. Which one suits your needs depends on where you find yourself in Figure 40, but they both rely on instance multiplicity. In other words, to deploy at low risk you want to be in one of the two right-most quadrants. This is because the basic premise of both techniques is to fall back on an instance (or instances) running a previous known-to-be-working version of the software. Recovering from a bad deployment in a single-instance scenario requires either downtime to shut it down, re-install and restart, or some live and typically improvised hotfixing – the sort of panic-induced hotfixing with which one will only dig oneself deeper into disaster with every change made.

One alternative, most applicable to the lower right quadrant of Figure 40, is blue/green deployment. The basic idea, as described by Martin Fowler [58], is to maintain two identical instances of the service – one "Blue" and one "Green" – fronted by a router, routing incoming requests to only one of them, as shown in Figure 42. In this case, let us assume that the Blue instance is the one servicing requests, while Green is on standby. At deployment, the new software is installed on the Green standby instance. Upon successful installation, the router then switches incoming traffic over to the Green instance, while Blue becomes the standby instance. At any sign of trouble, traffic can be switched back to Blue again, while the problem is analyzed in peace and quiet. For subsequent deployments the procedure is repeated, with Blue and Green constantly alternating between standby and live service.

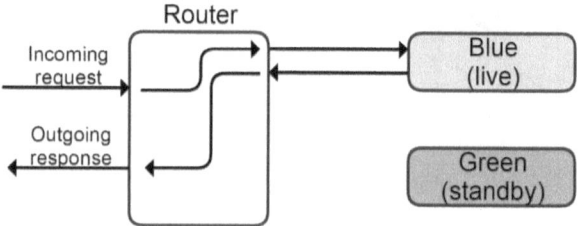

Figure 42: Blue/green deployment.

Particularly for stateful services, the following variant of the blue/green deployment pattern may prove useful: rather than routing requests to only one instance, both instances receive the exact same input. Instead, as shown in Figure 43, it is the output that is routed back from only one of the instances; while there is no difference from the client's perspective, this variant allows the standby instance to maintain an up-to-date state, avoiding data consistency issues.

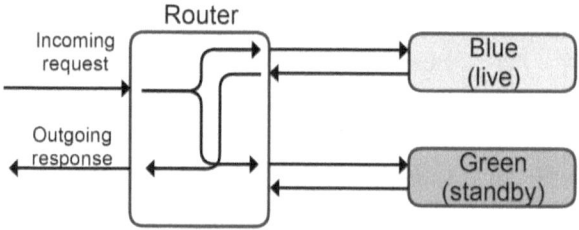

Figure 43: Blue/green deployment variant.

A second alternative to low risk deployment works best in the upper right quadrant, in a system of numerous small multi-instance services. It is based on the paradigm of cattle over pets, and hinges on the ability to bring instances down and up again without disruption to the overall service functionality. In such a scenario, software updates can be rolled out across the many instances in waves. At first only one or a few instances running the new software version are launched, making up a small minority of the total number of instances providing the service. If any issues are detected, those instances are quickly taken down again, and further deployment is aborted. If all goes well, on the other hand, another batch of instances is launched, and another one, until all instances have been updated. In this fashion, software updates roll across the production environment like waves. Indeed, in frequent deployment scenarios multiple such waves may be in progress at any given time, as depicted in Figure 44.

Note that this deployment pattern requires the ability to coexist multiple versions of the software in production, which in turn relies on interface management similar to what we outlined previously in this chapter. This pattern is sometimes referred to as canary deployment, briefly introduced in Chapter 2. It is aptly named after the historical practice of bringing caged canary birds into coal mines. Methane gas would easily build up to dangerous levels in the mines, threatening to kill the miners before they could detect the danger and evacuate. The canary bird, being more sensitive to asphyxiation, served as an early warning system: a dead bird meant it was time to get out of Dodge. Similarly, in canary deployment of software, only one or a few instances are used as an early warning system, detecting any fatal problems with the new software before the entire population is endangered by it.

For John's game and Bob's mobile device app, these deployment patterns aren't applicable, but Bob and his colleagues use canary deployments extensively in their web frontend, particularly coupled with monitoring and analysis of user behaviors to experiment with changes in interface design and layout.

If we turn to Mary's networking solution, we find that the system's technology stack unfortunately does not support the level of runtime modularization and rapid stopping and starting of services that would make canary deployments feasible, but she and her colleagues do make extensive use of blue/green deployments to safely roll out new network nodes.

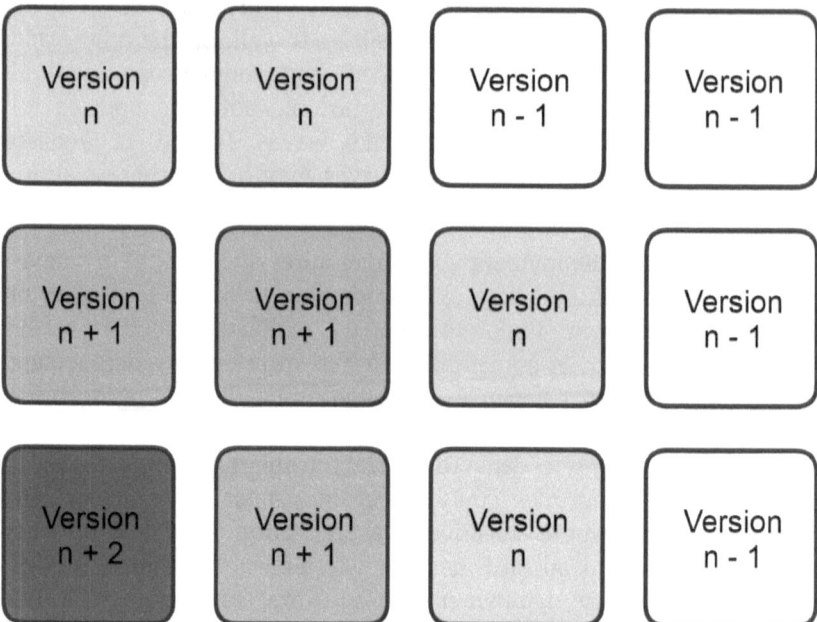

Figure 44: Multiple software versions running in parallel in a canary deployment scenario.

Tuning the Frequency

The previous success factors in this chapter take a relatively mechanistic approach to the problem of continuous deployment: the goal is to deploy rapidly and frequently, so here are the success factors for achieving that. There are situations, however, when the right frequency isn't "all the time" and the right speed isn't necessarily "immediately". In other words, there are cases where truly continuous deployment creates more problems than it solves, and it's better to find a cadence that is almost, but not quite, continuous.

This goes back to several of the contextual factors listed in Part II: Understanding Your Context. One is safety criticality (see Chapter 7), where for some systems there are simply times that are more suitable for deployment than others. Patching an aircraft while it's in the air or a network solution during peak traffic just isn't worth the extra risk it introduces – it's better to accept the delay, because the consequences of failure outweigh the benefits of immediate deployment.

Another situation where there is reason to put on the brakes is where the turn-around time for identifying, analyzing and correcting faults is significantly longer than the deployment frequency. This can be due to factors that have little to do with the development process or the pipeline, but that add lead time in a big way. Examples of this can be system complexity, fault reproduction difficulties or slow bug report routing within the organization. Committing to a deployment interval that is much shorter than the time it takes to fix the most pressing issues in the software might not be a big deal, or it might be a complete showstopper, depending on the type of relationship you have with your customers (see Chapter 8). Regardless, we highly recommend considering what a reasonable deployment frequency is in the individual case, rather than simply assuming that higher and faster is always better. It may be better, for instance, to adopt a step-wise approach where one strives to bring down fault correction lead times first, and only then speed up deployments, to avoid overreaching and consequent backlashes.

I have seen situations where too ambitious a continuous deployment agenda has backfired. When the turn-around time for fault corrections is several weeks, deploying once a day will just annoy your customer and erode their confidence in you. Taking a month to provide a patch that fixes the customer's critical fault may make you appear slow in their eyes, but sending out thirty daily patches that do nothing for them before you finally get it right will simply make you appear incompetent.

- Daniel

Calling Home

Last but not least among the success factors we list the importance of calling home. Safe, rapid and predictable deployment can never be feasible without transparency into the outcomes and consequences of those deployments in the target environment.

Under the heading of calling home we consider two basic types of information sent back home to R&D by the in-production software. The first is what we would label traceability data, which addresses the fundamental question of what is deployed where, and how it got there. Throughout this book we have returned to traceability in continuous integration and delivery pipelines, its importance and the benefits it can provide, so the concept should be a familiar one. Without belaboring the point, in continuous deployment traceability is about extending the graph of trace links from continuous integration and delivery (who made what change where, what it was built into, which test cases were executed verifying which requirements et cetera) to include which software is running in which target environment.

We strongly recommend using the same traceability framework for this purpose as for earlier stages of the pipeline, thus creating a seamless graph of trace links that can be analyzed from source change to production and vice versa. This allows you to build features into your pipelines, such as notifying individual developers who made changes in software versions that failed to deploy in a target environment. Conversely, this also enables developers to take full responsibility of their changes, as they can proactively monitor their deployment progress. This ability to connect individual source changes to in-service software is also a key enabler for the second type of information to send home.

This second type of information is various forms of runtime data: in-service performance, user behavior and other Key Performance Indicators. This is the data that allows you to analyze not only if the software could be deployed, but how well it serves its purpose. It is the data that allows you to amp up the benefits of continuous deployment by performing highly granular feature experiments and study the effects of each variant of the software.

The topic of such feature experimentation and the data driven engineering it leads to is both wide and deep, bit it is an area outside of the scope of this book and we will only mention it in passing. Even so, we consider it one of the major benefits of continuous deployment, and indeed a significant reason why one should consider adopting continuous deployment in the first place. We would also like to make a few observations.

First of all, if you're running a fairly standard operation (particularly a web service based one) you shouldn't have to develop your own feature experimentation technology from scratch. There are specialized frameworks that help you do that, and there is also literature dealing with this exact topic [60].

It is true that such software and literature primarily addresses the web service business, but the concepts are applicable as long as continuous deployment itself is applicable. We would argue that the reason these technologies and practices are – at the time of writing – predominantly focused on the web service market is mainly because those web services are amenable to continuous deployment. That does not mean the rest of the industry is out of scope, simply that it hasn't quite caught up yet – assuming, of course, that continuous deployment is even on the table to begin with; see Part II: Understanding Your Context for a more in-depth discussion on contextual factors and their implications.

Furthermore, large scale experimentation can be done not across manually entered changes in source code, but across more or less automatically generated variants, which means that the classic notion of a pipeline where every change is transformed from a source code commit to a packaged and ultimately deployed software update isn't quite true. Instead, one source code commit can result in multiple procedurally generated variants in deployment, in order to find the one most fit for purpose, resulting in a sort of evolutionary approach to software development. That being said, the basic principles of continuous integration, delivery and deployment as outlined in this book still hold.

The collection of this type of runtime data can be useful even without access to traceability data to complement it, but the reason we regard the latter as an enabler for the former is that this practice of carefully studying the effects of every minor change is impossible without it. After all, unless you know exactly which source code is running where, it's hard to tell which one provides the best service.

Calling home from the production environment isn't all that easy for all of our archetypes. Whether it is even an option first comes down to their distribution model (see Chapter 13). In a nutshell, insofar as they run their software as a service, they can do whatever they want in that production environment. This means that Bob is able to gather both traceability data and runtime data from his social media services, which is a prerequisite for the feature experimentation we mentioned previously in this chapter.

If that is not the case, it comes down to their customer relations and the balance of power in those relations (see Chapter 8). Where a powerful customer objects to the idea of sending any type of data back to the vendor – and many do – that effectively shuts the door on any ability to track the installed base and to monitor performance, usage and other characteristics.

That being said, attitudes in the industry do appear to be shifting on this topic. This is something Mary is experiencing first hand. Several of her customers are still highly skeptical of allowing any data to be sent back from the networking solutions they have purchased, while others have begun actively requesting it, so that Mary and her colleagues can better tune the product.

To conclude, we once again stress the importance of understanding one's business context, but also to plan ahead by ensuring the purely technical ability of calling home and collecting both traceability and runtime data, even if the attitudes in the marketplace currently seem to preclude it. Attitudes do change, and even customers who have not (yet) seen the light may be persuaded by a convincing demonstration of your secure and professional handling of their data, and the benefits you both stand to gain from collecting and analyzing it.

Summary

In this chapter we have outlined six success factors of frequent and rapid deployment of software: low risk deployment, rapid deployment, deployables as container images, runtime modularity, tuning the frequency and calling home. We have seen that there are multiple techniques that may be more or less suitable, depending on the type of software and the context, but in the end it all comes down to a handful of familiar principles: do it rapidly, do it in small steps, do it safely, and do it transparently so that you can tell whether it worked out okay or not.

We have also found that several of the success factors are highly dependent on software architecture, deployment topology and the software distribution model, to the point where continuous deployment isn't even a realistic option in certain cases.

In the next chapter we will look into how one goes about designing pipelines in a systematic fashion.

Chapter 21

Systematic Pipeline Design

So far in Part III: Building the Pipeline, we have looked into various challenges in software pipeline design and success factors to overcome them. Even so, as we noted in the introductory chapter to this part, any pipeline will be a more or less bespoke solution tailored to the software system it is producing. In this chapter we raise the level of abstraction a notch and consider methods for turning the design of that bespoke solution into a systematic and reliable process. We will consider how to model a pipeline using architecture frameworks, how to minimize its critical path, and how to design coupling and communication between its agents and activities. We will then end the chapter with a few words on security considerations.

Applying Architecture Frameworks

Designing and developing complex software systems rarely starts out by just writing some code and going on from there – or when it does, it rarely ends well. They require careful thought and purposeful architecture to meet their requirements and, just as important, to stay maintainable and evolvable. The systems we create to build, evaluate and deploy other systems are no exception.

There is a long history of tools and frameworks to assist the design and architecture of software. Prominent examples include the Unified

Modeling Language (UML[29]) along with well known architecture frameworks such as the 4+1 View Model [61] and the Agile influenced C4 model [62]. These frameworks help engineers visualize and analyze the anatomy, separations of concerns and topology of a system, or a would-be system.

As anyone who has ever attempted to visualize a software system can attest, however, it isn't enough to just draw up some lines and boxes. Any diagram can be interpreted in multiple ways, as there are multiple aspects of a software system that may be represented. A key feature of architecture frameworks is their ability to address those multiple aspects through distinct *views* on the same underlying system. For instance, the 4+1 View Model contains – as the name suggests – a total of five views: a development view, a logical view, a physical view, a process view and a use case view. Each view addresses a separate set of concerns, answering specific questions regarding the represented system.

From years of experience and research we strongly recommend using an actual architecture framework or modeling language to model and design any non-trivial software pipeline. It is possible to pick something highly generic (e.g. UML) and adapt it to the particular task at hand – the crucial point is to be very careful and explicit in what the models and pictures mean. It is all too easy to pick up a pen or open up Powerpoint and start drawing lines and boxes without properly thinking through what they represent. Are the edges causal relationships, dependencies, or consumption relationships? Are the boxes activities, servers, or logical processes? How does one find the critical path? How does one measure lead times? How does one find bottlenecks? Of the hundreds of pictures of pipelines, "software flows", production systems and test processes we have witnessed, few are ever able to clearly answer questions like these. Often, we find, because they weren't even considered by whoever drew the pictures in the first place – this is another benefit of using a thought out and proven framework: it will help you think in a structured way and point out important questions you probably want to consider.

Figure 45 shows an adapted example taken from industry of such an improvised visualization of a simple pipeline, manifesting several of the

---

29 http://www.uml.org

problems mentioned above. When studied in detail, it raises more questions than it answers. For instance, what does the edge connecting Developer to Build Activity mean? Does the developer manually trigger the activity, or does it represent the activity consuming software committed by the developer? If so, committed where, and triggered how? And does the edge connecting Build Activity to Test Activity mean that the latter is triggered by the former, or that it consumes its output? Or both? What types of tests are executed in Test Activity, where are they executed, what is their scope and what purpose do they serve? And is Deploy Activity triggered by the conclusion of Test Activity? If so, under which circumstances? Does the outcome of Test Activity matter? And where does Deploy Activity get the artifact to be deployed from? The list of unanswered questions goes on.

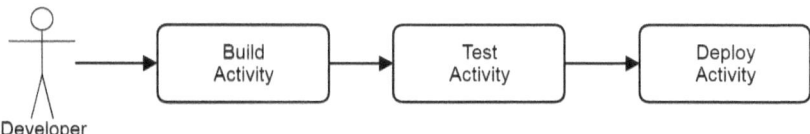

Figure 45: Improvised visualization of a simple pipeline.

One alternative to avoid these pitfalls is to use an architecture framework specifically tailored to the problem of representing software pipelines. Influenced by existing architecture frameworks for generic software systems and through extensive workshops with multiple companies, we have developed the Cinders framework [44] for this purpose.

Cinders provides four independent viewpoints from which any software pipeline may be regarded, based on a single coherent data model: the Causality Viewpoint, the Production Line Viewpoint, the Test Capabilities Viewpoint and the Instances Viewpoint. Each of these viewpoints has optional layers of data designed to answer specific questions. See Figures 46 and 47 for examples of the Production Line Viewpoint and the Test Capabilities Viewpoint, respectively.

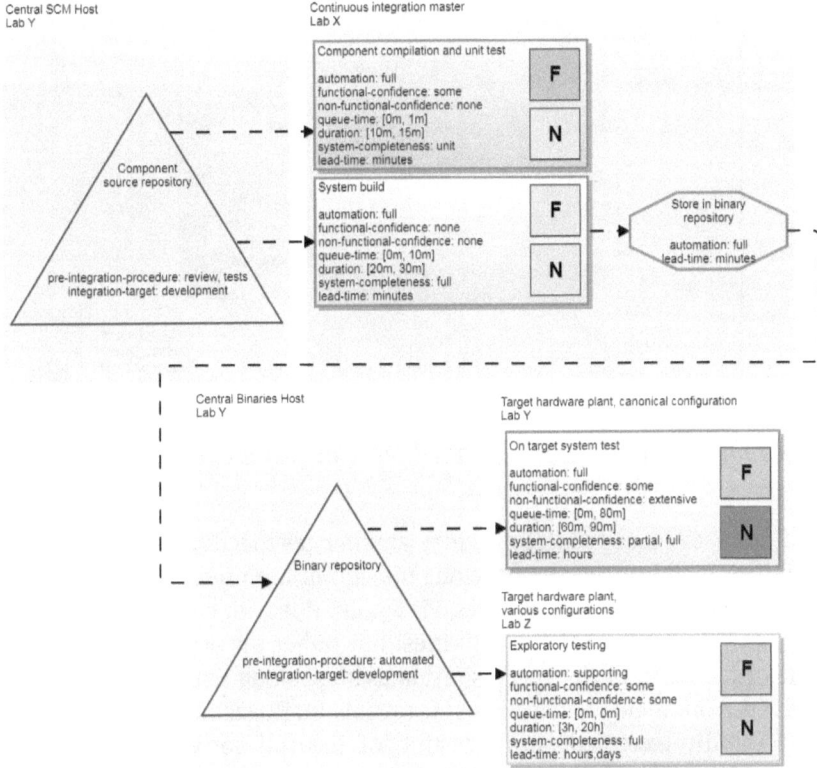

Figure 46: Cinders Production Line Viewpoint example.

The Production Line Viewpoint (shown in Figure 46) reveals how software is transported through the pipeline, while completely ignoring temporal or causal concerns. It shows how the System build and the Component compilation and unit test activities independently fetch their input from the same source repository. Whereas the latter is a dead end in this view (but may well serve other purposes revealed when studied from other viewpoints, such as causing subsequent activities to trigger), the System build activity then stores its output in Binary repository, from where it is then fetched by further downstream activities.

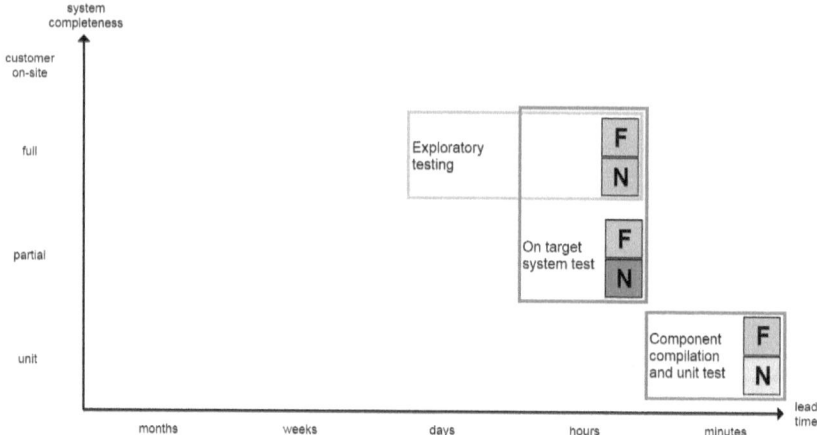

Figure 47: Cinders Test Capabilities Viewpoint example.

Figure 47, meanwhile, provides another perspective. Several of the activities visible from the previous viewpoint are present, but rendered differently. The Test Capabilities Viewpoint does not concern itself with the input and output of the activities, but rather the scope and the lead time of feedback of the various test activities, along with the confidence derived from them. For instance, it reveals that tests on a unit level are very rapidly executed, while testing of the full software product on target takes hours.

The Cinders framework is designed to enable automated collection and real time analysis of pipeline data (such as Eiffel events as described in Chapter 15). We have ourselves applied it in workshop settings in a range of organizations. We find that there are two important takeaways from that work. The first is that sitting down around a table for a few hours to agree on a single, unambiguous description of what one's pipeline actually looks like is a very healthy exercise. There hasn't been a single workshop where questions in the spirit of "Is that what it really looks like? I had no idea!", "Is that why it's so slow?" and "Why do we do it like that?" have not been raised, often followed by reflections such as "Now I finally understand why the developers keep complaining!". The second takeaway is that such exercises work best with a carefully selected mix of people of multiple roles. When a developer, a test manager, a project manager and a system architect sit down to agree on what their software production system looks like, interesting conversations are guaranteed to follow.

Minimizing the Critical Path

In Chapter 17 we introduced the concept of complementing automated tests in the pipeline with exploratory testing, but not making it a prerequisite for release and/or deployment. In other words, placing those manual and time-consuming activities outside of the pipeline's critical path, so as to reduce the time from source code change to production.

The concept of splitting feedback oriented activities away from gatekeeping activities and placing them to the side, outside of the critical path, may seem elementary, perhaps too elementary even to mention. All the same, I have again and again encountered companies and projects who protest that continuous deployment is not an option for them, because they simply cannot get away from their various manual test activities. Time and time again, the simple suggestion that they keep performing those tests, but consider whether they really need them as gatekeepers for every little change they make to the software has been received as a major revelation.

- Daniel

In this chapter we would like to re-emphasize this point, while also broadening it. The principle of minimizing the critical path of the pipeline applies not only to manual test activities, but to a wide array of test and analysis needs. For instance, every change to Bob's social media platform backend is subjected to an extensive battery of dynamic code analyses that monitor trends in network traffic, memory consumption, throughput, thread pool management, CPU load et cetera. A great deal of this monitoring is performed in production, but much is also carried out in dedicated test environments so as to not disrupt users.

While Bob and his colleagues pay close attention to these analyses, they do not consider them suitable as gatekeepers for deployment: they take too long, and any issues they identify are unlikely to be immediate showstoppers. Instead, they help the developers ensure that they don't inadvertently degrade performance over time.

Consequently, while not belaboring the point, we strongly encourage you to start small when designing your pipeline. Ask yourself what absolutely has to be verified before release and/or deployment: what are the non-negotiable gatekeeper activities? Then do what you can to prevent overly zealous quality managers, test managers and guardians of this and that to cram everything and the kitchen sink in there over time. It's always easy to add just one more test, but it's amazingly difficult to remove old ones.

Hooking up the Pipelines

A critical decision facing would-be designers of any software production system is how to hook up the various activities that make up the pipelines, and the pipelines that make up the larger pipeline network of the production system. To exemplify, when Alice checks in a new version of her electronic control unit (ECU), how does that trigger a build and test cycle of the ECU? And when a new ECU version has been built and successfully tested, how does that make it into a new baseline of the vehicle system?

There are three basic mechanisms to choose from: schedule, push and pull. Scheduled triggers are arguably the simplest to implement and occasionally necessitated by factors such as resource availability. They are easy because they require no direct communication between the activities. When running on a fixed schedule, the build activity constructing Alice's ECU has no need to query the SCM system or receive notifications from it: as depicted in Figure 48, each activity will simply execute when it is time to execute, but that is also what makes it

---

a poor solution. Even though Alice would like to get a new ECU version built, tested and integrated into the vehicle straight away, she'll just have to wait until the pipeline decides it's time, severely limiting the value of having a pipeline in the first place. Due to this, we find schedule based triggers to be the worst option of the three mechanisms.

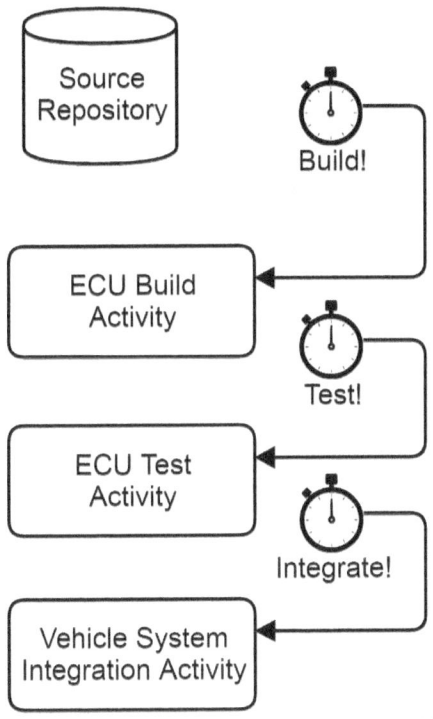

Figure 48: Schedule based activity triggering in Alice's ECU pipeline.

A push mechanism is slightly more sophisticated, in that it triggers downstream activities directly through some form of notification: a remote procedure call, a broadcast event or via a polling mechanism. This removes the delays introduced by (infrequent) scheduled activity executions, but it places the responsibility of determining downstream consequences of the individual activity. In other words, the ECU build becomes responsible for triggering test activities, and those test activities become responsible for triggering a system integration activity (see Figure 49). This works reasonably well in a more or less linear and kept together production system, but a library built and re-used by dozens or hundreds of distributed and possibly unknown consumers cannot be expected to instruct all those consumers under what circumstances to integrate the new version and rebuild – that is simply not its concern, and neither should it be its mandate. Similarly, when a new user comes along they shouldn't have to ask to be signed up on the trigger list. Besides, different users may have different policies, wanting to integrate new release candidates at different times and under different circumstances, depending on their own internal stability, their need for new features and whether they prefer a stable dependency or the latest build.

All of which is what makes pull based mechanisms the most flexible and extensible option. In a pull based system it is the downstream activity that determines when and how to act, depending on changing circumstances. Returning to Alice's case, this means that the vehicle system integration activity learns in real time that there is a new successfully tested version of Alice's ECU, and will react accordingly.

In other words, the difference between push and pull based triggers is not so much technical as it is conceptual. The underlying method of communication may be the same, such as polling or broadcasting events, but the distinguishing factor is where the decision to act is made. It's worth pointing out that this does not imply a *manual* decision made by a flesh and blood human being, nor does it imply a QA department only integrating new software on rare occasions, e.g. during a quarterly test activity. This would deprive the developers of their rapid feedback on how their software changes fare when integrated with other components and systems, and thus violates the basic principles of a continuous integration and delivery pipeline.

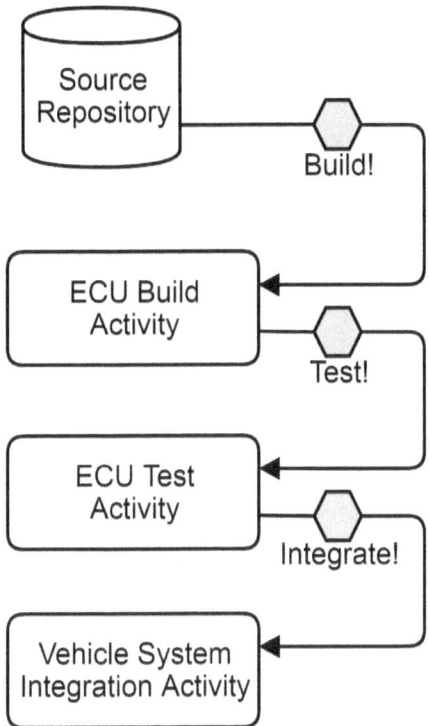

Figure 49: Point-to-point push based activity triggering in Alice's ECU pipeline.

In a push system, the downstream activity does as instructed, whereas in a pull based system, the downstream activity receives the relevant information – e.g. that Alice has committed a new version of the ECU source code – and then decides for itself what to do about it. In simple cases the difference is subtle, but in large networks of pipelines it is critical. On a related note, the same can be said for the difference between schedule based and push or pull based systems. A push or pull mechanism can be implemented via polling, which is technically a scheduled system that fires at very high frequently.

That being said, we find pull based mechanisms to work best when listening to broadcast events, as shown in Figure 50. This does away with the need of even being aware of upstream activities: Alice's

Vehicle System Integration Activity shouldn't even have to know that there is such a thing as an ECU Test Activity or an ECU Build Activity, and much less have to poll them for new results. Furthermore, Alice and her teammates are free to change their local ECU build and test activities any way they like without disrupting downstream activities, as long as they broadcast the relevant events. In other words, it behaves just as we would expect from a well designed loosely coupled architecture. Just as importantly, additional downstream activities can be appended to the pipeline without impact on upstream activities. To exemplify, Alice's company could introduce a new vehicle variant with its own composition of ECUs, and therefore its own independent Vehicle System Integration Activity. In a point-to-point push based system, as in Figure 49, Alice and all other ECU development teams would have to introduce a new call to this new integration activity whenever they have a new ECU version ready. In the event broadcasting and pull based system illustrated in Figure 50, on the other hand, there would be no impact on Alice and her colleagues.

Designing for Information Security

In previous chapters we have touched upon questions of information security, e.g. when discussing storage and distribution of pipeline event data. Here we would like to provide a few general pointers on security in context of software pipelines – pointers to keep in the back of your mind when considering what sort of pipeline or network of pipelines will fit your needs.

Information security is one of those subjects that many software engineers would agree is really important, but would rather not think too much about. It's a term that gets thrown around a lot – we are often told about the need for security, the lack of it and various products that will make our security concerns go away – but the questions of what, how and why are all too often left unanswered. In that spirit, let us break the concept down.

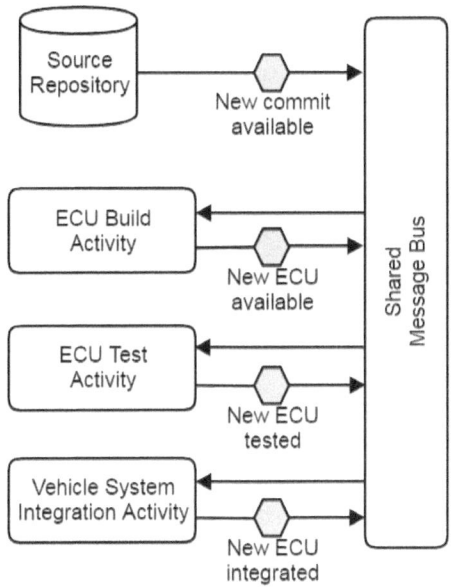

Figure 50: Event broadcasting and pull based activity triggering in Alice's ECU pipeline.

In literature, information security is defined as consisting of three core concepts: confidentiality, integrity and availability. These are often referred to as the CIA triad, or sometimes CAI [63].

Confidentiality refers to the ability to protect data from those not authorized to view it. It can be compromised in a variety of ways, e.g. through leaked passwords, malicious software attacks or misplaced laptops carrying sensitive data. Particular to continuous practices, a common source of vulnerabilities is the fact that a continuous integration and delivery pipeline connects software systems that previously might have been developed and maintained in separate environments. This new interconnectedness might unintentionally reveal source code or documentation to partners or to unauthorized personnel within the organization.

Availability, on the other hand, refers to the ability to access needed information, when it is needed. A common attack against availability is Denial of Service (DoS) attacks, distributed or otherwise.

The confidentiality and the availability of a pipeline ultimately comes down to the infrastructure and the tools used: the same threats and weaknesses hold as for any other computer system, and the same safeguards and solutions apply. Consequently, we leave these topics in more capable hands by recommending you to consider the confidentiality and availability requirements of your pipeline the way you would for any other tools or infrastructure in your organization, and consult with experts as appropriate.

That being said, we urge you to not underestimate the threat to pipeline infrastructure. For instance, continuous integration servers (such as Jenkins) are rarely considered high risk assets and consequently only provided perfunctory protection against malicious attacks. Due to their central role in an organization's IT landscape, however, it is common (but strongly discouraged) practice to store passwords to all sorts of tools and databases in their configurations. This asymmetry of weak protection and high value makes them prime candidates for attackers.

Integrity is different, however. Integrity refers to the ability to protect one's information from being corrupted or manipulated, intentionally or unintentionally, in an unauthorized or otherwise undesirable manner. The reason why integrity is different is that it not only comes down to the abilities of the tools used, but is an integral property of the pipeline design itself.

It is also different because an automated continuous deployment pipeline is a powerful thing, and could potentially cause a great deal of havoc if subverted: while there have been notorious incidents of virus infected software releases in the past, the sheer speed at which an automated pipeline can deploy to hundreds of thousands of targets only serves to amplify the threat. Indeed, at the time of writing, there is a strong trend of increasing attacks on software supply chains, with the aim of turning legitimate and trusted software into vectors for malware infection [64].

To determine the appropriate level of attention to integrity in your software pipeline, we recommend you to consider possible scenarios and their consequences by asking yourself three questions:

- What are the ways in which the pipeline might be intentionally or unintentionally subverted to deploy artifacts that were not intended for production, or even to deploy manipulated artifacts?

- What might the consequences of such deployments be?

- What are the ways in which a malicious third party might stand to gain from such deployments?

Answering those three questions serves to determine the appropriate level of response to the integrity concern. In our experience, however, careful consideration almost always reveals serious potential for harm. To exemplify, all five of our archetypes risk serious consequences in case of maliciously corrupted deployments – even ones that may appear relatively innocuous at first glance.

Perhaps most graphic are the disasters that may result if corrupted software was deployed to Alice's cars or Jane's military fighting vehicle, but the other archetypes also stand to cause major widespread damage: disrupting network traffic, leaking sensitive data and spreading malicious software to customers. Such malicious software may then, in turn, be used in further attacks, such as ransomware attacks or industry espionage. What's more, all of the five archetypes can easily identify capable third parties who would stand to gain, financially and/or politically, from such failures.

A crucial weak link in the pipeline is the automated agent performing the actual deployment of software, particularly in cases where such agents act remotely. This agent must ensure the integrity both of the instruction to deploy as well as the deployed artifact itself, preventing a man-in-the-middle or man-on-the-side attack from subverting the deployment, e.g. by injecting packets [65].

A tried and true method of achieving this is the strong distribution model of software. A strong distribution model is one that relies on asymmetric cryptographic key pairs and cryptographic hash functions to digitally sign and protect information from manipulation (or, more precisely, allow the recipient to verify that the integrity has not been compromised). An example of this at work is the possibility to include encrypted message digests in any Eiffel event, allowing any deployment agent to verify that it is acting upon information sent by a trusted source, even when communicating over an open and untrusted channel.

Another point of weakness is third party dependencies, as well as development tools, compilers or even build servers which may be compromised in order to inject malware into the product. In such cases, digital signing is not enough, as the software is already compromised at the point of signing. A strongly recommended protection mechanism against such attacks is the automated and mandatory malware scanning of all release candidates prior to digitally signing them.

On a closing note, even though we have focused on malicious attacks, it is equally important to remember the more mundane risk of accidentally deploying the wrong software artifact. The most ambitious and scrupulous test activities imaginable won't help the least if what ultimately gets deployed is not the artifact that was tested. Luckily, the steps prescribed above protect against accidental and intentional corruption alike.

Summary

In this final chapter of Part III: Building the Pipeline we have looked at success factors not so much related to specific challenges such as testing or deploying, but rather related to how one goes about effectively and efficiently designing a pipeline in more general terms. In that vein we have looked into the help that architecture frameworks may offer, how to think about the pipeline's critical path and inter-activity communication, followed by a few words of caution on security.

In the next part of the book we will leave the domain of the purely technical and bring up the arguably much more difficult question of onboarding the organization.

Part IV:
Onboarding the Organization

Chapter 22

Introduction

In this introductory chapter we will consider what onboarding the organization actually means for continuous practices. An effective software production system is about more than just technical issues and tooling; it involves human beings, and so it is about mindset, roles, responsibilities, skills and not least about motivation. In this regard, it is no different from any other software engineering problem. As Gerald Weinberg famously remarked, "no matter how it looks at first, it's always a people problem." [66]

Boiled down to its essence, the question is how to get people to behave the way we would like them to behave, in order to benefit from continuous practices. This raises additional, more detailed questions, such as how to enable and motivate developers to actually integrate frequently, how to support the software architecture discipline in a continuous practices context and how to balance a focus on speed against a need for high quality. We recognize that while continuous delivery and deployment are practices which can be decided upon and implemented top-down, continuous integration (being a developer practice) largely has to emerge bottom-up, as it's a behavior the individual developer needs to be motivated to adopt. Like Part III: Building the Pipeline, this part will touch on each of the three major continuous practices of continuous integration, delivery and deployment, but from the perspective that it's not really an engineering problem: it's a people problem.

Consequently, this part of the book focuses more the subjective perspectives of various stakeholders in the organization and what may incentivize or disincentivize them to change their behavior, and less on pure business aspects and potential benefits of continuous practices. In other words, it is intended more to support change initiatives in the particular case of continuous practices adoption, rather than as ammunition for selling that change in a board room.

With that said, we find that addressing this type of "soft" issues requires a slightly different approach from us as authors. Readers may find that this part is based on personal experiences and subjective observations to a greater extent than Part III, and to a lesser extent on objective, demonstrable facts. This is not least because human beings and their organizations are infinitely more complex than any software system in existence, and quite simply that much more difficult to understand and to generalize. Nevertheless, we wish to offer what lessons and advice we can in this area, so as to save others some of the pains those lessons are drawn from. We hope that this will provide you as a reader some nuggets of concrete value.

Understanding Human Motivation

Rather than just making random observations of how people behave – and sometimes more crucially, how they don't behave – we will look to two influential theories on job satisfaction and work motivation. We will alternate between these theories and use them as lenses through which we may better understand certain phenomena, and ideally how certain challenges may be overcome.

The first theory is the two-factor theory by Frederick Herzberg [67] (also known as the motivation-hygiene theory or the dual-factor theory). Herzberg argues that satisfying basic needs is not enough to motivate higher performance at work, an idea which builds on Maslow's hierarchy of needs [68]. Instead, meeting basic needs only serves to reduce dissatisfaction. To motivate increased performance, higher-level psychological needs must be satisfied, such as responsibility, recognition and/or advancement. Furthermore, unlike Maslow's hierarchy of needs, Herzberg finds that these factors do not exist in a single hierarchy, but are in fact separate. In other words, according to the two-factor theory, it is perfectly possible to increase satisfaction (e.g. via recognition) while not reducing dissatisfaction (e.g. due to unsatisfactory compensation). These types of factors are known as motivators and hygiene factors, respectively. While hygiene factors are important in keeping us from being *dissatisfied*, they are by themselves not sufficient to make us *satisfied* and thereby truly motivated to higher performance. Hygiene factors and motivators can also be thought of as extrinsic and intrinsic factors, respectively. When combined, hygiene factors and motivators form four quadrants, as shown in Figure 51.

	Low hygiene	High hygiene
High motivation	Employees are motivated, but have many complaints. The job is exciting and challenging, but conditions are not satisfactory.	The ideal situation where employees are highly motivated and have few complaints.
Low motivation	Employees are not motivated and have many complaints.	Employees have few complaints, but are not highly motivated. The job is just a paycheck.

Figure 51: Two-factor theory quadrants.

The second theory we will turn to is that of autonomy, mastery and purpose, as described by Daniel Pink [69]. Even though Pink himself doesn't mention the fact (and arguably makes certain other omissions [70]), the idea of autonomy, mastery and purpose can be seen as building on top of Herzberg's work on hygiene factors and motivators.

As Pink himself puts it, "carrots and sticks" – which, according to Herzberg's theory, we may regard as extrinsic hygiene factors – "are so last century". Instead, what is needed to truly motivate high performance in creative and cognitive tasks is autonomy, mastery and purpose. These intrinsic factors are about the desire for and satisfaction from self-direction, the urge to improve skills that are important to us, and the drive to be part of and contribute to something transcendent and meaningful beyond ourselves. This is based on repeated studies showing that rewards only increase performance in very narrow, mechanistic tasks, while they actually decrease performance in tasks requiring cognitive thought, problem-solving and/or decision-making. That being said, what Herzberg would have called hygiene factors are important to avoid dissatisfaction. This includes a satisfactory salary level that takes, as Pink puts it, "the issue of money off the table," but beyond that monetary incentives are ineffective or even harmful.

As we look into various behaviors supporting or counteracting continuous practices in subsequent chapters, we will use these theories of extrinsic and intrinsic factors to try to better understand their underlying causes and to identify possible solutions.

Identifying the Stakeholders

Before we proceed we need one more puzzle piece: we need to identify the stakeholders of continuous practices. The names of departments, teams and roles within an organization differ from company to company – sometimes even between units within a single company. Similarly, the way tasks and responsibilities are allocated also differs. Consequently, instead of discussing what, for instance, "the project manager" should do or what "the product owner" needs, we will focus on the stakeholder interests that all organizations must consider and address in order to benefit from continuous practices.

Some readers will note that we pay particular attention to large-scale cases in this part. While that is not our exclusive focus, there is good reason for this. Onboarding an organization is simply harder the larger that organization is; if it's just you and your two friends, then most of the challenges we will address in this part of the book probably will not resonate with you. That being said, when reading on, we encourage you to try to identify the various stakeholders of your pipeline in your own case.

In studies and interviews in multiple software companies, we have identified what we regard as five distinct stakeholder interests with regards to the continuous integration and delivery pipeline – interests that can be mapped to one or more roles within an organization. These are the stakeholder groups we will primarily focus on in this part of the book, though we will identify a few additional stakeholders once get into release and deployment of software in Chapter 25.

The first stakeholder interest is that of testing the quality and correctness of changes. In the organizations we have studied this is primarily a concern for developers or teams of developers: understanding whether committed software changes pass through the pipeline without causing failures, degraded performance or similar.

The second stakeholder interest is to safeguard the long term quality and integrity of the product, and to follow up on any unexpected impact on test cases. We also include ensuring that the product complies with architectural design, and stays evolvable and performant. This is related to the first stakeholder interest, but exists on a slightly higher level of abstraction. We should mention that we have not encountered this interest realized as an identified role in every studied organization, but in most, where it may involve typically senior engineers with titles that have words like "quality," "architect," "chief" and/or "system" in them.

The third identified interest is that of measuring project progress: what is the throughput, what are the lead times, when will features be completed et cetera. In most cases these are concerns of line managers, project managers, program managers and similar roles. In many organizations, these roles also cover the fourth interest, which is to verify requirements or related artifacts, such as usage scenarios, acceptance criteria or user stories. We have also seen the opposite, though, where this stakeholder interest is dedicated to particular roles, e..g technical managers or a product owner. Just to be clear, the fact that we identify this as a pipeline stakeholder interest is not to say that these people execute tests to perform that verification, but that they have an interest in the information provided by the pipeline for the purpose of determining whether requirements have been successfully verified.

Figure 52 shows these four stakeholder interests, categorized by whether their need for pipeline feedback is product centric or project centric (in other words, being primarily interested in the software product itself and its intrinsic quality, or in how it relates to project plans and other extrinsic artifacts such as requirements) and whether they take a short term interest (e.g. whether a commit has been integrated and tested okay) or long term interest (such as the trends in lead time from commit to deployment or whether requirements implementation is on track).

	Short term interest	Long term interest
Product centric	Testing quality and correctness of changes	Securing system health and integrity
Project centric	Verification of requirements and/or user scenarios	Measurement of progress

Figure 52: Software production system stakeholder interests.

In addition to these four, we have also identified a fifth distinct interest, although it does not overtly manifest in every organization. We say overtly, because we believe that it is a universal need that exists regardless of whether organizations are conscious of it and explicitly identify it: the optimization of tests and other pipeline activities. It is rather a special group of stakeholders, though, since it represents an interest in the pipeline for the purpose of improving the pipeline and does not derive any value for the product development itself. For this reason we have left it out of Figure 52, and speculate that this is also the reason it isn't clearly identified in every organization.

> It deserves to be pointed out that the people who build the pipeline infrastructure should also be users of that infrastructure, in the sense that the pipeline should build itself. In the ideal case, revision N of the pipeline should always be built and deployed by revision N-1. This is surprisingly often overlooked; I have seen more "pipeline teams" who do not continuously integrate, deliver or deploy their own software than I care to count. Drinking one's own champagne may seem like a platitude in this day and age, but it bears repeating.
>
> *- Daniel*

Again, as we have exemplified above, within each of these stakeholder interests there are multiple roles, the names of which vary from case to case. You will also find that we have refrained from describing any sequence for involving various groups or roles in a transformation to continuous practices. This is intentional; we could relate our own experiences from a number of companies, but we believe that there is no road map that will work for any situation. Instead, we will limit ourselves to identifying stakeholder interests with a clear stake in the network of pipelines and the feedback it can provide, and their respective needs and considerations.

On a final note, there are additional groups of people who are affected by continuous practices and who need to be onboarded, but who we would not consider as stakeholders in that they don't interact with, monitor or otherwise use the pipeline. We will consider these groups in Chapter 25, as we address frequent deployments.

Thus equipped with a scrap of psychological theory and a classification of stakeholders, we are ready to consider the elements of onboarding the organization.

Elements of Onboarding the Organization

Similar to how we broke the question of building the pipeline down into elements in Chapter 14, striving for a mutually exclusive yet collective exhaustive set of elements, a breakdown of how the organization can be onboarded is shown in Figure 53.

Just as we found in the case of building the pipeline, there is never a single way of breaking a topic down into its constituent elements. Here we have decided on a structure that is loosely mapped to the three practices of continuous integration, delivery and deployment, as they are defined in Chapter 2: enabling frequent integrations, achieving quality through the pipeline, and finally enabling frequent deployments.

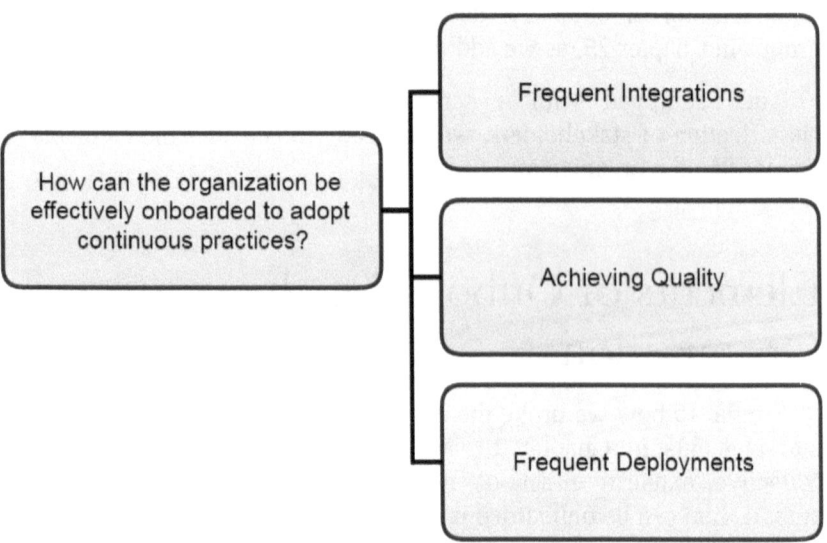

Figure 53: Elements on onboarding the organization.

In the following chapters we will address each element and its success factors in turn.

Chapter 23

Frequent Integrations

In this chapter we will present success factors for enabling and motivating frequent integration of source code. This means that the stakeholders in focus throughout this chapter are the ones in the upper left quadrant of Figure 52, the software developers themselves.

In study after study and in change program after change program we have encountered developers who simply do not commit their changes very frequently at all, despite the ambitions and the espoused beliefs of the organizations they are part of. We have been able to identify a number of reasons for this – reasons we may regard as hygiene factors and motivators, respectively. Depending on the background and the outlook of the individual developer, these may be more or less pronounced. In other words, it is common to encounter developers who would either like nothing more than to continuously integrate, but find it too slow, cumbersome or painful (i.e. lacking hygiene factors), whereas their colleagues in the same organization simply don't see the value in it (i.e. lacking motivators). This is why we find it critical to address both types of factors in Herzberg's two-factor theory, or some developers will inevitably be left behind and frustrated.

Work Planning and Breakdown

When asked what prevents them from integrating more frequently than they currently do, many developers speak of the fact that the work they need to carry out and the responsibilities they are given simply are not structured in a way that lends itself to small, frequent commits [34]. This comes down to several related issues: work items not being broken down into small enough parts, team structures encouraging larger and more infrequent changes, and the need for changes to be implemented in a certain order, thus creating coordination issues.

The problem of breaking down work items into small enough pieces is one of both technology and culture. Committing unfinished work can serve several purposes, such as giving early warning to your fellow developers that you're touching a certain piece of code and taking it in a particular direction, or as a way of getting regression test feedback on refactoring of the code in preparation of adding a new feature. Even so, committing only half of a new feature isn't necessarily a good idea, and when that new feature takes a month to develop, non-continuous integration follows.

The solution is not to have a project management or a systemization function break the work down into tiny pieces that the developers can swallow without chewing. Not only does such careful up-front planning add precious lead time, but it also takes the problem-solving out of the development and reduces the mastery and autonomy of the developers, something we will return to in the next section. Rather, there is an important hygiene factor at play: the product architecture must allow for partial, incremental implementation of new functionality, either via something like feature toggles or flags, or via modularity and interface version negotiation (similar to the techniques described in Chapter 20).

An engineer in a company I once worked with approached me to discuss how to introduce automated system testing techniques. Not far into that conversation it became clear to me that their actual problem was in fact not about automated testing, but rather how to coordinate updates of the numerous software components in their system to avoid integration conflicts. While it may be tempting to dive straight into solution mode, it's important to first consider what the correct question is. In this case it turned out not to be a question of technology, but rather of coordination and planning – or, as the case may be, how to avoid it.

- Torvald

Another important factor deciding the developers' ability to break a large chunk of work down is team structure, which also impacts the extent to which work has to be coordinated and sequenced. There are several schools of thought here. First, let us be clear on nomenclature. Cross-functional teams, in the sense of including multiple disciplines and competences in a single team in order to enable it to take greater responsibility, is generally seen as a good thing and we see little cause for controversy there. This should not be confused with cross-component or feature teams, however, where teams specialize in a type of features or characteristics of the system (or, for that matter, don't specialize in anything at all) and take responsibility for these entire features across the entire system. The opposite of a cross-component team is a component team, which specializes in a particular part of the product but takes responsibility for all types of features or characteristics in that part.

Deciding whether component teams are better than cross-component teams or the other way around is not easy. We would argue that each brings its own set of problems and its own need for coordination of work. Component teams can be great in that they foster ownership and a sense of responsibility for the local component, but they can simultaneously discourage engineers from taking responsibility for the entire system, and particularly for emergent properties which can not be cleanly mapped to any one component. They also drive the need for coordination between teams when features impact multiple components, particularly in not-so-loosely-coupled architectures requiring synchronized changes. Cross-component teams, on the other hand, drive the need for coordination between teams making parallel and sometimes conflicting changes to a single component. They can also lead to very poor code quality, as a lessened sense of ownership results in a tragedy of the commons type of scenario, where everybody's responsibility is nobody's responsibility. This is particularly the case when strong enforcement of coding style and quality is lacking.

All of this is relevant to continuous practices, because not only is the minimization of coordination overhead essential in allowing frequent integrations, but so is a well maintained code base that allows for small, rapid changes. In the end, we believe that the best an organization can do – if multiple teams are truly necessary – is to simply make up its mind and decide on one setup, while being conscious of and trying to mitigate its drawbacks. The worst case scenario is switching back and forth between the two.

> I have seen organizations that just couldn't seem to decide on a team structure. The pendulum would swing back and forth every two years or so, from component teams to cross-component teams and back again. The grass may well look greener on the other side, but once you get there you'll face a whole new set of problems.
>
> - Daniel

While on the topic of teams and organization, we would like to mention a sometimes overlooked issue, namely that of skills and competences. When we observe some organizations restructure their teams first this way and that in an attempt to get more out of them, we sometimes feel that by doing so they skirt the deeper and more uncomfortable root cause of their perceived inefficiencies, namely what Jurgen Apello aptly calls the Agile blind spot: "all software projects need people being smart, disciplined and attentive, [but when] you find out that your team consists of two trolls, a parrot and a hairdresser, and a relatively bright project manager, who happens to be deaf, blind and mute [no] amount of coaching will help" [71]. And neither will any reorganization, we would add.

John, our game developer archetype, is a good example of how being small enough to not have to worry about inter-team coordination can save you a lot of trouble. John and the other developers have never formalized any division of responsibility, but have grown into their respective competence areas in a more or less organic fashion. When assigning tasks they volunteer for work based on what they feel comfortable with, and when they feel out of their depth they usually try to solve that by pair programming. As the organization is small, so is the code base, and trying to break improvements down into small enough pieces to commit something at least once or twice a day has never been an issue.

Jane, on the other hand, works in a much larger organization, split into component teams. Early on in the product development, building the new platform and the architectural runway, she felt that this worked very well. Lately, though, as work has shifted towards implementing features cutting across the entire vehicle system, the amount of coordination meetings between teams has sky-rocketed, particularly as the components of the vehicle she's developing are very tightly coupled. As a consequence, Jane wonders whether cross-component teams wouldn't be a better solution, while some of her colleagues worry that this would lead to even more coordination work, only of another kind and involving slightly different people.

Developer Autonomy

Developer autonomy is largely a motivator – indeed, it's part of Pink's trinity of intrinsic factors – but we will also regard it as a hygiene factor.

As a motivator, developer autonomy is hugely important. Engineers want to feel ownership of something, where they can use their own skills and talents to make meaningful decisions and solve problems as they see fit, rather than mindlessly following orders. That ownership and autonomy doesn't have to be on an individual basis. On the contrary, as human beings we're great at sharing responsibility in a group, and often we derive even more motivation from collective ownership than from individual ownership of a domain. The problem is that this only works up to a certain group size: when the number of people who collectively own something goes from two to five to ten, a hundred or a thousand, somewhere along the way everybody's responsibility turns into nobody's responsibility. It would appear that the human mind just doesn't do as well identifying with too large a group.

This is why the two pizza rule works so well (see Chapter 16). If you are able to form small enough teams and give them clear ownership of something – be it a component, a set of features, a set of non-functional requirements or anything else – that will increase their motivation, not just to do a good job, but to do the job well. This includes behaving as "good citizens" in general, with frequent integration of changes and the maintenance of a high level of mainline quality.

It's worth pointing out that this delegation of ownership to teams implies a high level of trust. Sometimes we see organizations attempt to emulate this behavior, but as they don't fully trust the developers and the teams they will require external entities (architects, guardians, change boards, quality managers – they come in many shapes) to vet any meaningful decision made by the team, rather than embedding that competence and authority within the team itself. Needless to say, this quickly erodes the motivation of the developers.

The hygiene factor aspect of developer autonomy lies in a reduced need for coordination, and coordination is the bane of continuous integration. Almost by definition, a developer who has complete control over his or her domain doesn't need to coordinate changes within that domain with others. In practice it's not that simple, of course, as there are always dependencies to take into account. It's important to note that these are two distinct types of coordination, however: one is about obtaining permission or approval for a certain course of action, and the other is about managing concrete impact on parts or properties of the system outside of one's area of ownership. While any coordination is harmful to continuous integration and should be combated, the former type is largely political in nature and adds zero tangible value to the end product. The second type is necessary, but there are technical and architectural approaches to minimizing it (see Chapter 16 and Chapter 20). From a purely organizational standpoint, we recommend striving for a mutually exclusive, collectively exhaustive (MECE) split of responsibilities between teams, to avoid overlaps and consequent coordination needs between them, with the caveat that we have yet to see a flawless split of ownership.

Alice works in a clearly component oriented team, with responsibility for an ECU within the car. In theory, she and her teammates are free to make any change to the internal workings of the ECU, as long as external interfaces are unaffected (both syntactically and semantically). In practice, however, this means they can hardly do anything meaningful by themselves, as those interfaces are defined at a very detailed level. Moreover, she can't just handshake an interface change with the developers of dependent ECUs. Instead, she has to file a change request at a central architecture board controlling every ECU interface in the entire car – a process which typically takes several months.

Bob, meanwhile, has recently joined a feature team responsible for ad value on the social media platform. The team has complete freedom in making changes to any part of the software in order to increase the average value of ads, which is the main source of revenue to the company. This does mean that they sometimes affect the responsibilities of other teams, however. In particular, their changes often affect performance, but to not have to ask for permission from the team responsible for performance at every turn, the performance team has created automated tests that ensure that each part of the system stays within acceptable parameters. As long as Bob doesn't violate those boundaries, he is free to perform any experiment he can imagine to boost the company's revenue. Similarly, a large part of granting Bob and his teammates such freedom in experimenting with the company's revenue stream is the strict real time monitoring of any change in ad value: Bob himself can safely conduct experiments and quickly weed out anything negatively impacting the business, rather than having to ask for permission from senior colleagues.

Availability of Test Environments

Software engineers want to do a good job – they want to feel mastery. Most developers are conscientious people who want to craft high quality code – whichever way quality is defined – and they're uncomfortable checking in code they're unsure of. At least, that is the case when committing bad code has serious consequences (more on this in Safe Commits, further on in this chapter). Simply put, to enble developers to commit frequently, doing so must either be perfectly safe, or they must have ready access to appropriate test environments. When a bad commit stops 500 colleagues in their tracks and you only have a slot once a week where you can test your changes, continuous integration is just not a realistic expectation.

This is true not just for any particular part of the software, but for the entire system. As a rule of thumb, whatever the developer stands to impact through his or her changes must be possible to get test feedback from. There are several ways to provide that feedback. One is, as we have already discussed, to provide test environments where developers can try out their changes before committing. A challenge we often observe with this type of setup, however – particularly for large and complex systems – is that a lot of time is lost configuring the environment for the particular test at hand. This is especially painful where the test resources are scarce and engineers need to book a tight time slot: out of a precious two hour window to test one's changes, nobody wants to waste the first hour just preparing the environment.

Another approach is to have the pipeline provide the feedback, although this requires committing to be safe enough that developers don't hesitate to make use of the pipeline's tests as a regular, frequent source of feedback by committing early and without complete confidence. It also requires that the pipeline is responsive to the developers' actions, in the sense that it provides the feedback they need when they need it.

> I once studied a company which had adopted continuous integration on a component level, and also constructed a pipeline with tests on a system integration level. The problem, from the developers' point of view, was that the pipelines were disjointed. The system integration pipeline wasn't triggered when new component versions were published by the developers, but when it made sense to the system integration engineers. As a result, the developers had no control over when they would get feedback on their software in a system context, which frustrated the developers to no end. It was painfully obvious that this part of the pipeline was never built with the developer stakeholders in mind.
>
> *- Torvald*

A third, hybrid approach is that of Job as a Service, as introduced in Chapter 16, which allows developers to use the pipeline jobs for feedback without having to commit first.

These approaches are not mutually exclusive alternatives so much as they are complementary, and we encourage you as a reader to carefully consider which mix of testing opportunities that fit your case best. No matter which you go for, you should always assume that you will need more test equipment than you expect. Integrating frequently means testing frequently, and if the hardware isn't there to support it, the pace of development will inevitably suffer. Then it becomes a question of which is more expensive, more test equipment or developers unable to proceed at full speed. On a side note, this is an excellent example of how continuous practices are not just a developer concern or an R&D concern: you need to get whoever controls your IT infrastructure and test equipment budget on board from the outset.

As a developer of a game targeting standard PCs (and consoles), John can get the vast majority of testing of new features done on his development machine. For testing non-functional properties on multiple target variants he relies on automated test activities in the pipeline (as described in Chapter 17). Anything caught there shouldn't be a show-stopper, but even if it is the consequences are limited. Between himself and the two other developers, the pace of changes isn't so high that he can't manually revert a bad change before it becomes a serious problem.

For Jane the situation is very different. First of all the project is larger, so every time someone causes gatekeeping tests to fail on the mainline it has a tangible impact on the project schedule. Needless to say, it's not something anyone does if they can at all avoid it. Truly testing the impact of a change on the full system requires access to that system, however. In Jane's case this is a large, expensive, physical item of which the project has exactly one, and which can only be operated by specially trained personnel. Consequently, developers using it to test their individual changes on a daily basis is out of the question. The next best thing is a set of simulator environments, which can be booked for software testing. These are also in high demand and usually fully booked one or two weeks out, though, which means that they are mostly used for verification and prototyping of larger features with longer lead time and foresight than a continuously integrating individual developer. Jane's saving grace is another, pure software simulator she can run on her workstation. It isn't perfect, but it allows her to quickly test her software to a reasonable level of confidence before committing to the mainline.

Fast and Simple Tools and Processes

We have yet to see a tool or a process truly motivate anyone to improve and surpass themselves. They are critical hygiene factors, though: a frustrating process or a slow and unreliable tool will devastate a developer's readiness to commit frequently. This is particularly the case when they're forced to spend – or waste – time on what they perceive as not being their job. Developers are developers because they want to develop software, not because they want to spend their days in meetings, filing reports or wrestling with clumsy configuration management tools. If committing once a day means spending half of their time resolving merge conflicts without adequate tool support or updating architecture schematics in PowerPoint, most developers will simply avoid committing more than absolutely necessary.

Some will tell you that in the future, all companies will be software companies. Whether you believe that or not, it's an undeniable fact that a great number of traditional manufacturing companies today find themselves competing more and more on software, rather than on hardware. A common theme I have observed in these companies, who are used to building trains, washing machines, cars, lawn mowers, airplanes and power drills, is that they tend to apply the same product lifecycle management processes and tools to software, as they have always done to hardware. This has consequences from the merely silly, such as imposing versioning schemes designed for circuit board designs onto software components in parallel to the version control already performed by the SCM system, to the downright ridiculous, such as forcing engineers to register the weight, dimensions and number of units in stock for each piece of software.

- Daniel

In research, we have identified three vicious circles where inadequate tools and processes reduce the integration frequency. As shown in Figure 54, these are related to challenging software commit processes or tools, difficult merge conflicts and long software build times.

It's important to be wary of each of these vicious circles and ensure that tooling and processes are up to the job of enabling continuous integration.

That being said, in our experience from performing case studies and driving change programs, complaints about tools and processes are nearly ubiquitous. Interestingly enough, this appears to be the case almost regardless of the amount of investments that go into trying to improve them. A relevant question to consider is why that might be the case.

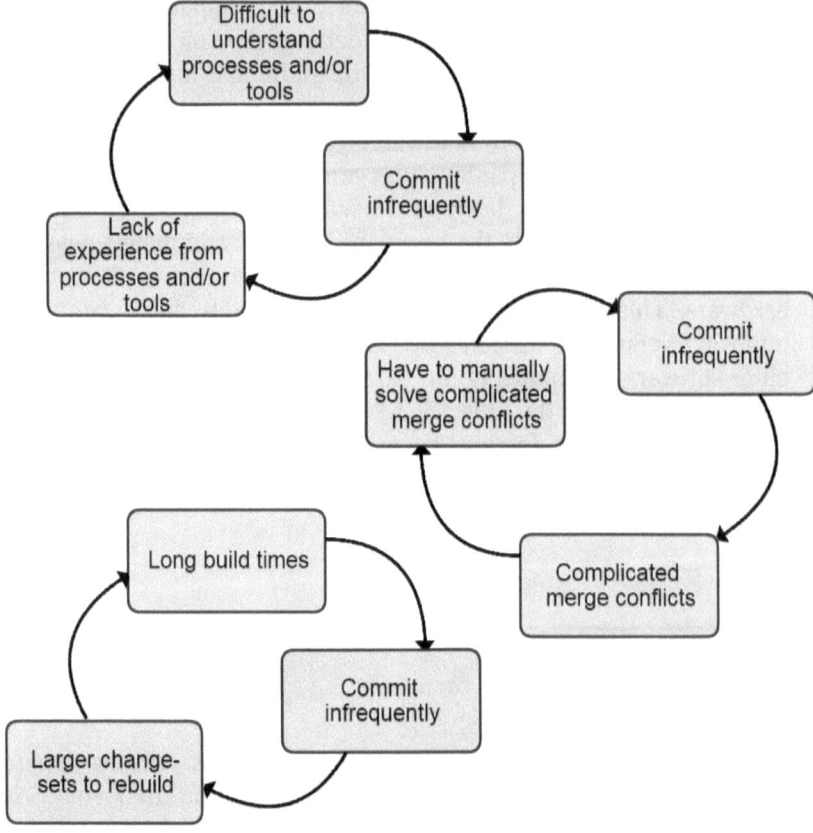

Figure 54: Three vicious circles of slow and cumbersome tools and processes.

We surmise that a strong reason is the central role such tools and processes play in the day-to-day work of software engineers. In general, people have a much higher level of tolerance for problems on the periphery, rather than at the core, of their work – and rightly so. In other words, as long as the tools and processes involved in committing software aren't perfect (and they never are) engineers will complain about them. It would be incorrect, however, to draw the conclusion that improvements in this area are consequently pointless, because those ungrateful developers will just find something to complain about no matter what. Rather, we find that a more accurate interpretation is that no matter how good things get, there will always be room for improvement.

> Sometimes I hear people say it's impossible to shorten build and test times. This is simply not true. It's all about how much effort you want to put into the performance of your build servers, decoupling in the product's architecture and improvements of the build and test process. Never accept "impossible" as an answer. "Too costly", on the other hand, is another story.
>
> *- Torvald*

A related question is how to organize the responsibility for these tools and processes. We have seen multiple variants of this, including large central units tasked with maintaining everything from integrated development environments, build jobs, SCM systems and test frameworks to review processes and quality management processes, the better to allow developers to focus on development. At the opposite end of the spectrum we have witnessed complete decentralization where every developer manages his or her own tools and every team their own pipeline.

Similarly to how any team structure comes with its own set of problems, either extreme is problematic. A highly centralized responsibility creates bureaucracy and overhead, where the people who best understand their own needs have to explain them to somebody else, argue for their prioritization and then wait for them to be implemented, rather than just fixing them by themselves. Apart from struggling to meet the basic hygiene requirements, such setups are very proficient at undermining any sense of autonomy the developers might feel. A completely decentralized responsibility, on the other hand, tends to cause problems in integration of a larger system, which requires a certain level of alignment to be efficient and possible to automate. Besides, a lack of central coordination can easily lead to runaway license costs for duplicated purchases of commercial development tools, and tools developed internally by the developers will also evolve without coordination, leading to waste when the same problem is solved over and over again at different places in the organization.

A better solution lies somewhere in between. To make a large system work, certain alignment and rules are necessary, but they shouldn't get in the way of local problem-solving. Just as in software application design, an organization optimizing for efficient software development in general and continuous practices in particular needs to strive for loose coupling by focusing on the interfaces and avoiding central control of what goes on behind those interfaces. In other words, establish common solutions to the things truly necessary to responsibly create the product: how software is stored, communicated and distributed, how traceability is assured, how compliance is demonstrated et cetera. Then allow engineers and teams to autonomously adopt or design the tools and processes that work for them, within those boundaries.

In Bob's current team, responsible for improving the ad value of the social media platform, there is no review process before committing. Instead, they value the ability to get experiments into production as quickly as possible, collect data, and then collectively decide which features to keep and which to scrap. This is a change of pace from Bob's previous team in the same organization, which often made changes to the backend platform and required any commit to be approved by at least two other team members before pushing it to the mainline. From a central point of view it makes no difference. All changes are built, tested and deployed in the same automated process – maintained by a dedicated team – but it's up to the individual team to decide on what they feel is a reasonable process for committing those changes in the first place.

Mary's experience is somewhat different. Earlier in the product development life-cycle she participated in a prototyping phase where she and the other engineers had a high degree of freedom in choosing their tools and ways of working as they saw fit. To her disappointment, once the prototype was concluded and turned into a "proper" development project, this became a whole lot more regulated. Corporate directives requiring documentation, reproducibility and configuration management were introduced. These are document driven processes centered around human authors writing for human readers, as opposed to the information driven processes she has grown used to from modern tools. As a consequence, she finds that the overhead of committing code is making her reluctant to commit more than she absolutely has to, as she would rather be writing software than filling out forms.

Safe Commits

There is a world of difference between trying to do the right thing, and trying not to make mistakes. Effective software development and continuous practices live and breathe the former – after all, if the overriding concern is to avoid mistakes, then the surest path to success is to do nothing at all – but all too often we see developers pushed forcefully towards the latter by reward and punishment structures. These structures may be more or less subtle, and may be created top-down or bottom-up, and may involve everything from lights and sirens going off when gatekeeping tests on the mainline fail, to product quality escalations to senior management and late night forced troubleshooting sessions. They are all by themselves well meaning and exist for seemingly good reasons, but taken together they can foster a very unhealthy defensive mindset where committing code becomes something to be dreaded, rather than something to look forward to.

This makes safe commits a crucial hygiene factor for encouraging frequent integrations. We see two sides of this coin. One is that the pipeline must be constructed such that the risk of serious harm to the business, to the work of colleagues, to innocent third parties, to the environment or to other assets is minimized. This means using tests as gatekeepers, sometimes at multiple stages in the larger network of pipelines: before integrating with a larger system context, before deploying to scarce and expensive test equipment, before conducting potentially hazardous tests, and of course before deploying to production. Simply put, a developer shouldn't have to worry that he or she will end up bankrupting the company or killing someone by committing bad code, barring gross negligence or malicious intent.

The other side of the coin is to not use the verdicts of tests and analyses to beat people over the head. Sounding a bullhorn and flashing the offending developer's name on giant screens may seem like games and fun to some, while profoundly unsettling to others. With that in mind we recommend everyone to carefully consider how to spread awareness without pointing fingers, and how to foster a sense of responsibility without spreading a culture of fear.

Playfulness has an important role to play here. Some go to great lengths to make feedback from the pipeline fun and interactive, including building a cute robot that rolls up to whoever checks in bad code [72]. Such efforts may seem like overkill, or like the silly pastime of underemployed engineers, but anything that helps create a healthy atmosphere where fun and responsibility are allowed to blend shouldn't be underestimated. Playfulness is serious business.

Mary sees the difference safe commits make to a developer's mentality first hand. The system she works on is split into a large number of components, continuously integrated into the full system context. Before being let in, new versions of those components are thoroughly tested. Some of these tests are notoriously flaky and produce a lot of false positives, but they are comprehensive. In other words, she isn't overly worried about introducing critical faults at that level. Mary works on one of the largest components, though, with some 500 developers all sharing the same source code (see Chapter 5). This means that the first point of integration and feedback is from a mainline on which half a thousand other full-time developers and a sizable development sub-project all depend. A set of gatekeeping tests on the mainline that stay broken for more than a couple of hours will have serious consequences with knock-on effects on project milestones and release dates. As a consequence, Mary really, really doesn't want to be the one identified as committing bad code, which also means that committing in the first place makes her really, really uncomfortable. This is the major reason why she and her teammates prefer to stay on a feature branch and make sure they have tested everything thoroughly before merging into the mainline – an event that happens once every week or two, on average. This is all very different from what Mary herself hears from colleagues working on the same product, but on a much smaller component. They work in a single team of five developers and are fairly carefree about their commits, as introducing failures in the component mainline for a few hours isn't a big deal, and they trust the automated system integration tests to weed out any critical errors before they get far enough to cause trouble to anyone outside of their team.

> The phrase "don't break the build" became popular at some point when continuous integration started to spread. Today, though, in a typical large scale implementation of the practice, your source code will not be integrated if the build process fails. I think "don't break the build" was quite a catchy slogan, but when new practices evolved it became obsolete. Therefore I try to avoid speaking in terms of "breaking the build" or "breaking the mainline", and instead prefer to speak of gatekeeping activities failing and causing blockages in the pipeline.
>
> *- Torvald*

Summary

In this chapter we have considered hygiene factors and motivators relevant to fostering frequent integration of sources by developers. We want to stress the importance of both, or one will inevitably end up either with engineers that are excited but frustrated, or just content but complacent (see Figure 51). In the next chapter we will turn towards success factors for achieving quality.

Chapter 24

Achieving Quality

Software quality is an elusive concept, tricky to define and even harder to quantify. There is a good case to be made that one shouldn't even try: any serious attempt to do so quickly runs into difficulties such as calculating the quality of two pieces of software added together, or determining the value of perfect quality. These are only some of many arguments for the concept of technical debt as a more practical tool. Nevertheless, in this chapter we are not out to measure or compare, but rather speak of quality as an abstract but desirable notion – the subjective impression that a piece of software is trustworthy, evolvable and fit for its purpose.

Achieving quality in software is difficult to do, not least because it is hard to define and lends itself to subjective interpretations. Consequently, we find that quality in a broader sense cannot be captured by requirements or tests. Narrow aspects of quality may be thus captured – e.g. absence of regression test failures or certain static code analysis measurements such as coupling or cyclomatic complexity – but beyond that it comes down to us as engineers cultivating a sense of responsibility for the software quality. In this sense, it is akin to quality of life: we all desire it and we all have a notion of what it means to us, but we can't measure it and we all have different understandings of it. The best we can do is to measure indicators we find to correlate with common perceptions of what people commonly think of as quality of life, such as absence of severe illness and suffering. Partly for this reason, it is ultimately up to the developer and his or her willingness to pursue and protect what he or she perceives as high quality. In other words, achieving quality is much more about motivators than it is about hygiene factors, at least assuming the engineers are not driven to the point where they simply don't have the time or mental energy to care about it. In this chapter we look into the success factors we have identified for nudging an organization in the direction of truly striving to achieve quality.

Pipeline Verdict Buy-In

As engineers we take pride in quality work, and in that regard software engineering is no different from any engineering discipline. The urge to create quality software plays directly to Pink's intrinsic factors of mastery as a motivator. A software pipeline is extremely potent in that it can augment and direct that desire by passing a verdict on our work: either it's good enough, or it isn't. But this power to pass judgment can be used to frustrate us just as easily as it can motivate us.

To serve as the motivator and certificate of quality that a pipeline verdict should be, it's crucial to gain buy-in from stakeholders that the tests and analyses are relevant and correct, working for them rather than against them. This is true for all stakeholder groups (as shown in Figure 52), but not least for developers, since the verdict on their latest commit directly influences their behavior in creating the next. In research studies we have encountered lack of credibility of pipeline verdicts in multiple cases, and observed the damaging effects it has on morale: when the only data point one has to go on isn't trustworthy, it should come as no surprise when engineers shrug their shoulders. Often the problem is that the test scope is regarded as bloated yet irrelevant (and not dynamic, as described in Chapter 17), with engineers relating how "we often run a lot of unnecessary tests", "we keep test cases too long" or "we execute a lot of test cases, but not necessarily the ones we should have executed" [34]. The problem may also be related to the flakiness of tests or to a general distrust of their ability to catch actual faults (in other words, false positives as well as false negatives).

In these situations, a golden opportunity to build on the desire for mastery is lost. Rather than representing that certificate of quality it ought to be, the pipeline verdict becomes just another arbitrary hoop to jump through in the day-to-day development process.

Another common example of this is targets for code coverage. We often observe pipelines that measure code coverage (typically in terms of lines of code) of automated tests, and fail release candidates that don't reach up to a certain percentage (or in some cases, that lower the percentage relative to the previous release candidate). We argue that such measurements at best serve as distractions from more relevant aspects of quality, but all too often they slow developers down by adding extra overhead and making them comply on paper while cursing under their breath, rather than encourage them to try for excellence. Besides, such metrics drive quantity in automated tests, and to earn the trust of engineers and promote software quality, pipeline tests need to be all about quality over quantity (pun intended).

As an example of this, in John's game development project one of the QA engineers pushed for a requirement of 90% unit test coverage for a release candidate to be considered good enough for delivery to QA. As a result, John and his developer teammates spent the better part of a week writing unit tests for class internal behavior and getters and setters, just to reach that target. Two months later, John silently removed the check from the pipeline and went back to just writing tests for behaviors he wanted to verify and protect from unintended changes, rather than writing them for the sake of racking up line coverage. Indeed, he ended up disabling most of the tests added over the last two months. In retrospect, looking at the data, there was no discernible effect on the number of bug reports filed by QA, but there was a notable spike in the time required by the pipeline to test every release candidate.

That being said, this is not automatically true for all stakeholders. Particularly those in the upper left quadrant of Figure 52 (page 235) may require high or even complete coverage in regulated environments (see Chapter 12) in order to demonstrate compliance, for instance through verification of behavior in all types of corner cases.

> As a general reflection on reaching arbitrarily set goals for one's pipeline, such as code coverage, there's a clear danger in a too narrow focus on speed and/or high frequency in continuous practices. If all one looks at is the speed and frequency of integrating and deploying software changes, without also considering the actual value delivered by those changes, it's easy to delude oneself into thinking one has this awesome software production system in place. In truth, though, it's more like revving the engine while not in gear: it makes a lot of noise, but the car isn't going anywhere.
>
> *- Torvald*

Fixing Broken Windows

The broken windows theory was introduced in social science by Wilson and Kelling in 1982 [73] and has been hugely influential to the understanding of vandalism and anti-social behavior, and how such behavior is affected by the environment. Its message goes beyond criminology, though, as it tells us something about the importance of norm-setting to how we judge our own actions. The theory poses that an environment that signals apathy towards disrepair and neglect (as where broken windows are left broken) is also an environment that discourages people from protecting property or other assets and values.

In this very general sense, the broken windows theory is widely applicable, and we can all recognize it at work in our day-to-day lives: we instinctively try to preserve what we perceive as pure and pristine, whereas we care little whether something already broken breaks a bit more. This is just as true in software development as in anything else.

Fixing broken windows in software requires developers to follow the stop-and-fix principle. I have seen terrible examples of the opposite, where developers respond to serious bug reports by explaining that they had their sprint planning the day before, so the current sprint is full, but they'll be happy to include it in their next sprint – which will conclude in six weeks. Sprint planning is all well and good, but there has to be room for responding to unexpected high priority incidents.

- Torvald

As we noted in the previous section, a software pipeline and the verdicts it provides have a powerful effect on how we perceive a project, its status and its quality. If lights flash red every now and then, or if builds fail more often than they succeed, none of us is going to feel motivated to walk that extra mile to safeguard quality. Because after all, what's the point? The code is clearly a hopeless mess anyway.

What we're saying is not that the pipeline should paint lipstick on a pig, showing green lights across the board no matter what, just to keep people happy and motivated. Instead, the message is this: pipeline verdicts should serve to draw our attention to what we truly need to care about, not distract us or discourage us by reporting problems we can't realistically do anything about anyway. Because we all have skeletons in our closets, but to help us stay motivated and focus our attention on our most urgent priorities, sometimes they just need to stay in the closet.

This becomes particularly relevant in the context of technical debt. An in-depth explanation of the concept of technical debt is outside of the scope of this book (a comprehensive introduction is provided by Eric Allman [74]). Briefly put, it represents the idea that making sub-optimal technical decisions can be likened to going into monetary debt: they will cause an overhead on further development, similar to paying the interest on a loan, and fixing them at a later date will require effort, analogous to paying the principal of that loan. But just as taking a monetary loan from the bank may be a sound decision, knowing full well that it will have to be paid back with interest, going into technical debt may be justified by short term gains. Clearly, technical debts need to be carefully managed to avoid complete bankruptcy, but the concept constitutes a useful tool for having constructive and relevant conversations about the costs and benefits of decisions in software architecture and design.

Because technical debt represents a conscious decision to – at present – not fix a given problem or go for the highest conceivable quality, it's important that the pipeline tests, measurements and analyses reflect that decision by not highlighting the issues you have chosen to set aside. In other words, the target against which the pipeline should measure your software needs to express the achievable wanted state you have decided to reach for here and now. If you have a group of flaky tests that you have classified and stored away as technical debt, don't keep executing them in the pipeline. If performance is not what it should be and you're well aware, but you just have bigger fish to fry right now, then adjust the performance tests accordingly to make sure that at least the problem doesn't get worse. Hanging on to broken windows you know you can't fix right now doesn't help anyone. Instead, focus on the ones you intend to do something about, and on making sure that all the windows that are still intact stay that way. This applies not only to developers, but also to stakeholders in the lower half of Figure 52 (page 235), particularly various managerial roles. If they are unable to see the forest for all the trees of blinking red lights, it's easy to wind up in a situation where they get the completely wrong idea of actual project status.

Some would consider me young and naive today, but in my even younger days I would happily set up all manner of visualizations of pipeline data, because it was cool, and why not? Little did I realize that high level managers soon began paying attention to those tables and graphs, and when they pointed in the wrong direction or showed the wrong color there would be emergency meetings and escalations – all because they misinterpreted the information, mistaking a benign change already under control for a major crisis. Much ado about nothing, which we could have done without.

- Daniel

As a case in point, the networking product Mary is working on has a long list of system integration tests that fail intermittently. There's a tacit assumption in the project that it's the tests that are flaky – similar failures have not been observed in production, yet – but no serious effort has been made to investigate the cause. Neither have they been explicitly classified as technical debt or removed from the pipeline test scope, as nobody wants to take responsibility for them. One obvious consequence of this is that release candidates frequently fail and are blocked from release, even though everybody assumes they were most likely just fine. A more insidious effect is that Mary and her teammates don't really pay that much attention to the system integration tests anymore. Some test or another is always failing, it seems, and the next release candidate will probably be fine. As a result, there have been several occasions where an actual fault has been introduced, but nobody really paid attention until half a day later after multiple consecutive failures. By that time, reverting to the last known good version wasted a lot of time and effort.

Identifying With the Customer

So far we have mostly looked into motivating through a sense of mastery – of the intrinsic drive to create quality work. Another motivator available for us to draw upon is what David Pink labels as purpose: the desire to be part of and contribute to something greater than ourselves. Depending on the domain and application of the software this may be easy, or it may be hard. If you would be writing software that helps aid workers locate victims in earthquake zones, then finding motivation in purpose would be easily done, whereas in most cases its not quite as clear-cut. Making more money for shareholders rarely does well at instilling a sense of purpose, particularly for those who are not shareholders themselves. This is one reason why corporations go to such great lengths in speaking of social responsibilities, and missions and visions of making the world a better place.

Of course, all of this has more to do with managing corporations and organizations in general than it does with continuous practices. Where continuous deployment in particularly enters into the picture is in its ability to strengthen that sense of purpose by giving the pipeline stakeholders – the engineers producing the software – a clear view of who the customers are, how they use the software, how it's working for them and how they feel about it, as well as the ability to rapidly and directly influence that customer experience. This requires traceability from the production environment, something that may be both technically, legally and/or ethically challenging, depending on the circumstances. Where those challenges can be overcome, the availability of such traceability data, both presented as statistics and as (anonymized) individual usage scenarios, can greatly enhance that sense of purpose as well as the ability to act upon it.

As an example of this, Bob's social media applications collect large amounts of real time usage data to be able to respond quickly to any changes in behavior among users. One such behavior is the number of private messages being sent, which one day suddenly begins to drop. The decline comes from web frontend users running a version deployed a couple of hours earlier (recall that there are always multiple versions running, exposed to different users at any given time, as described in Chapter 20, which is why the message count doesn't just fall off a cliff).

Tracing that version back through the pipeline to the source code repository, Bob's colleagues are able to identify the offending commit. They first roll back the bad version from production and then investigate the root cause, finding that a minor change to a stylesheet caused the messaging popup to render incorrectly in certain browsers. Twenty minutes later a new version containing the original change, but with a correctly rendering popup, is deployed.

There is a powerful interplay between the technical capabilities of the pipeline and the engineers' identification with the customers at work in this example. On the one hand, the data collection and pipeline traceability is an enabler for detecting and finding the fault, but what motivates the engineers to go into overdrive to fix the problem as quickly as humanly possible is their sense of purpose, because as active users of the application themselves they know who the customers are and what this bug means to them: the customers are themselves, their families and friends, who suddenly find themselves unable to communicate with one another as they are used to.

The situation would have been very different had there been no identification with the customer, despite all the technical capabilities and the information availability. Clearly the problem would have been fixed in time, but probably not in such a hurry, and it's not even certain that Bob and his colleagues would have known to prioritize it over whatever feature they were working on at the time, because they wouldn't have had the intuitive understanding of what the bug meant to actual flesh-and-blood users. All of which goes to say that data is great, but without context it will never have meaning. Even so, simply caring and understanding is not enough. Without the continuous deployment and the ability to rapidly fix the problem, that desire to help the user will result in little more than frustration.

Enabling Developer Responsibility

As we have stressed in previous success factors, most engineers want to build high quality products; the challenge is not so much making people care, as it is to draw on, augment and enable that intrinsic motivation. Similarly, most engineers have a sense of responsibility for what they develop. Most of the time, all that is needed is to not thwart it, but to enable it. Therefore this success factor will highlight extrinsic factors that need to be in place, even though we in the introduction to this chapter stated that achieving quality is mostly about motivation, rather than hygiene.

We identify two such important extrinsic factors. The first is traceability, and ready access to that traceability information. What we mean by that is that even if perfect information on everything that goes on in the pipeline exists somewhere, it's of little use to the developer unless he or she can have it presented in a format that is comprehensible at a glance. On that note, we would like to reiterate the point we made previously on playfulness in Chapter 23: consider not just how to make information accessible, but also the tone it sets. What is being represented is ultimately a judgment on people's work, and such judgments can be sensitive. With that said, a relevant question is clearly not just how to present data in order to enable developer responsibility, but what to present. A rule of thumb is always to present data on that which you want the audience to take responsibility for and act upon, but not more than that. That is not to say that other information should be restricted; people like to know what's going on, and a sense of being part of something greater is an important intrinsic motivational factor (one case in point being information on customer experiences and feedback in order to cultivate a sense of purpose, as described in the previous success factor). Instead, the point is to be very clear on the separation between what is "for your information", as opposed to "for you to act upon".

Deciding on what developers actually should be responsible for is our second identified extrinsic factor. It's not uncommon to hear managers speak of the importance of end-to-end responsibilities, but as we have noted previously, taking responsibility of something you can't see is easier said than done. Someone requiring others to take responsibility also needs to take the consequences of enabling that responsibility. Non-trivial questions to consider include how far through its life-cycle a developer should be responsible for a commit: until unit tests passed, until it successfully deployed to its production target, or somewhere in between? The answer clearly depends on contextual factors and software architecture. For instance, it makes perfect sense for our social media archetype, Bob, to take personal responsibility for any change he makes to any of the backend microservices, all the way through deployment. On the other hand, when Alice's change is batched with dozens or even hundreds of others into a vehicle system baseline, it's not as clear-cut. Another factor to consider is the contractual and organizational relationships of developers, dependents and other actors in the network of pipelines. To exemplify, a developer making an open source contribution to the bash shell[30], which is then integrated by an integrator, cannot be expected to take responsibility for any resulting issues in a particular Linux distribution. In a more centralized setup, such as typically seen in in-house commercial development, however, developers can be expected to take greater downstream responsibility.

To conclude, developers shouldn't be overloaded with information they can't or shouldn't act upon – unless it's very clear that it is strictly done for information sharing purposes – but at the same time they can't be required to take responsibility for more than what they can get clear and reliable data on. As an example, a developer who gets feedback from the test of a system function is unlikely to prioritize the issue if the problem is not repeatable and there is no recorded data. As a way of mitigating this, we have in research observed the benefits of having developers participate in the testing [45]. Then there is no handover between the tester who found the problem and the developer who will fix it. Indeed, this is also one of the fundamental principles of cross-functional teams (discussed in greater depth in Chapter 23).

Returning to Alice, she has been working together with the system integration engineers to improve feedback from system test to her and other ECU developers. Something she has noticed, though, is that having the latest system integration test verdicts flashed in her face isn't all that helpful, even if she can easily see that changes she made personally were included in the tested delta. That's because the tests are too infrequent, and so the deltas are too large for her to feel personally responsible. The idea that she and thirty other developers should throw themselves at troubleshooting a failure in a system baseline that they have all – independently and unaware of one another – contributed to strikes her as ridiculous. She would never get anything done that way. As a consequence, she has been talking to her teammates about removing the system test results from their team dashboards, despite the effort they invested in getting them there to begin with. When the test granularity is at a level where just she and maybe one or two other

---

30 https://www.gnu.org/software/bash

---

developers are implicated, then that type of immediate feedback makes a lot more sense to her.

Summary

In this chapter we have addressed organizational considerations and people issues in achieving quality in a continuous practices context. We find that while removing certain barriers preventing developers from taking greater responsibility is important, because of its subjective nature, achieving quality is largely about encouraging the intrinsic motivators of engineers, not least the desire for mastery and purpose.

Chapter 25

Frequent Deployments

Frequently deploying software is largely about technology and appropriate architecture, assuming a technology and business domain where it is even feasible (consider, for instance, the significance of distribution models as discussed in Chapter 13). It is also about achieving a conducive mindset, though, and not only in software development. Because of the way continuous deployment impacts the entire organization, in this chapter we will adopt an even broader perspective. Consequently, we will consider new stakeholder groups in addition to those described in Figure 52 (page 235).

It's also worth pointing out that this is not only about the internal mindset within the organization, but also the mindset of one's customers. That being said, in this chapter we will focus on the mindset in the organization. We will touch upon the problems of customer relations and dealing with customers who may or may not be enthused by the idea of continuous deployments. A thorough examination of this problem would have to be the topic of a separate book, however.

In doing so, we will cover both hygiene factors (such as making deployments safe enough) and motivators (for instance motivating operations personnel to reconsider their perceptions of their roles and responsibilities). We will also consider enablers for continuous deployment in the first place, as well as how potential side-effects of the practice can be avoided or mitigated.

Maintaining an Architectural Vision

In a traditional waterfall-ish project setup, the software architect has a well defined role, but as organizations shift into continuous practices, and continuous deployment in particular, we often observe architects who seem to lose their footing. When the upfront architecture phase disappears, it is no longer clear to them how to be architects, or even how to impact the evolution of the system in the first place. As a result, they are dragged along by the developers, trying to catch up and descriptively document what the developed software looks like, rather than prescriptively instructing it.

> I observed the lead architect of a major IT change program, one year into the program present the target architecture. The problem was that by then the program was well under way, with parts of it already implemented and deployed – without the guidance of any clearly defined architecture. As the document was presented, the architect's wording was revealing: rather than staking out a direction and explaining how it should be, he merely reported how he had learned the system worked. Granted, this description was not without value, but it failed utterly in its mission to steer the design of the system.
>
> *- Daniel*

The problem is not so much caused by continuous practices, as it is highlighted by them. Rather, the problem is about architects who are unable to act as leaders – as individuals to whom engineers will instinctively turn for support and guidance – in a process that does not provide them a well defined space in which to operate. In other words, there are two ways to look at the issue: either it's the architects who need to carve out a new role for themselves and lead informally, or it's the process that needs to be formalized in order to enable them.

To the extent that it works at all, the former can work very well, but as any process that merely relies on people being all-around great, it will never be predictable or reliably replicated. In effect, we once more end up in the Agile blind spot (see Chapter 23). Conversely, the latter perspective is one where hygiene factors are required for architects to do their job effectively.

At a project meeting one of the system architects was asked to summarize the status of an important issue related to his system. He came back with a list of design decisions he "had heard of" and a summary of a design meeting the week before where he himself had not even participated. I see this as a sad example of an ivory tower architect with visions and plans, but clearly no rapport whatsoever with the developers. He was simply bypassed.

- Torvald

It has been argued that the idea of architects and software architecture is outdated, and that in the continuous paradigm one should instead embrace the organic, adaptive evolution of the software. We believe that nothing could be farther from the truth. As we have noted in Chapter 20, continuous deployment relies on particular architectural patterns to be successful. Furthermore, developers tend to find that regardless of component or cross-component teams, one easily gets into a "Too many teams, too many chefs in the kitchen" situation without proper systemization and careful architectural design [34]. In other words, in continuous integration and deployment, architects serve an important role as traffic planners by creating a software structure that enables the effectiveness and autonomy of developers, thereby ensuring manufacturability in the sense introduced in Chapter 16. This means

---

that architects have a critical role to play. Helping them find that role and a place in the organization from which to do it is a critical concern.

That is not to say that an upfront detailed architecture phase is called for, though. While there are many other sources on how to combine the software architecture discipline with Agile processes in general, the particular advice we would offer is to involve product architects in the design of the pipeline (or network of pipelines, as the case may be) from day one. This is because of its (often underestimated) ability to control the de facto structure and behavior of the produced software, making it an infinitely more powerful tool for steering software design than any slide deck can ever hope to be. When breaking architectural rules prevents you from integrating your source code, those rules tend to be followed.

While Bob and his fellow developers share a vision of a loosely coupled architecture of microservices, they have no rules on the interface design, communication methods or formats for telemetry, logs et cetera. At first, this felt liberating, but as time wore on and the system grew it became increasingly problematic. With each little microservice having its own style, its own programming language, its own interface version control mechanisms and its own persistence solutions, getting features implemented across multiple microservices is more difficult than it seems like it ought to be, not to mention the many heated ideological arguments over software design that flare up. Lately, Bob has found himself wishing for somebody with the authority to just establish some basic ground rules.

Mary's experience is different, yet reminiscent of Bob's. She also wishes for some more structure, even though there is a whole team of dedicated architects in the project. Her problem is that she sees very little of them. At some unit meetings there are slides shown of the product architecture, but truth be told she doesn't recognize it from the actual source code. The boxes and lines on those slides seem to describe some platonic ideal of a software product that has little bearing on her day-to-day work. Instead, what appears to have happened is that the component she's working on has grown from a fairly small and contained piece of software to an enormous spaghetti monster – not through any one conscious architectural decision, but through a long series of accidental and/or reactive choices made along the way. Recently the architects seem to have woken up to the fact, and are reportedly working on splitting the component into multiple parts, with automated tests verifying compliance with interface specifications – both syntactic and semantic. Mary has yet to see the results from that work, but she remains cautiously optimistic.

Transforming Competences

Continuous deployment is not always well received by the engineers whose job it is to install, maintain and upgrade software services. This is because it ultimately turns that craft into another form of software development and automates it. One response to such reluctance to embrace new ways of working is to brush it off as dinosaurs fretting over their inevitable extinction, or as a form of luddism. Another, arguably more constructive way of viewing it is through the lens of mastery and purpose.

When you remove a significant part of what up until that point was another person's professional identity, as continuous deployment does (and cloud platforms, more generally, do), then you're in effect telling them that the skills they have been honing for years are not longer relevant. The impact of that on a person's motivation and sense of worth should never be underestimated. To add insult to injury, the operations profession offers plenty of opportunities to be the hero who saves the day by scrambling to set up new servers just in time or tweaking the in-production database settings to stabilize a failing service. In a world where new hardware is not only provisioned automatically when needed, but fiddling with the production environment is explicitly prohibited, those opportunities disappear and a very real sense of purpose is lost. Therefore it should come as no surprise when operations engineers become seriously demotivated and thoroughly uninterested in taking on new roles, e.g. as software developers.

It is worth pointing out that continuous deployment by no means spells the end of operations as a discipline. On the contrary, it is arguably more important than ever, but it does require new skill sets and a new frame of mind. In this regard, it has many similarities to testing and configuration management: if anything, continuous practices highlight their importance, even though the testers and configuration managers who used to embody those disciplines in a waterfall-ish project may not be the most suited to take them forward into the future (with testers being tasked with developing automated test suites, discussed in Chapter 17, as a prime example).

Needless to say, different people react in different ways to such disruption of their professional identities, depending on their own individual propensities, experiences and state of mind. Some will jump at the opportunity to finally change how things are done around here, whereas others will find the change profoundly unsettling.

We firmly believe in the importance of not being judgmental about this. To the extent that engineers can rediscover purpose in a new role and be motivated to master new skills, that is great, but for those who can't it's usually better to help them find other opportunities than to try to shoe-horn them into something they have no desire for (with the caveat that depending on local labor laws, that may be more or less straight forward). The toxic effect on morale of a disgruntled employee who has been robbed of all motivation and been forced into a new role they have no interest in is not to be taken lightly. That being said, it's important to keep in mind that there is no reason to assume that an individual engineer's lack of programming skills should keep them from effectively contributing to software development. Thinking slightly out of the box of mapping developers to keyboards on a one-to-one basis, and instead trying out techniques such as strong-style pairing [75] or mob programming [76] to leverage the knowledge of non-developers, can help these engineers find a new purpose while at the same time giving them a joyful way of broadening their competence.

For several of our archetypes, the very concept of operations is inapplicable. John the game developer, for instance, publishes games that run on end user desktop computers and consoles, while Alice sells cars, also operated by the end users themselves (the current trend towards Car as a Service aside).

For Bob, on the other hand, the question of how to optimize operations is always high up on the agenda. In the early garage start-up days of the company, cloud services weren't as mature as they are today, and their first application ran from a single on-premises server. Back then they were lucky to hire Greg, a brilliant operations engineer who saved them through several crises as the demands on that server grew rapidly. As they eventually migrated to a cloud hosting service, those skills and instincts were difficult to transform into software, since Greg lacked anything but the most rudimentary development experience. They soon figured out that by applying strong-style pairing, Greg could help produce operations and monitoring software, as well as support developers in creating operations friendly services, while rapidly expanding his own skills. Three years later, Greg has found his niche and is still regarded as one of the key competences in the company.

Safe Deployments

Safe deployments are the in-production mirror of safe commits (addressed in Chapter 23). Just as developers shouldn't be expected to commit often if they're uncomfortable doing so, engineers shouldn't be expected to practice continuous deployment unless they feel perfectly confident performing those deployments. We have all experienced, witnessed, or at the very least heard of nail-biting horror stories of disastrous deployments, emergency all-nighters and ruined weekends. When that is the reality of deployment, it is not only callous toward the engineers to push for continuous deployment, but irresponsible to the customers or whoever else might be on the receiving end of those deployments.

To the extent that deployments are dreaded by the organization, turning that around needs to be a top priority. This is a critical hygiene factor for enabling continuous deployment – deploying should be fun and rewarding. It would be tempting to say that it should be a cause for celebration (albeit not in the sense of "Oh thank heavens we made it through"), but even that would be to miss the point. Instead, deployments need to be taken for granted as something that is entirely matter-of-course.

This shift in mentality, from thinking of deployments as significant yet scary events, to not really thinking about them at all, can scarcely be overemphasized. Only when that has been achieved is it fruitful to push for more frequent and eventually continuous deployments. This shift in mindset is separate from the purely technical enablers (see Chapter 20), but at the same time serves as a useful litmus test for them. An organization that has the infrastructure, test coverage, fallback mechanisms and the software architecture to enable safe deployments is also an organization where engineers feel good about deploying – mindset and technology are not independent variables.

This phenomenon was recently evident in Mary's organization. For years there had been a strong push towards continuous practices in general, with great advances in automation and reduced time to market as a result. But when high level managers extended their ambition to not only continuous delivery, but continuous deployment, and began setting targets for deployment frequencies, this quickly backfired. In the interest of meeting these new targets, engineers were forced to skip many of the precautions they had previously taken, such as on-site pre-testing and manual integration into the customer environment of each new product version. It's important to understand that these precautions had not been implemented because of lack of imagination, but because the tools at hand and the quality of the software necessitated them – the product had simply never been designed to be plug-and-playable, and quality was not up to scratch for truly hands-off deployments. This led to a series of incidents caused by failed deployments, forcing the project to dial down the pace again. Instead they instituted a recurring survey, asking engineers how confident they felt in software deployments and asked them to identify their top three causes for concern. By focusing on these identified issues they were able, over time, to slowly nudge the survey responses in the right direction. Today they are once again increasing the deployment frequencies, but from a much more robust position.

Onboarding Sales and Marketing

Continuous deployment (or continuous release) can never be an end in and of itself. It will always be a means to an end. Sometimes that end may be increased value for the user – either directly, or via the improved ability of developers to make informed design and prioritization choices – but most of the time, user value is also not an end, but a means.

To the extent that the software is commercial (which does not preclude it being free), customer and/or user value is only valuable to the extent that it can be turned into revenue, and that requires involvement from the sales and marketing organizations. Here we use the terms sales and marketing in their broadest sense, regardless of the particular business models and revenue streams in the given case: sold licenses, subscriptions, advertisements or anything else.

Sometimes this is less of an issue, and sometimes continuous practices adoption is even driven by sales and/or marketing. Sometimes, on the other hand, getting the sales side of the house on board and cognizant of the opportunities requires substantial effort, not least in terms of education. If unsuccessful, there's a high probability that they will be caught unawares by the shenanigans of R&D and unable to effectively capitalize on the change, or even be harmed by it. As we noted in Chapter 2, adoption of continuous deployment can be prompted either by business needs or by a desire to improve software development, or both. Either reason is perfectly valid, but understanding one's own incentives is always a good place to start when embarking on a transformation journey.

That being said, even if continuous deployment is driven by the desire to improve the development process (e.g. by enabling feature experimentation) it's crucial to understand that continuous deployment will always affect not only R&D, but has a significant impact on the business. Consequently, adopting continuous deployment requires a clear business decision on which products to continuously deploy, how and why. In this regard, continuous deployment is very different from continuous integration and delivery.

A sales manager I once interviewed related how continuous deployment in the early days had caused them a great deal of headache. It had been driven primarily as an R&D initiative, with little involvement from sales, and so they kept signing contracts stating that upgrades would be performed and paid for on an annual or semiannual basis even while R&D were speeding up from yearly to monthly, weekly and eventually daily deployments. Since sales hadn't been involved from the outset they were forced to play catch-up and rethink their entire business model, while missing out on revenue for software updates they were forced to deploy for free. In the end, the R&D initiated engineering transformation resulted in a complete business transformation, but in retrospect the ride could have been a whole lot smoother if only sales had been on board from day one.

- Daniel

This is because continuous practices are, in the vast majority of cases, driven by software engineers. It is the engineers who understand software development, understand the improvement potential, and who stay up to date with the latest trends in how to develop, distribute and deploy software. None of this should come as a surprise. Perhaps as a surprise to non-engineers, though, a lot of the time they also think about how the software and the ways in which it is distributed and deployed can boost revenue. Unfortunately, what all too often happens in large organizations – and sometimes in not-so-large ones – is that these engineers don't talk to the people whose job it is to create those revenue streams, if they at all know how to get into contact with them. As a result, the opportunity for developing a joint strategy informed both by R&D's understanding of the engineering opportunities, and by sales and marketing's understanding of market realities, is lost.

Recommending that the separate departments of a business communicate better is unhelpful, bordering on tautological. The problem goes both ways, though. Not only do R&D need to consult with sales and marketing to understand how, or even if, continuous deployment and/or release may be financially sound. Likewise, without a basic understanding of the software engineering discipline, the sales and marketing side won't even know the questions to ask. Many authors, speakers, bloggers and deep thinkers have contributed their views on how to break down silo barriers, and so there is little need for us to go into great depth on the topic here. That being said, we do believe that the solution is not to be sought in communication or coordination, so much as in actual collaboration. This may sound like an inane piece of advice, but one software engineer embedded in the sales organization and personally facing the day-to-day realities of that line of work stands a much greater chance at finding conducive solutions than do ten of his or her colleagues abstractly discussing the issue in meetings.

As described in Chapter 5, John's company seeks to strike a delicate balance between frequent enough updates and content packs to maintain a high level of interest in their game, yet not so frequent as to be annoying to the customers. Awareness that such a balance even exists was reached the hard way, though. Just after the release of their previous game, the developers read a series of blog posts on continuous deployment and, without reflecting on the implications of differences in distribution models between themselves and the cases in those blogs, decided to automatically ship the latest release candidate tested by QA every day. More importantly, they did so without reflecting on whether to do that was even an engineering decision to begin with, or whether it was actually a sales and marketing strategy decision. As a result, players wound up having to update their games every time they wanted to play, and many were inconvenienced by incompatibility issues that arose and the back and forth changes that resulted from fine tuning of the game mechanics. Not only was there a backlash among their customer base, but the company's head of marketing was furious. The frequent updates undermined the value of the purchasable Downloadable Content (DLC) business, which generated the majority of the company's revenue. Now they have settled on free updates of game mechanics and minor features every few weeks, and larger releases of purchasable DLC packs every few months, which appears to hit the current sweet spot of their customer base.

Summary

This chapter has listed success factors for onboarding the organization with regards to frequent deployments. Whereas previous onboarding success factors have focused on the stakeholder groups shown in Figure 52 (page 235), in this chapter we have gone further and also looked into onboarding sales and marketing. This is because while integration of software is largely a developer concern, its distribution and deployment has much greater implications and involves more parts of the organization – including non-engineers.

This sums up Part IV of the book. So far we have considered context and explored continuous practices success factors; in the fifth and final part we will turn these insights into tangible improvements as we move forward.

Part V:
Moving Forward

Chapter 26

Introduction

We are now approaching the end of the book. So far we have looked into what continuous practices actually are, the contexts in which they operate, and the success factors that make them work – and work well enough to meet our expectations on a modern software pipeline. As interesting as all of that may be from a purely academic point of view, it is of limited value unless we also succeed in applying it, turning insights into improvements.

To help you do that we will spend the next chapter on this particular problem, drawing on our own experiences of driving changes in general, and pipeline improvements in particular.

This is only one perspective on what it means to move forward, however. In contrast to the challenges and opportunities of the individual case, there are also challenges and opportunities facing the software industry at large. There are two distinct sides of this coin. We will begin by reflecting on the general trends and possible futures of software engineering: how our software products change, how we go about constructing them and how that may then influence continuous integration, delivery, release and/or deployment. With that in fresh memory, we will then wrap up this part and indeed the book as a whole by gazing into the crystal ball and speculating on what the future of continuous practices will bring – the questions we struggle with but have yet to find satisfactory answers to, as well as the questions we have yet to clearly phrase.

Chapter 27

Improving the Pipeline

In this chapter we turn to the challenge of improving the pipeline: finding out what, when and how to improve. To that end we consider four equally important questions in turn: where you are, where you want to go, how to plot a path from here to there, and how to follow up whether you're on the right track.

Figuring Out Where You Are

Before considering how to plot a path towards a wanted position, the first step is to accurately assess one's current situation. Some maturity models and similar tools for this purpose exist, but experience teaches us to be wary of oversimplification. The question of how well one is doing is simply too complicated to be boiled down to a plain score or a position on a diagram. Unlike the ultimate question of life, the universe, and everything, 42 is not the answer you're looking for.

This is not only because continuous practices are multi-faceted and their implementation requires both quantitative and qualitative descriptions to be captured, but also because of the many differences in context outlined in Part II: Understanding Your Context. What in one case may be considered a critical shortcoming of the pipeline may in another be perfectly fine, or the best that can be expected given the circumstances.

All the same, without a firm understanding both of one's current position and the wanted position it's impossible to plot a path to get from one to the other. Through Parts III and IV of this book we have listed a number of success factors that we have encountered over years of experience practicing, studying and researching continuous integration, delivery and deployment. We encourage you to carefully consider and in one or two sentences phrase what your current situation is with regards to each one of those success factors (by yourself or in a workshop setting together with your coworkers). When doing so, remember to be very clear on the scope you are addressing. There are two equally important aspects of scope to consider. The first is whether the subject is a single pipeline, or a larger network of pipelines (see Chapter 6). The second is which questions and possible solutions are even on the table – this scoping is strongly interdependent with the participants of the workshop. If you are part of a large organization, try doing it as a group exercise involving multiple roles, similar to the Cinders workshops described in Chapter 21. Also try to bring in individuals who, if not able to make necessary decisions themselves, are at least capable of bringing any output of the workshop to responsible parties. Remember, not all of the success factors may be applicable to your particular case. That's fine, though, just skip those and focus on the relevant ones.

For reference, we include a complete list of success factors addressed in this book, grouped by elements. Please regard them as topics for consideration, with the text in Parts III and IV as supporting material to provide context and guidance.

Visualizing and Analyzing the Pipeline
Collecting Data from Every Pipeline Actor in Real Time, page 106
Collecting Data from Across the Network of Pipelines, page 112
Aggregating and Analyzing the Pipeline Data in Real Time, page 116
Visualizing the Pipeline Data, page 120
Integrating with the Enterprise Landscape, page 123

Producing Release Candidates
Integration Time Modularity, page 127
Archiving in a Definitive Media Library, page 134
Meta-Data as Source, page 137
Job as a Service, page 144

Fast and Simple Tools and Processes, page 248
Safe Commits, page 253

Achieving Quality
Pipeline Verdict Buy-In, page 257
Fixing Broken Windows, page 259
Identifying With the Customer, page 263
Enabling Developer Responsibility, page 264

Frequent Deployments
Maintaining an Architectural Vision, page 269
Transforming Competences, page 272
Safe Deployments, page 274
Onboarding Sales and Marketing, page 275

To help anchor this in practice, let us consider our archetype from the automotive industry, Alice. As we described in Chapter 5, she and her team develop an electronic control unit (ECU) which is then picked up and integrated into the vehicle. Alice and her colleagues refer to this as Vehicle Integration, where a specific version of every component in the vehicular system is identified as part of a composition, whereupon that composition of components is verified.

To decide whether they may improve their current ways of working, Alice calls her teammates to a short workshop to identify some prioritized activities to put on their backlog. The first order of business, however, before even scheduling the workshop, is to decide on the scope of the improvement work. It could be the breadth of the entire vehicle – the entire network of pipelines – and the entire depth from source code changes to certified software running in a customer's car, or it could be the ECU pipeline itself, or anything in between. This scope not only affects the type of questions one will be able to address and the level of detail at which one can discuss them, but also the people who need to be in that workshop in the first place. In this case, the scope is the ECU pipeline specifically and its connection to Vehicle Integration. Given that, Alice decides to bring one fellow developer from the ECU team who is also responsible for its configuration management, a project manager and a team leader from Vehicle Integration.

With everyone in place, Alice begins to step through the success factors one by one, asking her colleagues to collectively describe in a few brief sentences what the current status of the ECU pipeline is for each of them. Some of them turn out to be non-controversial, where as others result in intense debate as to what the current de facto practice is in the company. The end result is shown in Figure 55 (although the complete spreadsheet would be much too large to include in its entirety).

Alice's ECU Pipeline Path Forward		
Success Factor	Current Position	
Collecting Data from Every Pipeline Actor in Real Time	Test framework and ECU build jobs emit Eiffel events. No data from CI server or SCM systems.	
Collecting Data from Across the Network of Pipelines	Vehicle Integration results only available in spreadsheet format or verbally communicated.	
Aggregating and Analyzing the Pipeline Data in Real Time	Test events aggregated into requirement	

Figure 55: Alice's assessment of the current state of her ECU pipeline.

With Alice's spreadsheet all filled out, she turns their attention to their wanted position.

Figuring Out Where to Go

The exercise described above can be valuable in itself, as it tends to trigger reflection; it can be thought of as a light-weight alternative to e.g. building a full Cinders description of the pipeline. To plot a path forward, however, repeat the same exercise, but this time phrase a wanted position at some defined time in the future. Pick a time that is relevant to you – in a year, in three years, or the planned launch date of your killer application. The exact time interval is not important, as long as it is close enough to be tangible. A date fifty years into the future would be of limited value, as it's impossible to tell what the world will look like by then. The important thing is that it provides a clear time frame for improvements. For each success factor, briefly, in one or two sentences, describe the wanted position. Strive for the ambitious, but realistic.

To achieve that balance between ambition and realism, we recommend setting the scene by quickly considering context of the pipeline in question. By discussing and collectively acknowledging your own position in each of the dimensions listed in Part II: Understanding Your Context, you gain a shared perspective on what is both feasible and desirable in your particular case. This is crucial in order to accurately determine what your wanted position is, as this is completely dependent on the contextual factors that define your case. In particular, a good understanding of your context facilitates a focused conversation on what is achievable, by closing off inapplicable or unrealistic options. Similarly, consider which types of potential solutions correspond to the functions and roles of the individuals participating in the workshop. To exemplify, solutions requiring a financial investment decision at a higher level than the workshop participants can effect – directly or indirectly – would arguably constitute little more than wishful thinking. That being said, this should not only be thought of as a restriction, but also as an important consideration with regards to who should be invited. Clearly, the ideal scenario would be to have all the relevant individuals participating in the first place, to be able to make any relevant decisions there and then, but in our experience this can be easier said than done.

As a general note on these types of multilateral conversations and workshops, it's important as a moderator to ensure that every voice is heard. Try to invite every participant to share their views and actively seek out opposing viewpoints – if you find yourself struggling, there's no shortage of guides and literature on facilitating creative group discussions.

As for deciding on the wanted position to strive for, this is clearly not a trivial task. What it represents, in reality, is a series of decisions on organizational and indeed sociological issues, and not least architectural design. While Philippe Kruchten has observed that "software architecture is a long and rapid succession of suboptimal tactical decisions, mostly made in partial light," [77] there are methods that offer some guidance. Ultimately, the decision of whether to use them comes down to the amount of effort one is ready to expend. The fastest approach would be to simply make those decisions based on the expertise and experience of the people available in the workshop. For a more thorough approach to finding the pain points and opportunities for improvement in a pipeline, we have positive experiences from applying the Enable More Frequent Integration of Software (EMFIS) model [78].

The EMFIS model is designed to find pain points that prevent engineers from adopting continuous behaviors, and particularly emphasizes the distinction and differences in perspective between the engineers who *depend* upon the tooling and infrastructure to produce their software, and the *enabling* engineers who construct and maintain the tooling and infrastructure that support continuous practices.

By interviewing both groups, asking them to assess how well e.g. regression tests, product architecture or test environment availability is working, the EMFIS model provides a more nuanced view of the currently most pressing issues in a way that a single, small workshop is not positioned to do. Furthermore, the EMFIS model reveals any opposing views between the two groups, as shown in Figure 56, such as whether the tooling is actually fast and simple to use. Such differences may otherwise remain undetected, unless the two views of the two groups are intentionally separated as prescribed by the EMFIS model.

It is worth highlighting that while the EMFIS model specializes in finding pain points to help guide improvement efforts and prioritization, it does not reveal a wanted position. In this way it is a great support in figuring out where to go, but in itself it is not enough.

Returning to Alice's workshop, the four participants draw the seven contextual dimensions described in Part I of the book on a whiteboard and then note individually where they would put the ECU pipeline in each of those dimensions. Comparing the results, in most cases they are close enough to simply be acknowledged, whereas two warrant further discussion: Power Balance (see Chapter 8) and Distribution Model (see Chapter 13).

	Developers' assessment		Enablers' assessment	
Activity Planning and Execution				
Work breakdown	2.5	⚠	3.0	
Teams and responsibilities	3.0		4.0	≠
Activity sequencing	3.0		3.0	
System Thinking				
Modular and loosely coupled architecture	4.5		4.0	
Developers must think of the complete system	4.0		4.0	
Activity Planning and Execution				
Tools and processes are fast and simple	2.0	⚠	4.0	≠
Availability of test environments	4.0		5.0	≠
Test selection	4.0		4.0	
Fast feedback from the integration pipeline	3.5		4.0	
Confidence Through Test Activities				
Test before commit	3.5		3.0	
Regression tests on the mainline	3.0		4.0	≠
Reliability of test environments	1.5	✖	4.0	≠

Figure 56: EMFIS model of current status in Alice's ECU pipeline.

In the case of Power Balance, from the point of view of the ECU pipeline they agree that the "customer" in this case is Vehicle Integration. As it turns out, the ECU developer and the Vehicle Integration team leader disagree on their mutual relationship and their respective mandates over when and how ECU software should be published, as well as the types of testing they should be subjected to prior to publishing. Rather than pursuing what is turning out as a confrontation rather than collaboration, Alice acknowledges the differences in perspective and asks the participants to hold their thoughts and focus on how they would *like* that testing and publishing to be carried out so that an agreed solution might be reached, regardless of formal role descriptions and mandates. Similarly, Distribution Model – interpreted as distribution of software to customer vehicles – is outside of the scope of the workshop. Interpreted as how the ECU distributes its software to consuming pipelines, such as Vehicle Integration, on the other hand, is something the engineers present in the room can actually decide upon themselves, and so they decide not to spend time splitting hairs over how their current process might be classified.

Having established their context, Alice and her colleagues proceed to consider what their wanted position in twelve months would be, for each success factor in turn. To facilitate this step, Alice has conducted an EMFIS assessment of the current status of the ECU pipeline. The scope is not large enough to allow for extensive interviews with large numbers of engineers, but that is not Alice's purpose. She has simply asked two of the developers and the one engineer responsible for the pipeline infrastructure to rate on a Likert scale [79] from 1 to 5 what they perceive to be working well, and what they perceive as being in need of improvement. The result provides a backdrop against which Alice and her colleagues in the workshop can better identify the areas that require improvement (see Figure 56). This not only indicates areas of major difficulties in the pipeline (via warning and error icons), but also highlights the difference in awareness of these difficulties between engineers (via inequality signs), underlining the importance of involving multiple roles in the improvement work.

Following an assessment of realistic targets per success factor, partly informed by Alice's EMFIS assessment and partly by the individual experiences and expertise of the workshop participants, the resulting wanted positions are entered into Alice's spreadsheet (as shown in Figure 57). In most cases these are incremental improvements of what they already have in place. In other areas they envision more radical changes, while in some cases they are happy where they are and don't see any need for improvements in the coming year.

Alice's ECU Pipeline Path Forward		
Success Factor	Current Position	Wanted in 12 months
Collecting Data from Every Pipeline Actor in Real Time	Test framework and ECU build jobs emit Eiffel events. No data from CI server or SCM systems.	Eiffel events emitted from SCM system upon commit to mainline, with references to addressed issues.
Collecting Data from Across the Network of Pipelines	Vehicle Integration results only available in spreadsheet format or verbally communicated.	Vehicle Integration automatically publishes compositions and test results, preferably as Eiffel events.
Aggregating and Analyzing the Pipeline Data in Real Time	Test events aggregated into requirement	Real time dashboard show status per commit, from source code change

Figure 57: Alice's wanted position for her ECU pipeline.

Plotting a Path

After establishing both the current and the wanted position, the third step is plotting a path from here to there. This can be done by looking at the delta – if any – between the two, represented by the two columns in Figure 57. For each success factor, this delta can then be broken down into work items to be estimated, prioritized and planned according to your favorite methodology.

Alice decides to simply add a third column to her spreadsheet and enter brief slogans for the items of work that need to be done to reach the wanted position (see Figure 58). They spend the remainder of the workshop identifying the top ten items to start working on, prioritize them internally and play planning poker to estimate them. The project manager then brings them into the larger development backlog to be prioritized against other ongoing activities.

Alice's ECU Pipeline Path Forward			
Success Factor	Current Position	Wanted in 12 months	Work items
Collecting Data from Every Pipeline Actor in Real Time	Test framework and ECU build jobs emit Eiffel events. No data from CI server or SCM systems.	Eiffel events emitted from SCM system upon commit to mainline, with references to addressed issues.	- Review system plugin deployed - Commit message syntax established
Collecting Data from Across the Network of Pipelines	Vehicle Integration results only available in spreadsheet format or verbally communicated.	Vehicle Integration automatically publishes compositions and test results, preferably as Eiffel events.	- Needs explained to Vehicle Integration - Communication interface agreed - Collection and visualization of Vehicle Integration data
Aggregating and Analyzing the Pipeline Data in Real Time	Test events aggregated into requirement	Real time dashboard show status per commit, from source code change	- Visualization solution candidates evaluated

Figure 58: Alice's path forward for her ECU pipeline.

Following Up

Whatever development and/or project planning methodology one subscribes to, we recommend using the same process for planning and executing pipeline improvement work as for everything else. Then the same methods of following up and tracking progress – of which there is an infinite number – can naturally be applied.

That being said, we encourage you to consider repeating the workshop once or twice before reaching the time of the wanted position. These would typically be shorter sessions, giving you the opportunity to reflect again on your current and wanted positions. Perhaps your position has changed, due to improvements, new challenges or changing circumstances (one would hope that *something* has changed as a result of the planned improvement work!), or perhaps your wanted position has changed due to shifting market trends or business strategies.

Ideally, such follow-up sessions would be planned well in advance on day one, to prevent them from slipping and sliding when good intentions meet the reality of congested calendars. In this spirit, the very last thing Alice does before wrapping up her workshop on pipeline improvements over the coming year, is to schedule two follow-up workshops four and eight months out, respectively, to give herself and her colleagues the chance to touch base and re-assess their situation.

Summary

In this chapter we have considered one aspect of moving forward: improving one's pipeline. Equipped with the understanding of contextual factors and success factors in both pipeline design and processes from earlier in this book, we have turned that into a light-weight yet systematic approach to analyzing and planning improvements. In the next chapter we wax speculative, as we consider the challenges we see facing the software industry just around the corner.

Chapter 28

Trends in Software Engineering

Predicting the future is a popular pastime amongst software engineers, and indeed amongst human beings as a species. Unfortunately, that doesn't mean we are any good at it. You should treat anyone – regardless of titles or credentials – claiming to predict the future with the greatest skepticism. Even so, we will endeavor to spend this chapter contemplating a set of possible futures, and what they might imply for continuous practices.

Systems of Systems

Throughout this book we have taken pains to emphasize that – even though we often use the term ourselves – the idea of a single pipeline is really an oversimplification. Consequently, in Chapter 6, we introduced the concept of networks of pipelines, feeding one another in a complicated (and sometimes complex) system not unlike the food chains of a wildlife ecosystem. This phenomenon can be viewed as both a manifestation and a consequence of the trend towards systems of systems (SoS) in the industry.

A system of systems can be described as "a super system comprised of other elements which themselves are independent complex operational systems and interact among themselves to achieve a common goal" [80]. Examples of systems of systems include the

Internet, swarms of robotic drones, military C4I (Command, Control, Computers, Communications and Information) systems, interconnected computerized systems of government, and transportation fleet management systems.

To a fair degree, large networks of software pipelines are a direct consequence of the rise of systems of systems. The trend towards systems of systems has been observed for decades [81]. As interconnectedness increases, so does the need for integration and verification of that integration. It is no longer enough to merely test all the software that makes up a military vehicle – sizable as it may be – but its interaction with command and control systems must also be tested. Similarly, it is no longer sufficient to only test a router or a car or a website in isolation: their correct behavior in interactions with their collaborators may be just as mission critical as their internal functionality, and must therefore be thoroughly tested before release and/or deployment.

This is why the network of pipelines producing each respective system in a larger SoS context will tend to mirror that larger SoS context, in the sense that each system's collaborators will feed into its continuous delivery pipeline. This pattern is depicted in Figure 59. In runtime (to the right side of the dashed line) System X collaborates with Collaborators A and B, forming part of a larger system of systems context. In order to verify correct interaction, however, the latest releases from Collaborators A and B are picked up from their respective pipelines and used in automated regression testing of System X. This way, the actors found on the right hand side of the figure also show up on the left hand side as dependencies in the network of pipelines. As noted, converse may also be the case – that System X releases are fed into regression tests in the pipelines of Collaborators A and B, respectively – but for reasons of simplicity no such relationships or deployments of those collaborators are included in the figure.

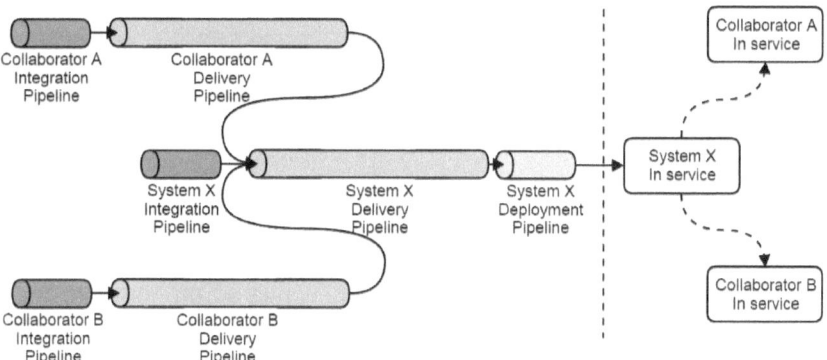

Figure 59: A system of systems network of pipelines.

It's important to emphasize that while this is true for systems of systems, it isn't necessarily true for simply large systems which consist of various integrated subsystems. The key difference is that in the case of SoS, each constituent system is partially independent and has value in and of itself, and therefore has its own pipeline. This is where treating collaborators in the SoS context as dependencies to that pipeline comes into play.

As we come from different backgrounds, when Daniel first broached this subject of pipeline networks mirroring the runtime topology of systems of systems, I had a hard time understanding where he was coming from. In my experience, building large and complex, yet self-contained systems, this just seemed convoluted: in my mind, there was one pipeline integrating and testing one system. But when you think of it in terms of a multitude of semi-independent systems with their own life-cycles, possibly provided by separate and perhaps even competing companies, this way of thinking about the problem makes a lot of sense.

- Torvald

The increasing trend towards systems of systems has been observed for many years, along with an uptake in interest from the engineering and researcher communities with regards to their particular challenges and opportunities, such as the coordination, interoperability and synergy of the many semi-independent systems that make up the larger SoS context [80].

The type of collaboration required across not just enterprises, but within entire ecosystems of organizations cooperating to construct and evolve these systems of systems, places demands on the ability to collaborate and make joint plans, but also on continuous practices. Particularly, it requires an effective and efficient means of communication between the interdependent pipelines in the network, allowing frictionless orchestration of activities as well as traceability. This is true whether the needed frequency of integration between two pipelines in the network is once a minute, once a month or anything in between. Consequently, we see a steadily increasing need for solutions that allow pipelines to communicate across organizational boundaries without manual coordination, similar to the technologies such as Eiffel (introduced in Chapter 15).

Another feature of increasingly complex systems – systems of systems or otherwise – is presence of emergent behavior and properties. An emergent behavior or property of a system is generally understood as one which is not apparent from studying its individual parts, but which appears as a result of their interaction. The concept as such is value-neutral, in that such behaviors may be either beneficial or detrimental to the purposes of the system, but they pose additional challenges to continuous practices in that they are by definition unplanned and as a rule unexpected.

This brings us back to the major weakness of automated execution of test scripts discussed in Chapter 17: you can only design test cases for what you're aware you ought to be testing. In a sense, emergent behaviors are "unknown unknowns"[31]. The potential for unplanned emergent behaviors in complex software systems constitutes an additional argument for retaining a certain degree of manual evaluation of release candidates, and not growing over-confident in automated test

---

31 Although (unintentionally) popularized by Donald Rumsfeld in 2002, the concept as such is valid and rooted in psychology research.

coverage. The human brain is extraordinarily skilled at spotting patterns and divergent behaviors. That ability needs to be exploited to support the software pipeline, while taking care not to let its slowness obstruct it, as described in Chapter 17.

Artificial Intelligence

Artificial intelligence is constantly breaking new ground, demonstrating capabilities matching or surpassing humans in increasingly complicated cognitive tasks – tasks recently thought to be well outside the reach for many years, or perhaps even our lifetimes. To understand the implications of this revolution it is important to understand how the way in which computers manage these tasks has changed.

An illustrative example of this change is how AlphaGo (Alphabet Inc's Go playing artifical intelligence program) in 2017 beat Ke Jie, the world's top ranked Go player. Prior to this victory, Go had long been considered a much more difficult problem to solve for a computer program than chess, where the reigning world chess champion Garry Kasparov was defeated by IBM's Deep Blue in 1997. The reason is that even though Go's rules may appear simple in comparison to chess, it's much more complex in that it involves a greater number of possible moves [82]. This is important, because while Deep Blue relied on evaluating the move most likely to lead to victory for any given state of the game, based on very large numbers of recorded games (and a great deal of bespoke algorithms for special positions). In contrast, this approach is not feasible for a game like Go, where computer programs need to rely on more dynamic approaches that do not require domain knowledge or expert input (particularly neural network based machine learning combined with the Monte Carlo Search Tree algorithm) [83]. This development has allowed artificial intelligences to make considerable leaps in very short time, conquering areas long believed to be out of reach for the foreseeable future.

This example demonstrates how artificial intelligence is not only growing more powerful with increasing hardware resources at its disposal, but also becoming capable of solving completely new sets of challenges in ways that increasingly resemble the human brain. This means artificial intelligence can be employed to make the sort of judgment calls we would otherwise only entrust a human being with, but doing so at speeds that humans could never match.

Software pipelines are rife with such potential decision points where we currently implement simple algorithms to determine behavior. For instance, in Chapter 17 we have discussed techniques for dynamically selecting test scripts to execute at any particular time for any particular release candidate. Such selection can favorably be implemented using relatively straight-forward algorithms, but there is significant potential for more sophisticated and/or intelligent methods. Other potential future scenarios include neural networks trained to make judgment calls on which components to pull into a given system composition, managing and scheduling build and test environments, or predicting in-production behavior based on historical data and test outcomes.

Clearly, all of this is assuming that artificial intelligence doesn't progress *too* far. The day we hit the singularity, chances are the software engineering profession as a whole will be obsolete.

Virtualization

In its broadest sense, virtualization is the process of creating a non-material version of some asset, such as networks and computer hardware. The virtualization trend that has been observed over the latest decade and which profoundly affects the applicability and nature of continuous practices is that of migrating software functions from custom hardware and/or embedded systems in the field into cloud environments. This has in turn been enabled by the increasing connectivity of devices, as part of the larger societal trend of Internet of Things.

The impact of virtualization on continuous practices is related to the importance of proximity to hardware (see Chapter 10). A virtualized production environment not only affords mature tooling and infrastructure, but enables the containerization and the rapidity in deployment that are crucial success factors for continuous deployment (see Chapter 20).

At the time of writing, we see parts of the software industry reaping the full rewards of continuous deployment. These are predominantly found in the web and Software as a Service domains. Meanwhile, others, typically software-intensive embedded systems, strive to achieve the same practices, but struggle to do so. This situation has come to a tipping point, but it's far from clear which it will play out.

One likely scenario is that the virtualization trend will continue unabated, placing the vast majority of currently embedded software functionality in cloud environments, enabling continuous integration under the same circumstances as any other software. It is also possible that virtualization doesn't live up to the high hopes, leaving significant parts of the software industry tightly coupled to bespoke hardware platforms, e.g. for performance or security reasons, but that those platforms mature to better support the success factors of continuous deployment. Or, perhaps neither of those two scenarios will come to pass – a future very similar to the current situation is entirely possible, where embedded systems remain non-virtual and unable to support continuous deployment, effectively forcing us as a community to acknowledge the fact that the practice is not fully applicable to every software context.

Summary

There are multiple trends, or movements that may or may not develop into trends, in the software engineering community. Furthermore, what constitutes a trend and what doesn't is largely in the eye of the beholder. Which ones will pan out and to what extent they will impact continuous practices is inevitably subject to a great deal of speculation. In this chapter we have taken a closer look at a handful of trends that we currently perceive, and which hold the potential to change the way we think of continuous practices in the future.

Chapter 29

Trends in Continuous Practices

While the previous chapter discussed trends in the software industry at large and their potential impact on continuous practices, this chapter focuses on what we may expect from the field of continuous practices in the future. This largely draws upon the challenges we are currently facing as practitioners in the industry, and on the opportunities we glean in current research.

Achieving Continuous Integration at Scale

Previously in this book we have presented scale as one of the contextual factors that determine the feasibility and applicability of continuous practices (see Chapter 11) and described detrimental effect on continuous practices. One can speculate with regards to the emergence of new, unforeseen paradigms that completely change the playing field of software versioning, merging and development in general. For instance, it's always possible to wave one's hands and speak vaguely of phenomena such as artificial intelligence and machine learning, but it's difficult to see a convincing argument for how the effects on scale can be effectively mitigated in the foreseeable future. Consequently, we speculate that the rise of continuous practices effectively spells the end of large, monolithic software systems, at least in competitive commercial segments.

Historically, there has arguably been little reason *not* to combine every part of a very large system into a single source monolith. Indeed, there are clear benefits: developers have easy access to and can change anything in large, atomic commits, and everything is versioned as a single entity avoiding overhead in configuration management. Even in a very large such monolith, as long as every individual doesn't commit too frequently, the pace of change can be manageable.

Continuous integration changes that, however. When the size of those monoliths become the critical factor that impedes the ability of developers to continuously integrate, as we have found in research [29], then the benefits are not as appealing anymore. As a consequence, we observe a clear trend towards modularized architectural styles, both in integration time and in runtime (see Chapter 16 and Chapter 20, respectively).

Test Environment Stability

In Chapter 17 we discussed test flakiness and the damage it wreaks upon continuous practices. As problematic as troubleshooting flaky test cases can be, working with flaky or otherwise unstable test environments is even worse. While in principle there is no such thing as a completely reliable environment, in pragmatic terms test environment stability is rarely an issue as long as one stays within the confines of a single machine. As soon as the environment involves distributed systems and networking configurations, on the other hand, all kinds of fascinating and unexpected things happen, e.g. related to timing aspects of dependencies between different versions of subsystems. The larger and more complex the system, the larger and more complex the test environment tends to be, and the larger and more complex the test environment is, the greater the likelihood of failure.

This is because the chances of successful environment configuration decreases for every component – in other words, for every source of potential failure – introduced into it. It would be tempting to say something in the vein of how a test environment is only as reliable as its most unreliable component. Unfortunately, this is a common misconception, whereas the truth is actually much worse: the chance of avoiding failure in the complete test environment can never be higher than the chance of success in each constituent component multiplied together. A test environment of twenty interacting components, each with a 99% chance of not failing, will not fail 1% of the time. Instead, it will fail closer to 20% of the time (assuming independence of failure modes between components).

This problem is particularly pronounced where bespoke test equipment, such as emulators and simulators – often complex systems in their own right – are used in an active development phase, where both the item under test and the test equipment is constantly in flux with little time to stabilize either of them.

One perspective on this is that such instability should be embraced, and the software made robust enough to withstand it (see e.g. chaos testing, discussed under Open Ended Testing on page 167), but we must keep in mind that different types of testing serve different purposes. Chaos testing is excellent for testing the robustness of the item under test, but not for verifying its functionality or measuring its performance. While an unreliable test environment will let you test the robustness of the item under test to that particular type of unreliability, for other types of testing it will only introduce noise in the data: you will get false positives in your testing, leading to overhead, lead times and wasted effort.

It would be very rewarding to present a silver bullet solution to this problem, or at least a direction in which to search for it. Alas, the advice we can provide amounts to applying the same architectural principles to achieve performance, predictability and repeatability in test environments as in commercial products. Admittedly, this is not very different from simply recommending that people do a better job – all of which is well meant, but arguably of little concrete help to the individual engineer struggling here and now under punishing time and budget constraints. Simply put, the software industry sorely needs new and innovative approaches to constructing reliable test environments for large, distributed software systems.

Holistic Testing of Continuously Deployed Large-Scale Systems

Writing stable and efficient end-to-end tests for large systems is hard. So hard that many developers don't do it at all, or restrict such testing to a minimum, preferring in-production testing and monitoring [84]. As we noted previously, that can be a viable strategy if one's context allows it. If it does not, e.g. for reasons of safety criticality (see Chapter 7) and/or regulations (see Chapter 12), effective end-to-end testing strategies need to be devised.

Already today we note the importance of a shared objective and vision in Agile software development. Even so, it is something for which we find there is limited support in the standard set of Agile tools and methods. This is particularly true in very large scale development, and consequently we predict that as interconnectedness and systems of systems become ever more prevalent (see Chapter 28), that importance will only increase.

This challenge becomes even more pronounced when collaborating in an ecosystem of organizations, all contributing in a more or less organic manner and with more or less governance by a central authority. This is because in such scenarios, engineers may not even know their collaborators, or ever come into direct contact with them.

At the same time, continuous deployment of large-scale systems is challenging, because in practice it is impossible to execute a complete and detailed test scope for every single version being deployed. This leads us to the conclusion that we must find better approaches to testing than the repeated verification of detailed requirement specifications on the inner workings of systems for every release candidate.

This is particularly the case in the ecosystem context described above. By ecosystem, in this context, we refer to networks of "businesses, suppliers and customers" not only exchanging goods and services, but also "information and knowledge sharing, inquiries, pre- and post-sales contacts, etc" [85]. The reason this is particularly challenging is that in a typical ecosystem setup, the resulting "system" is impossible to define. As an example, consider your phone. Nobody has verified that the exact combination of hardware, operating system and apps on your particular phone functions correctly. In fact, it is not unlikely that that particular combination – or that particular system – exists nowhere else in the world, except in your pocket. It is a unique snow flake. This clearly poses a problem to the company or ecosystem of companies who develop the software that constitutes that system. Clearly, they have a more or less well defined vision of how the phone will be used – particularly the developers of the basic framework holding the ecosystem together, such as the phone's operating system – but there is no way for them to predict or test your personal user experience.

These factors come together in a very clear future direction. For software companies to use continuous integration, delivery and deployment to verify a comprehensive list of requirements is not feasible. Instead, those pipelines need to be used to focus on the verification of user experiences or system scenarios at a very high level of abstraction, without spending valuable time and resources verifying precisely how those experiences and scenarios are realized. In the example of the phone ecosystem, for instance, this may be done by utilizing a limited set of reference applications in testing. There are two main reasons for this. First, the software company or organization conducting those tests may not have complete control over or even access to all of the parts that eventually make up the larger system. Second, the nature of the system will change rapidly over time, and therefore the ways in which those user scenarios are realized also changes, making too fine-grained low-level tests obsolete.

That being said, this is more than just a coping mechanism. Precisely this type of high level tests stands to provide the sort of shared objective and vision required to align large-scale distributed development. This is particularly the case when the outcome of those tests is not binary, as in merely passing or failing, but able to assess the degree to which the objectives are achieved. In essence, this is a way of amplifying the pipeline's ability to provide feedback and guidance to developers, effectively turning it into a pole star for the larger system development effort.

This is a concrete example of how there are more objectives to consider in pipeline design than merely achieving high speed and frequency, and that not all activities need to be on the pipeline's critical path. As we have touched upon multiple times in Part III: Building the

Pipeline, the challenge lies in choosing the right type of test activities for the given purpose and that one's toolbox contains more than just automated test scripts – manual tests performed by skilled engineers have a place in there, just as open ended testing techniques (see Chapter 17). We predict that overcoming this challenge will be a key factor in separating the leaders from the pack in tomorrow's software industry.

Applying the Right Test to the Right Job

In this book we have occasionally touched upon the fact that there are different types of tests, and that one isn't necessarily inherently better than the other. We believe that this realization, or rather a lack of it, poses a grave threat to the future validity of continuous practices.

For that reason, an important area of future research is the mapping of distinct types of tests to the various needs of different stakeholders. When we as engineers are able to not merely write more automated test scripts to generate increased coverage of lines of code, requirements or whichever metric we're using, but rather think in terms of satisfying a stakeholder's specific need and selecting the right tool for that particular job from a well ordered and thoroughly understood toolbox of alternative approaches, then we can multiply the value we derive from our software pipelines. Until then, as long as all one has is a hammer, every problem will look like a nail.

To be clear, the type of research we suggest is not into testing techniques or test automation per se, but into how various types of testing can be applied in order to, for instance, satisfy the developer's need to verify a source code change, for a product owner to assess overall product quality, for a project manager to assess progress, for an architect to identify prioritized areas in need of refactoring et cetera. It's also worth pointing out that this is different from the problem of dynamically and intelligently selecting test cases to execute for any given release candidate, as we have described in Chapter 17. Such selection is an important part of optimizing test execution, but in the larger scheme of things only represents optimization of one particular type of testing. What we call for is a broader framework that allows for the informed selection of entire testing approaches, with predictable results for specific ends.

Summary

In this chapter we have considered future trends and needs specifically related to continuous practices, as opposed to the software industry at large. With that we have reached not only the end of the chapter, but the end of the book.

In ways of parting words, we hope that you have found some nuggets of value hidden among these pages, and that you remember to keep an open mind and keep learning. Even though continuous practices have been with us for twenty years, we are convinced that we have only seen the beginning of what they have to offer the software engineering discipline. Never before have as large and complex software systems been created as efficiently, predictably and rapidly as today. Therefore we would be very surprised if the last word has been said – or the last book written – on continuous practices. But regardless what new technologies, business models or methods we might apply tomorrow, we ask you to remember this: excellence begins not by attempting to copy somebody else's success, but instead by appreciating your own context. Given that context, understand where you are, decide on where you want to be, analyze how to get there, and then execute.

We wish you good luck on your journey!

Bibliography

1. Booch, G. (1994). Object-oriented analysis and design with applications, 2nd edition. Addison-Wesley Longman.

2. Beck, K. (2000). Extreme programming explained: embrace change. Addison-Wesley Professional.

3. Rodríguez, P., Haghighatkhah, A., Lwakatare, L. E., Teppola, S., Suomalainen, T., Eskeli, J., & Oivo, M. (2016). Continuous deployment of software intensive products and services: A systematic mapping study. *Journal of Systems and Software.*

4. Ståhl, D., & Bosch, J. (2014). Modeling continuous integration practice differences in industry software development. *Journal of Systems and Software, 87,* 48-59.

5. Ståhl, D., & Bosch, J. (2013). Experienced benefits of continuous integration in industry software product development: A case study. In *The 12th IASTED International Conference on Software Engineering,* (pp. 736-743).

6. Ståhl, D., & Bosch, J. (2016). Industry application of continuous integration modeling: a multiple-case study. In *Proceedings of the 38th International Conference on Software Engineering Companion* (pp. 270-279). ACM.

7. Humble, J., & Farley, D. (2010). *Continuous delivery: reliable software releases through build, test, and deployment automation.* Pearson Education.

8. Duvall, P. M. (2007). *Continuous Integration.* Pearson Education India.

9. Beck, K. et al. (2001). The Agile Manifesto.
    http://agilemanifesto.org
    Online; accessed 2017-01-24.

10. Fitz, T. (2009). Continuous Deployment.
    http://timothyfitz.com/2009/02/08/continuous-deployment
    Online; accessed 2017-01-24.

11. Ståhl, D., Mårtensson, T., & Bosch, J. (2017). Continuous
    Practices and DevOps: Beyond the Buzz, What Does It All
    Mean? In *43rd Euromicro Conference on Software Engineering
    and Advanced Applications*, (pp. 440-448).

12. Google Trends (2017).
    https://www.google.com/trends/explore?
    date=all&q=continuous%20delivery,continuous
    %20deployment
    Online; accessed 2017-01-25.

13. Fowler, M. (2006). Continuous Integration.
    http://martinfowler.com/articles/
    continuousIntegration.html
    Online; accessed 2017-01-02.

14. Fowler, M. (2013). Continuous Delivery.
    http://martinfowler.com/bliki/ContinuousDelivery.html
    Online; accessed 2017-01-02.

15. Phillips, A. (2016). Interview on Software Engineering Radio.
    http://www.se-radio.net/2016/01/se-radio-episode-247-andrew-
    phillips-on-devops
    Online; accessed 2017-01-26.

16. BlazeMeter (2015). 5 Things You Should Know About
    Continuous Deployment... by the Man Who Coined the Term
    https://www.blazemeter.com/blog/5-things-you-should-know-
    about-continuous-deploymentby-man-who-coined-term
    Online; accessed 2017-01-31.

17. Humble, J. (2010). Continuous Delivery vs Continuous Deployment.
https://continuousdelivery.com/2010/08/continuous-delivery-vs-continuous-deployment
Online; accessed 2017-01-31.

18. Edwards, D. (2012). The (Short) History of DevOps.
https://www.youtube.com/watch?v=o7-IuYS0iSE
Online; accessed 2017-01-31.

19. Rapaport, R. (2014). A Short History of DevOps.
https://www.ca.com/us/rewrite/articles/devops/a-short-history-of-devops.html
Online; accessed 2017-01-31.

20. Searle, W. (2016). A Brief History of DevOps.
https://turbonomic.com/blog/on-turbonomic/a-brief-history-of-devops
Online; accessed 2017-01-31.

21. Lwakatare, L. E., Kuvaja, P., & Oivo, M. (2015). Dimensions of DevOps. In *International Conference on Agile Software Development* (pp. 212-217). Springer International Publishing.

22. Mueller, E. (2010). A DevOps Manifesto.
https://theagileadmin.com/2010/10/15/a-devops-manifesto
Online; accessed 2017-01-31.

23. Tilkov, S. (2015). The modern cloud-based platform. *IEEE Software, 32*(2), 113-116.

24. Cohn, M. (2010). *Succeeding with agile: software development using Scrum*. Pearson Education.

25. Ståhl, D., Hallén, K., & Bosch, J. (2016). Achieving traceability in large scale continuous integration and delivery: Deployment, usage and validation of the Eiffel framework. *Empirical Software Engineering*, 1-29.

26. Leffingwell, D. (2010). *Agile software requirements: lean requirements practices for teams, programs, and the enterprise.* Addison-Wesley Professional.

27. Scaled Agile (2016). Scaled Agile Framework. http://www.scaledagileframework.com Online; accessed 2017-03-02.

28. Mårtensson, T., Ståhl, D., & Bosch, J. (2016). Continuous Integration Applied to Software-Intensive Embedded Systems– Problems and Experiences. In *17th International Conference on Product-Focused Software Process Improvement* (pp. 448-457). Springer International Publishing.

29. Ståhl, D., Mårtensson, T., & Bosch, J. (2017). The continuity of continuous integration: Correlations and consequences. *Journal of Systems and Software, 127*, 150-167.

30. Forbes (2013). Cars That Can Last For 250,000 Miles (Or More). https://www.forbes.com/sites/jimgorzelany/2013/03/14/cars-that-can-last-for-250000-miles Online; accessed 2017-05-11.

31. Shih, W. C. (2015). Does Hardware Even Matter Anymore? *Harvard Business Review.*

32. Roberts, M. (2004). Enterprise continuous integration using binary dependencies. In *International Conference on Extreme Programming and Agile Processes in Software Engineering* (pp. 194-201). Springer Berlin Heidelberg.

33. Rogers, R. O. (2004). Scaling continuous integration. In *International Conference on Extreme Programming and Agile Processes in Software Engineering* (pp. 68-76). Springer Berlin Heidelberg.

34. Mårtensson, T., Ståhl, D., & Bosch, J. (2017). Continuous Integration Impediments in Large-Scale Industry Projects. In

IEEE International Conference on Software Architecture (ICSA), (pp. 169-178). IEEE.

35. Conway, M. (2012). Conway's Law. http://www.melconway.com/Home/Conways_Law.html Online; accessed 2017-09-15.

36. U.S. Department of Health and Human Services (2002). *General Principles of Software Validation; Final Guidance for Industry and FDA Staff.*

37. U.S. Department of Health and Human Services (1999). *Guidance for Industry, FDA Reviewers and Compliance on Off-The-Shelf Software Use in Medical Devices.*

38. Chevallier, A. (2016). *Strategic Thinking in Complex Problem Solving.* Oxford University Press.

39. Fowler, M. (2014). BoundedContext. https://martinfowler.com/bliki/BoundedContext.html Online; accessed 2017-06-12.

40. Cairo, A. (2012). *The Functional Art: An introduction to information graphics and visualization.* New Riders.

41. Few, S. (2013). *Information Dashboard Design: Displaying Data for At-a-Glance Monitoring.* Analytics Press.

42. Ware, C. (2010). *Visual thinking: For Design.* Morgan Kaufmann.

43. Van Der Storm, T. (2008, April). Backtracking incremental continuous integration. In *12th European Conference on Software Maintenance and Reengineering, 2008* (pp. 233-242). IEEE.

44. Ståhl, D., & Bosch, J. (2016). Cinders: The continuous integration and delivery architecture framework. *Information*

and Software Technology.

45. Mårtensson, T., Ståhl, D., & Bosch, J. (2017). Exploratory Testing of Large-Scale Systems – Testing in the Continuous Integration and Delivery Pipeline. In *International Conference on Product-Focused Software Process Improvement (pp. 368-384)*. Springer.

46. Luo, Q., Hariri, F., Eloussi, L., & Marinov, D. (2014). An empirical analysis of flaky tests. In *Proceedings of the 22nd ACM SIGSOFT International Symposium on Foundations of Software Engineering* (pp. 643-653). ACM.

47. ArsTechnica (2012). Exclusive: a behind-the-scenes look at Facebook release engineering. https://arstechnica.com/information-technology/2012/04/exclusive-a-behind-the-scenes-look-at-facebook-release-engineering Online; accessed 2017-08-23.

48. Kaner, C. (1988). *Testing computer software*. Tab Books.

49. Kaner, C., Bach, J., & Pettichord, B. (2001). *Lessons learned in software testing*. John Wiley & Sons.

50. Gregory, J., & Crispin, L. (2014). *More agile testing: learning journeys for the whole team*. Addison-Wesley Professional.

51. Hendrickson, E. (2013). *Explore It!*. Pragmatic Bookshelf.

52. Whittaker, J. A. (2009). *Exploratory software testing: tips, tricks, tours, and techniques to guide test design*. Pearson Education.

53. Netflix (2011). The Netflix Simian Army. http://techblog.netflix.com/2011/07/netflix-simian-army.html Online; accessed 2017-06-29.

54. Alvaro, P., Rosen, J., & Hellerstein, J. M. (2015). Lineage-driven fault injection. In *Proceedings of the 2015 ACM SIGMOD International Conference on Management of Data* (pp. 331-346). ACM.

55. Atkinson, R. (1999). Project management: cost, time and quality, two best guesses and a phenomenon, its time to accept other success criteria. *International journal of project management, 17*(6), 337-342.

56. Hamilton, J. R. (2007). On Designing and Deploying Internet-Scale Services. In *LISA* (Vol. 18, pp. 1-18).

57. Newman, S. (2015). *Building microservices*. O'Reilly Media, Inc.

58. Fowler, M. (2010). BlueGreenDeployment. https://martinfowler.com/bliki/BlueGreenDeployment.html Online; accessed 2017-05-30.

59. Nickoloff, J. (2016). *Docker in Action*. Manning Publications Co.

60. Siroker, D., & Koomen, P. (2013). *A/B testing: The most powerful way to turn clicks into customers*. John Wiley & Sons.

61. Kruchten, P. B. (1995). The 4+ 1 view model of architecture. *IEEE software, 12*(6), 42-50.

62. Brown, S. (2013). Software Architecture for Developers. *Coding the Architecture*.

63. Andress, J. (2014). *The basics of information security: understanding the fundamentals of InfoSec in theory and practice*. Syngress.

64. Wired Magazine (2017). Software Has a Serious Supply-Chain Security Problem. https://www.wired.com/story/ccleaner-malware-supply-chain-

software-security
Online; accessed 2017-09-22.

65. Wired Magazine (2013). Our Government Has Weaponized the Internet. Here's How They Did It.
https://www.wired.com/2013/11/this-is-how-the-internet-backbone-has-been-turned-into-a-weapon
Online; accessed 2017-08-03.

66. Weinberg, G. M., & Shay, P. (1985). *The secrets of consulting.* Dorset House Publishing Company, Incorporated.

67. Herzberg, F. (1959). *The motivation to work.* Wiley.

68. Maslow, A. H. (1943). A theory of human motivation. *Psychological review, 50*(4), 370.

69. Pink, D. H. (2011). *Drive: The surprising truth about what motivates us.* Penguin.

70. McQuarrie, F. (2013). Daniel Pink's 'Drive': A Short Journey on a Tiny Piece of Road.
https://allaboutwork.org/2013/04/11/daniel-pinks-drive-a-short-journey-on-a-tiny-road
Online; accessed 2017-09-26.

71. Appelo, J. (2011). *Management 3.0: Leading Agile Developers, Developing Agile Leaders.* Pearson Education.

72. Ablett, R., Sharlin, E., Maurer, F., Denzinger, J., & Schock, C. (2007). Buildbot: Robotic monitoring of agile software development teams. In *The 16th IEEE International Symposium on Robot and Human Interactive Communication, 2007.* (pp. 931-936). IEEE.

73. Wilson, J. Q., & Kelling, G. L. (1982). The police and neighborhood safety: Broken windows. *Atlantic monthly, 127*(2), 29-38.

74. Allman, E. (2012). Managing technical debt. *Communications of the ACM, 55*(5), 50-55.

75. Llewellyn Falco (2014). Llewellyn's Strong-Style Pairing. http://llewellynfalco.blogspot.se/2014/06/llewellyns-strong-style-pairing.html
Online; accessed 2017-10-20.

76. Zuill, W., & Meadows, K. (2014). Mob Programming: A whole Team Approach. In *Agile 2014 Conference.*

77. Kruchten, P. (1999). The software architect. In *Software architecture* (pp. 565-583). Springer US.

78. Mårtensson, T., Ståhl, D., & Bosch, J. (2017). EMFIS – Enable More Frequent Integration of Software. In *43rd Euromicro Conference on Software Engineering and Advanced Applications*. IEEE.

79. Allen, I. E., & Seaman, C. A. (2007). Likert scales and data analyses. *Quality progress, 40*(7), 64.

80. Jamshidi, M. (Ed.). (2008). *Systems of systems engineering: principles and applications*. CRC press.

81. Osmundson, J. S., Huynh, T. V., & Langford, G. O. (2008). Emergent Behavior in Systems of Systems. In *INCOSE International Symposium* (Vol. 18, No. 1, pp. 1557-1568).

82. Los Angeles Times (2016). AlphaGo beats human Go champ in milestone for artificial intelligence. http://www.latimes.com/world/asia/la-fg-korea-alphago-20160312-story.html
Online; accessed 2017-09-02.

83. Burger, C. (2016). Google DeepMind's AlphaGo: How it works. https://www.tastehit.com/blog/google-deepmind-alphago-how-it-works

Online; accessed 2017-09-02.

84. Clemson, T. (2014). Testing Strategies in a Microservice
    Architecture.
    https://martinfowler.com/articles/microservice-testing
    Online; accessed 2017-09-08.

85. Bosch, J. (2009). From software product lines to software
    ecosystems. In *Proceedings of the 13th international software
    product line conference* (pp. 111-119). Carnegie Mellon
    University.

Index

Vici, 122
visualization, 122
electronic control unit (ECU), 38,
39, 45, 76, 85, 95, 133, 143, 180,
220, 286
Enable More Frequent Integration
of Software (EMFIS), 289, 291
environment,
as container, 187, 188
build, 145
dependencies, 167
development, 76, 145, 251
flakiness of, 158, 303
learning, 42
management, 27
production, 19, 21, 28, 30, 39,
42, 54, 70, 71, 84, 144, 150,
154, 170, 207, 212, 263, 272
reliability, 145
selection of, 166, 167
simulated, 35, 63, 65, 67, 71,
189, 190, 248
stability, 303
target, 16, 21, 43, 55, 61, 63,
65, 121, 132, 133, 144, 210
test, 71, 76, 119, 144, 145,
154, 156, 158, 160, 171, 187,
188, 220, 246, 300, 303
traceability, 126, 161
variability, 166
event sourcing, 117, 120
exploratory testing, 153, 154, 168,
170, 219
Extreme Programming, 2
extrinsic factors, 232, 233, 265
feature flag, 147
frequency, 10, 12, 35, 46, 83, 98,
103, 108, 151, 154, 190, 193, 194,
208, 209, 213, 249, 259, 298, 306

gatekeeping, 157, 168, 219, 220,
248, 253, 254, 255
graphics processing unit (GPU),
166, 167, 186, 187
hardware, 27, 36, 38, 39, 45, 47,
66, 67, 69, 71, 72, 73, 74, 75, 76,
77, 90, 144, 148, 162, 189, 191,
193, 203, 247, 249, 272, 299, 300,
301, 305
hierarchy of needs, 231
hygiene factors, 232, 233, 239,
240, 243, 244, 248, 253, 257, 268,
270, 274
Information Technology
Infrastructure Library (ITIL), 134
infrastructure, 4, 12, 26, 35, 60,
62, 75, 80, 93, 203, 226, 236, 247,
274, 289, 291, 300
integrity, 80, 225, 226, 227, 234
interface,
enforcement, 132
GUI, 136
human-machine, 35
integration, 4
management, 38, 200, 207,
252
negotiation, 63, 80, 200, 240,
245
network, 76
of the pipeline, 107, 113, 116
physical, 36, 69, 72, 73
specification, 66, 67, 85, 207,
271, 272
testing, 54
versioning, 80, 132, 133, 240
intrinsic factors, 232, 233, 243,
257, 263, 264, 265, 267

www.ingramcontent.com/pod-product-compliance
Lightning Source LLC
Chambersburg PA
CBHW031819170526
45157CB00001B/117